THE MAN FROM TISHBE

THE PEAK OF THE PROPHETIC SPECTRUM

By

KEITH LANNON

Copyright © *Keith Lannon,* 2025
All Rights Reserved

This book is subject to the condition that no part of this book is to be reproduced, transmitted in any form or means; electronic or mechanical, stored in a retrieval system, photocopied, recorded, scanned, or otherwise. Any of these actions require the proper written permission of the author.

Table of Contents

Foreword: 1

Introduction 10

PART A GETTING TO GRIPS WITH THE NATURE OF THE PROPHETIC GIFT 31

    1 An Introductory Portrait Of The Man From Tishbe............................. 32

    2 Defining The Spiritual Package That Constitutes The Prophetic Gift....... 43

    3 An Aerial View Defining The Wild Animal That Is The Prophetic Gift. (From A Prophet's Perspective.) 49

    4 A Ground Level View Defining The Harassing Pest That Is Prophecy. 59

    5 The Divine Encouragement For All Christians To Seek To Prophesy....... 64

    6 The Differing Frames Of Reference Of Prophets Has Always Been. 76

    7 The Overarching Experiential Truths Marinating Every Prophetic Activity Of Elijah.. 83

PART B THE DYNAMICS OF PROPHECY 90

    8 Defining The Dynamics Of The "Prophetic Spirit". 91

    9 Inspiration Is An Event, Not A Slow Growing Awareness. 100

    10 A Conscious Awareness Of Heavenly Authority. 107

    11 "Man Shall Not Live By Bread Alone, But By Every Word That Proceeds From The Mouth Of God."(Matthew 4:3. Deuteronomy 8:3) 112

    12 The Agency Of God In The Earth As Seen In Elijah's Prophetic Ministry. 120

    13 Taking Authentic Responsibility For The Sins Of The Nation............. 129

    14 Elijah Aligned Himself Totally With Yahweh..................................... 136

PART C ELIJAH IN THE SACRED SCROLLS. REAL-TIME. 140

    15 The Historical Setting Of Elijah's Arrival. (1 Kings 1-16)................... 141

16   The Real-Time Delivery Of Elijah's Revolutionary Prophetic Word. (1 Kings 17:1) 152

17   Let's Just Stop And Stare For A Moment At This World Shaking Three Seconds Of History. (No Rain Until I Say So…) 164

18   Self Isolation And With Nothing Else To Do? (1 Kings 17:2-4) 175

19   Elijah, The Healer Of A National Trauma. 188

20   Seeing, Hearing And Experiencing Other Dimensions.(1 Kings 17: 8-9) 195

21   Prophetic Authority Over Life And Death. (1 Kings 17:10 -24). 205

22   Darkness Confronted By The Light Of The Prophetic. (James 5:17)..... 223

23   The Call To Demonic Confrontation. (1 Kings 18:1-15)................... 230

24   The Mindset Of Ahab Against Elijah's Paradigm. (1 Kings 18:16-19) . 234

25   The Legitimacy Of Twenty-First Century Prophecy........................ 240

26   The Benchmark Demonstration Of Prophetic Power. (1 Kings 18:20- 40) 251

27   Closure To The Prophetic Baalistic Conflagration – Validating Divine Victory. (1 Kings 18:40-45) 258

PART D THE AFTERMATH OF THE INITIAL PROPHETIC DELIVERY. 265

28   The Rise And Fall Of The Schools Of The Prophets......................... 266

29   The Exhausted Prophet Flees Wanting To Die. (1 Kings 19:1-9) 295

30   The Word Of The Lord Came Again. (1 Kings 19:10-18)................. 299

31   The Recommissioning To Anoint Two Kings, And A Kingly Prophet. . 303

32   Elijah Goes Looking For Elisha (1 Kings 19:19-21)...................... 310

33   Elisha Who? From Where? 314

34   Benhadad Threatens Ahab And Israel - A Prophet Speaks. 318

35   Elijah (With Elisha?) And Naboth's Vineyard (1 Kings 21) 322

36   The Removal Of Elijah. The Succession Of Elisha (2 Kings 2:1-18) 327

37   Twice As Much Of Your Spirit. (2 Kings 2:9-10) 332

PART E   LEGACY AND REFLECTION 336

    38   Resurrection In The Old Testament 337

    39   The Revolution That Was The Hebrew Prophets. 340

    40   Destiny And Fate. 347

    41   Does One Have To Be Eccentric And/Or Lose Commonly Accepted Normalcy, Or Othodoxy In Order To Change The World? 354

    42   Why Should Christians Read The Old Testament?............................ 372

    43   What's The Takeaway ? 377

PROPHETS THROUGHOUT THE HEBREW BIBLE. 380

BIBLIOGRAPHY 387

FOREWORD:

OUTRAGEOUS FAITH. INTRUSIVE CONVICTION. INVASIVE STRATEGY.

Get ready to let your jaw drop, and for the hair on the back of your neck to stand on end. Goose pimples all over maybe. We are going to negotiate a rather bohemian gentleman by the name of Elijah. Nothing else. No surname in biblical days. He came from a place called Tishbe. This man is known and recognised by biblical scholars and historians as; "Elijah the Tishbite". And nobody has a clue where Tishbe is – or was. There are various clues, but nobody can claim certainty.

What went on in Tishbe that helped to develop Elijah the Tishbite? By the time you have read all these pages, I have failed if, at the very least, you have more than a few little clues how a baby in mom's arms feeding on his mother's breast turns out to be the giant history-changing man. A man that never died…..seriously! Factually and actually, not allegorically. No valley of the shadow of death for the man from Tishbe.

This man did a few things that are so utterly amazing that some scholars and Christians find it hard to believe it happened, as reported. Some bible reading Christians even think that he is like Superman or Spiderman i.e.: just a legend. Bah!

Well! I believe it to be historically true. So there! And that's what these pages are all about. We are about to thoroughly explore where Elijah came from – and I am not referring to the place where he erstwhile lived, where he was when he was changing the world – and again, I do not refer to his house number or postcode, and where he was going – and I do not mean heaven or a place name.

We have no clue as to whether he was a genius or educationally challenged. Whether he was nice to talk to or intimidating to all as some of his activities suggest. His dress sense was utterly bohemian. One could very well describe the biblical description of his appearance as a biblical "Tarzan". Leather belt and hairy (camel) skins is all we are told.

But here is the rub. The big one.

He took charge, for three and a half years, of the weather that covered the whole Levant – and who knows how much further beyond those borders. He took charge of the life and death register, bringing a dead person back to life. He took a 15 to 30-mile run at one point of time and was faster than a horse and chariot. He dialogued with angels. I am not at all making this up. "No more rain until I say so" was his most notable prophetic phrase. Methinks he was undoubtedly laughed at and mocked until the months passed by after his drought announcement and the normal weather patterns were stultified. My goodness! The penny had to drop in the psyche of the middle Eastern masses. There was no rain for 42 months. That is Three and a half years. This utterly profound and unique statement not only illustrates Elijah's status as a prophet, a spokesman of God, and a spiritual giant but also highlights the complexities of prophetic responsibility in the divine-human relationships shown in each of the Old Testament Hebrew prophets. By asserting control over the weather, and that for a few years he adventures out into carrying a responsibility that fundamentally resides within God's sovereign domain. My goodness! What are we talking about?

Whether you are a Christian or atheist - whatever your worldview may be, You cannot argue with me when I say that there has to be abnormal changes in the skies, the winds, the sea currents, the cloud creations, and a thousand other atmospheric and stratospheric moves and changes that gather together in order to create drought, especially in a geographic location which, as long as mankind could remember, had regular rain periods. That is why the Levant has always been a wonderful corner of the earth for farming production. Elijah, by his classic and outstanding brief sentence (see 1 Kings 17:1), actually and truly took on the burden that forever had belonged purely to God alone. But it was here where God Himself shared the responsibility of controlling the geographic climate of Israel. This writer was, and is, desperate to get hold of the micro details of how Elijah got to apply and qualify for such a job and how he expertly managed the responsibilities that had forever been on the job description of God Almighty alone.

THE BLURRED LINE BETWEEN DIVINE AUTHORITY AND HUMAN AGENCY.

Elijah's declaration serves as a pivotal moment in the historical narrative of prophecy, of Israel, indeed, in the narrative of the entire Old Testament, marking a dramatic shift in the displayed relationships between Yahweh and His most intimate friends. The divine intimacy Yahweh enjoys with Elijah also exhibits a revelation of Yahweh's desire to fellowship with His Covenantal people, i.e. the two Hebrew states of the day, Israel and Judah.

800 years later, Jesus Christ did tell twelve fellows who had followed him for circa three years, that they would do greater things than he did. It seems to me that Elijah knew and acted upon those words before Christ touched down on planet earth. These pages purposefully and intentionally wish to declare all the reasons why Christ following, Bible-believing people can do the stuff that Jesus did, and Elijah practised as his "normal day at the office."

In ancient Israel, the rain was viewed (as it still is, of course) as a blessing from the Almighty, essential for agricultural prosperity and human and animal survival. By claiming authority over rain, Elijah positions himself as an intermediary between God and the Israelites. However, this act raises significant questions about the nature of prophetic responsibilities and human agency. Elijah speaks in a way that makes the rains in Israel totally his personal responsibility.

Of course, theologically, the ultimate responsibility for providing rain and sustaining life rests with God. The Scriptures consistently affirm that God controls the elements and determines the fate of nations – apart for the dangerous damage that the fall of man has begotten on the planet. We reap what we sow. A fallen world – which includes the planet itself– clearly acts outside of God's will and prerogative sometimes. However, in allowing Elijah to take on this authoritative responsibility, God Himself surely risks His divine character being misrepresented by allowing a human being to actually state, "No rain until *I* say".

Really Elijah?

His exercise of hitherto unseen power and unnoted authority in the voiced statement above implies not only a command over the natural world but also a judgment against the people of Israel for their idolatry and unfaithfulness. While Elijah acts as a faithful servant of God, his declaration blurs the lines between divine sovereignty, God's word, and human prophetic agency.

THE WEIGHT OF PROPHETIC RESPONSIBILITY.

Elijah's boldness is admirably astonishing. He stands against a corrupt and idolatrous society, calling the people back to faithfulness towards God. Yet, in doing so, he assumes an immense personal burden. The drought that follows is not merely a natural phenomenon but a profound spiritual crisis that affects the entire nation and beyond. This situation illustrates the mind-boggling weight of responsibility that Elijah bore: he, like other prophets highlighted in the Hebrew Bible, is tasked with conveying God's thoughts, calling for repentance – that is a total 180-degree turn round, and then personally navigating the potential fallout of his declarations.

Elijah's actions reflect a bottomless depth of commitment to his God, and in that commitment demonstrates the awesome, intimidating act of overstepping the natural and normal boundaries of human responsibility. He talks with the tone and timbre of the divine. "No rain till *I* say so." By claiming authority over rain, he creates the impression that God's blessings are contingent upon Elijah's personal will and word. This understanding (or was it a misunderstanding?) could lead to nationwide despair and confusion who might see Elijah as the source of both their future suffering and their hope. What on earth happened in Tishbe? What took place in Elijah's hometown? Will somebody take me to Tishbe? I desperately need to examine the evidence.

A CALL TO HUMILITY

The tension inherent in Elijah's declaration serves as a reminder of the need for totally absorbing humility in prophetic leadership and prophetic exercise. While prophets are called to speak truth and stand for righteousness and tend to be envisaged as somewhat spiritually above the majority of the population, they must also recognize their limitations. The ultimate responsibility for the natural order and human fate rests with God. Spiritual leaders must humbly seek God's guidance, acknowledging that their authority is derived totally from the divine will and selection. The absolute mindset before god demands the complete denial of personal ambition for the water of their message delivery to be pure, fresh and lifegiving.

Moreover, this narrative of the man from Tishbe highlights the live-or-die importance of faithfulness in the face of intimidating uncertainty. Elijah's declaration sets the stage for a series of events that test not only his faith but also the follower's faith of the entire nation. In their time of drought, the people are Divinely invited to reflect on their relationship with God, leading them to either repentance or further rebellion. This dynamic underscores that while prophets may bear responsibility for delivering God's message, the ultimate outcome lies in the choices that the nation's millions decide.

Elijah's declaration in 1 Kings 17:1 encapsulates the ultimate moment of intricate interplay between divine authority and human agency when negotiating the Divine Word. By taking on the ultimate responsibility for climate and rain, Elijah embodies the weight of prophetic duty while illustrating the potential dangers of misrepresenting God's sovereignty. Like the man crossing Niagara Falls on a tight rope without a safety net or safety belt, Elijah needed absolute accuracy in each step he made. This narrative invites us to consider in devotional moments on our knees the nature of our own responsibilities, urging humility, faithfulness, and a deep reliance on and faith in God. In recognizing this, we can better navigate our roles in the world, serving as faithful stewards of God's message while trusting in His perfect will. We also all walk a tightrope. But when our tightrope walk is only a few inches above the fallen world, people will not be traumatised if we lose balance. Imagine the scenario we are spectating with the man from Tishbe who must have been envisioned by Israelis as above the highest archangel.

Stellar influences precipitate solar output that influences our little planet more than we know. If we assume that the sun's energy is significantly intensified during a period of heatwave and drought, it would lead to higher temperatures across various regions. An increase in solar irradiance would exacerbate heat and minimize moisture, creating an environment ripe for drought.

Noting that Elijah is speaking with the authority and release of Yahweh Himself, the declaration of "no rain" would precipitate a shift in the atmospheric conditions prevalent at the time. An increase in greenhouse gases, hypothetically due to human activities or natural events, could trap heat more effectively, raising temperatures and disrupting traditional precipitation patterns. This would create a feedback loop where rising temperatures would lead to reduced rainfall.

Then, the cultural practices and land use during Elijah's time would have influenced local climates. If deforestation or overgrazing occurred, it would diminish vegetation cover, reducing transpiration—the process whereby plants release moisture into the atmosphere. This would further lower humidity levels and contribute to drought conditions. Oh Elijah! Have you the slightest idea what you have released with your confrontational order you gave to the cosmos of planet earth. "No rain till I say"?

Then there is the mighty sway and influence of the Mediterranean Sea being a critical climate driver for the region, playing a major role in the stultification of the Levants climate. The state of the oceans, particularly sea surface temperatures, influences atmospheric circulation and precipitation patterns. If ocean temperatures rise, this enhances evaporation but could also disrupt normal weather patterns throughout the locality beyond even the Middle East, typically bringing rainfall to the area. An increase in sea surface temperatures could have led to a breakdown in the climatic systems necessary for precipitation over Israel and Lebanon. Did the man from Tishbe know how the cosmos was moving itself just because he challenged the king of Israel.

A prophetic word, if truly speaking the thoughts of God, is quite literally speaking as God. The phrase "Thus says the Lord" or "This is what God says" appears over 400 times in the Old Testament". The phrase is a technical term indicating that the ensuing quotation is the exact word of God. The big shock of meeting the man from Tishbe is that he is never recorded as saying, "This is what God says." He just says that he is in God's presence. And from that location, "There will be no rain till I say so." Are you getting the picture. Elijah was not only from Tishbe, wherever that was, but his language had fed him from God's throne room, wherever that may be. Please tell me, dear reader, that I am making you hungry. Prophetic lesson 101 is that by living 24/7 in the presence of God, ultimately, the Holy Spirit may dominate your spirit to the degree that you are aware of what God Himself is saying.

The cessation of rain at his command symbolizes a powerful interaction with natural forces, where the spiritual realm directly influences climatic conditions. Activities of God that are tangible and impacting in the physical world are compelling to the rational observer. If Elijah's opening salvo in 1 Kings 17:1 exhibits the fact that God's revealed words impact the natural causes of planet earth, does it not also reinforce the idea that human immoral actions can affect nature as well as culture and mass human conduct?

Yes indeed! Reflecting on Elijah's initial declaration brings forth profound ethical considerations. The consequences of such a drought would have been dire, impacting agriculture, water supplies, and the livelihoods of countless millions. The potential for harm is immense, and the interconnectedness of Earth's systems means that localised changes could have far-reaching global effects. Oh, Elijah! Did you not have any inward consideration of what you had unleashed upon the planet.

This proclamation, while rooted in spiritual and moral motivations given by Yahweh and Elijah, can be examined through a scientific lens to understand the mechanisms behind such a prolonged period of drought and heat. To say that Elijah had opened mountains and deserts full of worms and side issues is not an understatement.

The interconnected nature of Earth's weather systems means that localized alterations, as in the Levant, could have far-reaching impacts, potentially affecting global weather patterns and climate systems. With the immoveable and unchangeable rock of the revealed fact that "God is love" and never ceases to be love, we press on taking grasp of the divine goal and purpose in the fallout from Elijah's short prophetic statement, a statement he will have heard in heaven and repeated on earth.

So this writer demands of himself to query Elijah's whys, wherefores and how's. To pursue his foundations of a lifestyle that changed his world and his people deeply. Come with me, and let's dig deep and not be afraid to find out the negatives and lacks concerning our own faith. Just how does a man get to that intimacy with Almighty Yahweh? That is what these pages are all about. I want to get my heart and hands on Elijah's outrageous faith, his intrusive conviction, as well as his divinely created extreme strategy.

Keith Lannon Saturday 7 December 2024

INTRODUCTION

ONE WAY TICKET TO TISHBE PLEASE.

Circa 2,800 years ago, a certain man hit the headlines in Hebrew Canaan, then known as Israel, up north, as opposed to Judah down south. Not that they had any newspapers, of course, but whatever the equivalent was, this man caused the Beatlemania or the Taylor Swift equivalent of the day, apart from one thing. He was not a singer or a comedian but a man of God. There were lots of Godless idol worshippers. The place was full of "gods" but void of "God." This man was seriously Godly. Totally non-religious but Godly to a level that you and I have not seen or, imagined, or even conceived of. It started in a place called Tishbe.

He was considered (and still is) so important that the official historian-narrative-writers of the day stopped writing about the long cacophonic list of Hebrew kings that were born, reigned, did good and/or bad and then died. During what we call the real-time of the two books of Kings in the Hebrew Bible, the scribes of the day refrained from the conventional chronicle listing and homed in purely on this man as well as his chosen successor. Imagine if you can, that for several decades, the official historians of the day had no story to tell but the narrative of these two men. I am telling you that these two men were something else. Yes! Thirty per cent of the books we refer to as First and Second Kings are devoted almost totally to these two characters of God, who were prophets.

NO SMALL TALK IN TISHBE.

The first of these two giants – and giants they were - was the man from Tishbe, Elijah, who, unlike any of the other Old Testament prophets, had a known, direct successor to what he was doing. Elisha, mentored by Elijah, carried on as the national prophet from the very moment Elijah left this world. It was two men, yet it was one wave of divine selection. One ministry. One mission. Two men. Minimal dialogue, yet maximum impact, was Elijah's style. Elijah's dialogue in scripture is all short, sharp and to the point. No small talk.

NO RELIGIOSITY IN TISHBE.

The deeds, words, and influence of Elijah and his successor are like some sort of fantasy world of miracles, struggles and engagement with hellish obstructions, always resulting in their total and absolute victory. So far did these men live in, "another world" (or what Walter Brueggemann refers to as "the elsewhere") while they walked among men, that I find writers, preachers, and teachers tend to discuss them as almost unreal - comic figures nearly. Like Superman or Spiderman. Everything about these two prophets reads like some surreal graphic novel (that's a posh euphemism for a comic). These two heroes of the faith were full of God, and yet totally lacking in religiosity. I have never read a book or heard a sermon concerning Elijah or Elisha, that encourages me to emulate the heights of what they both soared to. There is a reality of other worlds constantly in the eye, presence and psyche of this duo that we seriously need to explore, yet sadly only theorise about. Having never read a book that satiated my thirsty heart concerning them, I have chosen to write the volume that satisfies my heart myself. Allow me to share my thoughts and convictions. However, I have to say that I am talking about a venture that reveals my lack of thought and conviction rather than my positive assertions about prophecy and its intrinsic attributes. I want to go and visit Tishbe – if you know what I mean euphemistically.

NO MEDIOCROTY IN TISHBE.

Elijah the Tishbite and Elisha of Abel- Meholah were just plain wild. Wildly Godly, that is. Unrestrained, with outrageously boundary-breaking-theology of the limits of God and practical faith, and more fearfully and righteously dangerous than small-minded kings, queens and dictators. Pure "100% proof" Godliness is dangerous you know. You may be sure of that. And we have no indication that they were steadied or stabilised with a few year's dosage of university or book learning helping them to sanitise the God of the Bible. Mediocrity was a filthy swear word to these two.

NO REDACTION OF SCRIPTURE IN TISHBE.

Western institutionalised Christianity is a vastly redacted animal and quite an extensive distance from the spirit of the text-scrolled narrative that it claims as the validation for its own existence. The Middle Eastern text of both Testaments is, in the West, of course, commonly interpreted from the viewpoint of Western worldviews and European and American paradigmatic presuppositions by Western theologians and Western scholars and philosophers. Even the sanitised, packaged, western mainstream theology has more relevance to Europeans and the so-called Western developed world than to the rest of the globe. Elijah spoke Hebrew, the language of the sacred scrolls. Nothing was, therefore, lost in translation or interpretation.

NO "PLAYING IT SAFE" IN TISHBE.

William Golding, the British novelist, was quoted as saying, "Marx, Darwin and Freud are the three most crashing bores of the Western World. Simplistic popularization of their ideas has thrust our world into a mental straitjacket from which we can only escape by the most anarchic intellectual violence." He says this on the grounds of a philosophical perspective that states when all the bees, worms or whatever are released from a tin, it is impossible to put things like Marxism, evolution, and or Freudian paradigmatic philosophy back in the theoretical euphemistic tin, away from the public mind. That straitjacket has somewhat reached and impacted Christianity in the aforementioned Western world. Secular rationality, so-called intellectual enlightenment, and Freudian psychology have rocked the stability of the good ship "Gospel Faith". Eastern Christianity does not properly relate to the contemporary Western template. Russian, Greek, Ethiopian and Coptic Orthodoxy have little bearing on Western Christian dialogue, even though it seems they have captivated a greater percentage of their national followers than the Western brand ever has. There was no attempt at balance or safety with the man from Tishbe.

NO SANITISED YAHWEH IN TISHBE.

Elijah has no sanitised or redacted Yahweh. Elijah is a wild, giant, dangerous prophet. Yahweh is a wild, infinitely giant, dangerous God. He is too big for any box or tin. Too wild for any attempts to tame Him or redact Him, and too dangerous to dilute what he has revealed to mankind in the person of Jesus Christ. Incredible cathedrals, embellished gowns, mitres and surpluses do not bring majesty or reflect his glory. Elijah carried the intrinsic danger of having met God face to face and was transformed somewhere along the road into the fearful, awe-inspiring, God-carrying human being that he was. He was conscious and aware that "Nothing is impossible" and that the received and believed word from God, when spoken out with faith, was the source of life, death, and/or creation and/or destruction. Life and death are in the power of the tongue. This was an eternal factual truth that Elijah carried with him. God was raw with Elijah, totally without any sanitising of the Divine.

NO WESTERNISATION OF YAHWEH IN TISHBE.

Translating the Hebrew and Aramaic Old Testament as well as the Greek New Testament should, of course, render such a product as what we could refer to as a secretary's job. However, it is phenomenal how Western rational logic can dilute "purer translation" of ancient Hebrew and Greek, redacting the biblical thrust of some of its meaning. Middle Eastern Elijah read Middle Eastern interpretation of what needed to happen.

NO LIMITATION BORDERS FOR VISIONARY POSSIBILITIES IN TISHBE.

By this Western "dampening process", the presentation of the biblical deity is generally sanitised, diluted and adapted for Western cultural normalcy. The wild, untamed Lion that is the Bible, with the equally unfettered and undomesticated God who inhabits the text, is incarcerated securely behind the bars of the prison of "balance" and "rationality" and left in the zoo of religiosity. Like all wild animals caged by man, the Lion still roars, the Gorilla still thumps his superior chest, and the elephants still trump loudly. But it has degenerated to a false roar, a benign thump, and a penny whistle of a trumpet. The beasts are ruling zoo paddocks of denominationalisation instead of the vast jungles and planes of their nativity, calling for nothing but to be fed by their keepers. Instead of roaming across many miles and acres each day, they have ten square metre kingdoms while they lose their majesty and natural vocation. They are free monarchs of God's creation, placed in restricted quarters to be watched and studied, while the visiting humans cry "Ooh!" and "Aah!" at the wonder of the sight of majestic divinely created monarchs of different areas of the planet being visited in their tiny boxes and cages of prison, being nought but a spectre of what they are in the wild. The Old Testament, probably the wildest of the two Divine volumes, is commonly dampened down more amongst Western Christian "zookeepers", as Yahweh seems far too wild for many "sophisticated" minds of "non-easterners" who live with the delusion that "We always know better," while all previous generations, empires and nations were just superstitious ignoramuses. There were no borders to those to whom the scriptures came. Zarapheth was way beyond the understood barriers.

NO TAMING OF THE ALMIGHTY IN TISHBE.

God is wild. In the Old Testament, he is multi-voiced, highly complex, and, according to Brueggemann, "irascible and self-conflicted." Like that classic line in C.S. Lewis's writings where Mr Beaver tells the children about Aslan the Lion (a characterisation of Christ). "He's wild, you know. Not like a tame lion. But He's good!" In the Narnian stories of Lewis's Lion, Aslan won world-shaking battles simply by roaring. God has a similar roar.

So, yes! Western Christianity is undoubtedly somewhat redacted from the original raw biblical brand. The bible does not need rewriting, just rereading, re-understanding, and even occasionally re-translating without the bias of twenty-first century paradigms.

NO TIPTOEING AROUND THE WORLD ISSUES IN TISHBE.

My meditations and thoughts into Elijah's character show how Elijah was a completely eccentric fundamentalist in his interpretation of the sacred scrolls. We will see how he accepted, believed and acted upon some of the most incredible divine statements in the books of Moses that it would seem nobody had taken seriously, or at least thought Moses was simply writing poetry that exaggerated Yahweh's anger at idolatry. Elijah read the scrolls, feared God, and acted on some of the most "far-fetched statements that Moses ever wrote. There was no "Documentary Hypothesis" playing with his mind and giving him wooden legs to walk on, robbing him like spiritual Thalidomide of the arm and limbs of his will to serve God.

NO MEANINGLESS CERTITUDES IN TISHBE.

In the dark offices of the "Rewriting of Christianity Department," let me explain how false revolution becomes accepted as the norm, precept by precept, and line by line. The idea that biblical paraphrases lead to "redacted Christianity" suggests that when biblical texts are paraphrased or simplified, essential meanings and nuances may be lost or altered. This can lead to a version of Christianity that is less faithful to the original texts. There was no constitutional set of beliefs in the small print on the Hebrew Bible scrolls to create prepared theology systems. I have several paraphrased copies of the Bible on my bookshelves. I read them. I accept them. But when I am reading paraphrases, a red flashing light continues to distract me like at the operating theatre at a hospital, or a recording at a TV studio. "Beware Paraphrase".

Paraphrases lead to and create interpretation variabilities. Paraphrases involve interpretation that messes with the meanings of translation. That is the only reason for creating them. "Let's make an eastern mystical document as acceptable to western thought and secular mindset as we possibly can." Such a goal cannot possibly be achieved without introducing biases and/or personal agendas. This may result in a version of Christianity that reflects the paraphraser's beliefs rather than the trajectory of the original texts. Paraphrases may also adapt to the paradigmatic demands of western culture.

NO LIMITATION - BUILDING PARAPHRASES IN TISHBE.

Paraphrases end up with a loss of Depth. The original language of the Bible is rich with meaning, symbolism, and cultural context. Paraphrasing can strip away these layers, potentially leading to a superficial understanding. The intricacies of the ancient Hebrew are fertile with parabolic wisdom.

Because paraphrases are birthed with a burden to make a statement by the authors (yes! I said author, deliberately placing its source as human, while the Hebrew was more clearly divinely inspired) and their selective emphases are sure to be made with intentionality. All paraphrases highlight certain themes while downplaying or omitting others. That is the whole point why people write paraphrases. These selective emphases can shape theological perspectives and practices.

When accepted as "the version to be read" in any particular group, church, stream or denomination, and the novelty of a "new version" wears down, and congregations state, "Let's see what the Word says," they will be all opening a paraphrase to depend on for specific truths on delicate issues. Paraphrases will have impact on Doctrinal issues. Over time, undoubtedly, widespread use of paraphrased texts can influence community beliefs and practices, potentially leading to doctrinal shifts that diverge from traditional interpretations that came into being before the word "paraphrase" was heard of or utilised.

Paraphrases create unintentional tensions between cultural relevance and faithfulness to the inspired text. While paraphrases may make biblical texts more accessible, there is a tension between making scripture relatable to the everchanging modern language and maintaining strict faithfulness to its original message.

In summary, while paraphrasing can help people engage with biblical texts, it is important to be aware of its potential to alter the core tenets of Christianity. Engaging with multiple translations and commentaries can help provide a more rounded understanding of the scriptures and the Eastern culture in which they were created and written in. Paraphrases are useful for reference and street language interpretation of difficult passages.

NO "WOKE" THINKING IN TISHBE.

Once upon a time, there appeared in the Book shops, next to all the historic translations of scripture (and there were not too many of them in the late sixties and early seventies), "The Living Bible". This volume clearly and proudly declared itself to be a "Paraphrase." It was good. We knew what it was. A "paraphrase of any book is made to be a restatement of a text in different words, usually created to aid its meaning to would-be-readers. Question: Why would we need a restatement of the Bible? Answer: Because of its Eastern mysticism and parallelisms that the Westerners on the streets aren't too good at following. On top of that, it was polled that Bible reading was on the decrease. For this reason, certain Christian scholars produced Bible paraphrases. I remember being told that Kenneth N. Taylor created "The Living Bible" so that it could be understood by his little Granddaughter in 1971. He used the American Standard Version as his base text.

Fantastic! Great idea! The greatest and most profoundly impacting presentation of scripture ever written was redacted for the sake of a granddaughter. With that, I have no problem. It is not the real thing. It is a paraphrase. We welcomed it – and rightly so, methinks.

As a single piece of trivia illustrating my caution of paraphrases, it was understood that because Taylor did not believe in prophecy in the church today, the word "prophecy" in the New Testament was paraphrased to "inspired preaching". Pentecostals didn't like it, but Taylor was, like any self-respecting Grandad, desperate to win his Granddaughter. Other words and concepts throughout the volume were redacted to Taylor's own belief system. Christians accepted such flaws - *because it was accepted as a paraphrase.* That was 1972.

The Living Bible was a million-seller. I mean, seriously worldwide. Even Pentecostal evangelists like TL Osborn wrote a book entitled, "The Good Life" about Christian living, written with possibly hundreds of "scripture quotes" validating every statement he made in the volume. The quotations were 100% ALL from the Living Bible (TLB).

Unfortunately, TLB was such an incredible project, that book publishers everywhere wanted to jump on the publishing bandwagon. Then came 1976. "The Good News Translation". (GNT) Sold with the rarely read "introduction" saying it "was a paraphrase'" but with "Translation" written on the cover. Followed by "Today's English Version" (TEV). "Version" on the cover, paraphrase in the small print. Then the Adventists came out with "The Clear Word", another paraphrase. God's Word?

To cut the story short all this was followed by "Contemporary English Version", "God's Word" etc, and even "The New Living Bible" which is a paraphrase of a paraphrase.

What's my point? My point is that the basic philosophical bent towards dynamic equivalents instead of stricter translation trajectories gives room for personal opinions, a western rationalisation to be used in the name of "helping the biblically illiterate westerner to read the Bible", redacting the strict, and at times vital, biblical concepts to softer and less revolutionary significance. All paraphrases, to a degree, contain various indistinct and indefinite verbiage that is full of uncertainty, personal viewpoints, and dissonant concepts of the faith.

Let me shout it out loud. I am definitely **not** against paraphrases! Lord, give us more! What I am calling for is that the word, "Paraphrase" is part of the large fonts on the cover. The Western biblical illiteracy, rampant in the occidental world, is enhanced by teaching the population that scripture is almost a "Western production."

Redacted Christianity may increase recruitment in churches, putting bums on benches, but softens discipleship and conceptualisation of the Gospel message.

THE WESTERN PAROCHIAL NATURE OF REDACTED CHRISTIANITY CAN LEAD TO CULTURAL DILUTION OF THE FAITH – BUT NOT IN TISHBE.

It is generally accepted that the deep faultline in the presentation of God in the eighteenth and nineteenth centuries that spread from Europe and later from the USA was the respective cultures of the overseas evangelists and missionaries, cultures which were exported with possibly more emphasis than that of the biblical concepts learnt from the sacred scrolls. In sweet ignorance, westerners assumed that global Christianity, as defined above, was the divine norm of what needs to be shared and grafted in and around the planet. Redacted Christianity was then nuanced also by the culture of British Imperialism and western values in general. Yes, western Christianity is now clearly global. Yet we are, generally speaking, still convinced that we are the mature, correct, divinely guided section of the church, and so we need to build all of the hemispheric southerners and easterners into clones of the west – to be just like us.

It is a painfully accepted point of history that a huge amount of Western missionaries did more to "Anglicise" Africa and the East as we did to Christianise them.

But note: the Eastern church has arisen far beyond Western orthodoxy. Eastern Christian orthodoxy is much more embedded in their respective societies as a whole than Christianity is in the West. Westerners don't like the thought of the "younger ruling the elder" in this context. However, it is true they are getting bigger and purer than anything the West has to offer. We (Western Christians) have acted like the world's spiritual policeman of the faith, damping down on excesses and spiritual explorations because "that isn't how *we* do it". Historical events like Paul Yonggi Cho's million-member Korean church in the eighties, African and Eastern prophets that far exceed their equivalent in the West, manifestations of healing amongst the masses, and news of witch doctors becoming powerful ministers of God are more rampant than anything we witness in our "superior" west. Holy Spirit power, grace and far-reaching far-seeing prophets are in abundance throughout Africa and the East, leaving the West behind. They seem to be doing a better job of emulating the man from Tishbe and his successor from Abel-Mehole. And they clearly seem much more straightforward than high-posted church leaders debating, "Did Moses really write the Pentateuch?"

Western Christianity continues to sentence "the prosperity gospel" to a torturous heretic's death, refusing to differentiate the character of the high-profile people that push the teaching to a hideous, ungodly perspective on life, ignoring the valid texts of scripture that present the God of provision. The fact that some gruesome statements along the lines of, "Send me $500.00 today, and God has told me you will be blessed," suggests worldly criminal manipulation of the vulnerable, which is surely damnable and to be abhorred and denounced. However, the comprehensive viewpoint of the scriptures, like the blessings of Deuteronomy 28:1-14, 2 Corinthians 9:8, and similarly pointed texts, get painfully ignored by so-called "balanced" ministers of the word, avoiding those biblical statements like the plague for fear of being labelled "prosperity preachers" themselves. I despise any teaching that is used to manipulate the vulnerable out of their livelihood, yet without any shadow of a doubt, Moses, Paul and – wait for it – the Lord Jesus Christ Himself, had a tinge of "prosperity teaching", as seen in a body of similar scriptures that tend to get neglected (i.e., Luke 6:38). In an attempt to curtail mischievous ungodly practices, the truth is ignored for "decency" and reputations sake. The pastor who initiated me into the Bible told me fifty years ago that, "The answer to bad use of scripture is not no use, but proper use." Non-use always produces redacted Christianity carrying redacted Bibles infusing redacted faith and leaving the redacted destiny of life. Some people are simply off balance on the subject of balance.

All the concepts and promissory loaded statements of Christ around His teaching that lays on us the idea of "give and it will be given unto you," suggest that our condemnation of the so-called, "prosperity preachers" and their message is an out-and-out disposing of the heavenly baby of truth being dumped along with the absolutely filthy bathwater of its main prosperity proponents. Orthodoxy, as is generally understood in the West, is merely a set of rules that can, when clung to too tightly, prevent spiritual exploration. I prefer the whole package of biblical truth as my level of orthodoxy.

MENTALLY NEGOTIATING UNREDACTED BIBLICAL VISTAS IN TISHBE.

I have read and browsed many books, commentaries, and study collections on the subject of "Elijah and Elisha", and I am flummoxed. These two men were outrageously astonishing in their work as prophets, and their understanding of the cosmos and their conscious control over, and handling of, the awesome and infinite power of God. Most writers have created devotional or doctrinal statements encouraging us to "follow in their footsteps" as tidy, correct moral believers. Yet my take on these two men is that their godliness, view of God, courage when facing danger, and personal vision of the kingdom of God goes light-years further than the devotional reads I have come across throughout my life. We are universally encouraged to follow Elijah and his faith and boldness, yet preachers, teachers, book writers and film-makers almost unanimously are silent on his command to "slay the 450 prophets of Baal". Diluted message for the sake of Political Correctness.

NO EXPECTED OLD TESTAMENT LEGALISM IN TISHBE.

The lives of these men of God were extraordinarily exciting and astonishingly revolutionary in the society they lived in. Over many years I have sought after commentaries, devotionals, historical books, articles, university dissertations and recorded teachings and sermons on the Tishbite and the man from Abel-Meholah, but none has ever satisfied me as having grasped the full stature of who and what they were and their relevance to Christianity today. Activities, words, and prayers that brought the visible, powerful, impacting agency of God into people's lives and the direction of nations, were, it seems, a normal day at the office for these two fellows.

To properly negotiate the text on the biblical scrolls that itemise all we have about these two men, one must raise the bar – update the software – get a new model of receptor on one's worldview, paradigm, or belief system – whatever epithet the reader uses to define his ontology – and start as a child from the beginning of things. I promise you that the "elsewhere," from which Elijah and Elisha gathered their beliefs and insights, and the norms of their daily reality are mind-blowingly non-western and filled with conceptual realities that stun universal secular (and religious) thought.

When these two men are thoroughly examined, one can only conclude that they took prophetic practice to a new expansive border. They brought divine provision in the midst of hardship 800 years before Christ Himself. They both lived with such an intimacy with Yahweh that at times, it is difficult to define whether they were doing what God asked of them or whether God was doing what they spoke off the cuff. Their understanding of God's active and real agency in the world was beyond anything Israel had experienced since the

Exodus and the forty years wandering. They were also beyond where Christian cosmology is perceived today.

Views on the reality of life and death, sickness and health, heaven and hell, relationship with God and many other topics that arise within the various modules of the narrative concerning the two men who took faith and God-given authority to planes that many have failed to touch, are faced squarely. In fact, apart from Christ Himself, the machinery of faith within these two men was of a calibre that extremely few have stepped into. Where these two men lived is so extreme in the spectrum of things spiritual that many simply concede defeat and are reduced to talking about how "this could not happen today." There we go …biblical redaction. Some even strain at a gnat and swallow a camel by suggesting, "It is so astounding it couldn't happen at all". I pity such thought patterns presented in the name of Christ by readers of the biblical scrolls.

I believe in prophecy, healing, miracles, and the agency of God in the world today in the worldwide church of Jesus Christ. I believe that in all times, eras, dispensations, and epochs from the fall of man to the present day, (and on into the future until who knows when), divine prophecy has been current and is to be expected and sought after. Although a little farmer in the Hebrew Bible named Amos stated in the eighth century before Christ that, "Yahweh does nothing without telling his prophets", it does not mean that it was true for his lifetime alone. There were prophets in the real-time of the Genesis narrative many generations before Amos, and God told them what He was about to do. There are prophets to impact the world yet future in the closing chapters of the book of Revelation, where God tells them what is about to take place. There are prophets in the world today who are hearing God about what has happened, what is happening, and what will soon be happening. There have always been non-canonical, non-biblical prophets and prophecies. By that, I do not mean that they are anti- or contradictory to anything that is contained in the bible. (We shall discuss this point later.)

THERE IS A SPECTRUM TO MOST SPIRITUAL THINGS – TISHBE IS THE EXTREME.

All prophets are on a spectrum. All prophecy is also on a spectrum. A spectrum means a gradient. With all prophecy there is deep, deeper, and deepest. There is coming soon, later, and latest. There is clear, clearer, and clearest. There are some prophecies that are weightier than others. This has always been literally, factually true. There are some serious load-bearing revelations in the Bible. There are others that seem to be vague, creating more questions than answers. Some contemporary prophecies may not even seem to be prophecies at all to the ear of the cursory cynic.

The gift of prophecy within the context of the "gifts of the Spirit" is explained in 1 Corinthians 14:3 where it states, "the one who prophesies speaks to people for their **strengthening, encouraging and comfort.**" Those three criteria are good and valuable. We thank God for such prophetic input from church members in the gathering. However, the letter to the Ephesians talks of people who don't just prophesy, but who are God given prophets, gifted to the church and who **lay the very foundations of the faith and character of the church they are part of**. Ephesians 2:19-20 talks of believers being "fellow citizens with God's people and also members of his household, built on the foundation of the apostles and prophets, with Christ Jesus himself as the chief cornerstone." That is a huge distance away from the 1 Corinthians 14:3 parameters. Prophecy, when delivered by a prophet who is a gift of Christ, is laying spiritual foundations into the body of Christ. That is two hugely different points on the prophetic spectrum than strengthening, encouraging, and comforting. In this very area of spiritual exploration, the apostle encourages every Christian to get their feet on the first rung of the prophetic spectrum, and thereafter to climb with it. I Corinthians 14:1 calls to every Christian that has ever lived; "Pursue love. Desire spiritual gifts, but especially that you may prophesy." There must always be more! I shall enlarge on this in a later chapter.

This ultimate "Elijah/Elisha peak" of prophetic performance violently challenges much long-held general evangelical theology. As one reads their narrative, one is even forced, at times, to ask, "Is this the will of Elijah, Elisha, or God?" "Has God given away His sovereignty?"

THE WIDE SPECTRUM OF THE POWER OF THE SPOKEN WORD - ULTIMATES IN TISHBE.

Let me make note that when Christ walked throughout Israel and cursed a fig tree, that tree withered within 24 hours. When it was brought to His attention his response referred not only to his own actions but explained the words and actions of the likes of Elijah and Elisha. Jesus said, "Have faith in God. (Some prefer the phrase to be, "Have the faith of God") Truly I tell you, that if anyone says to this mountain, "Go, be cast into the sea," and does not doubt in their heart but believes that what they say will happen, it will be done for them." Elijah and Elisha had a good and well-practised understanding of Mark 11:22, 800 years before Christ uttered it in real-time. Christ was saying stuff that was new to the disciples but was an ancient ever-present truth since the world began. It was the knowledge that Elijah and Elisha walked in. From where did Elijah and Elisha learn this stuff – and I don't mean academically, as learned from a book. I mean learned at the coal face by doing it and experience. Mark 11:22 in exposition of the statement and its context, cannot escape from the point that Jesus was saying, "Any of you 12 may follow this principle." And thereafter it must logically apply to anybody who reads the Bible and believes it Today.

NO SAFETY NETS FOR PROPHETS OR MINISTERS IN TISHBE.

My point with all this is to help us grasp what is happening when Elijah says to 50 soldiers, "If I am a man of God, let fire come down from heaven and consume you." He said this three times to three different groups of fifty soldiers, and immediately having stated it, fire from heaven killed each 50. Was this really God speaking? Or was it Elijah's own frustrations? He virtually said, "If I am what you address me as", and they had spoken without really believing the title with which they addressed him, "let fire come down and consume you." I say again, one is clearly forced to debate with oneself as to whether God was following Elijah? Or did God inspire Elijah to make such a statement? We cannot and must not redact what it says. By all means, the issue must be open to debate. There is a detail on the dynamics of prophecy that is not perceived by the masses. The intrinsic wild beast's roar is in the elusive detail.

NO ORTHODOX PREDICTABLE MINISTRY IN TISHBE.

Something similar happened in later years with Elisha in full prophetic flow. The Shunamite woman had encouraged her husband to build an extension to her house for Elisha to stay whenever he passed by (which seems to have been quite often). In essence, Elisha was so pleased with her generosity he asked her what he could do for her. She expressed to him that she lacked for nothing and left the room. However, after she had left the room, his servant said to Elisha, "She is childless". He quickly, spontaneously, told the servant to recall her. As she re-entered, on this spur of the moment thought, Elisha told her that she would have a son twelve months hence. She begged him not to mock her. As if he would! A year later, she had the promised child in her arms. Question! Was that spur-of-the-moment thought, Elisha's or God's? On the surface of the scene painted by the scriptures, it was simply Mark 11:22 in effect. The creativity of the Word of God in a man's mouth is awesomely powerful – to move even mountains. The Old Testament talks of power and life and death in the tongue. This needs to be understood and mastered.

It is my purpose, while highlighting the biblical narrative of Elijah, that his lifestyle and mission among people was rational, necessary, and needful then, as much as it is today. I have met, talked with, and witnessed prophets in the world in our generation. Alph Lukau (South Africa), Shepherd Bushiri (Malawi), T.J. Thomas (India), and others.

I have heard these men as a conversational aside to people, ask a personal preference, and responded without as much as a "Thus says Yahweh," saying, "OK! If that is the detail you prefer, you shall have it as you prefer." I am talking of several prophetic words that I have witnessed and heard, like being present and hearing a prophet say to a barren couple, "You shall have a child". The husband, interrupting the proceedings, exclaimed, "But prophet, my wife is 40 years old, and she wants three boys!" "Really! Then you shall conceive and have triplets," was the happy spontaneous response. The whole thing occurring with laughter, spontaneity and lightness. Nine months or so later, the couple turn up in the church with the afore promised triplets. We have to engraft into our hearts a worldview and theology that grasps this kind of phenomena easily. It is part of the Elijah lifestyle. It is him we are after to emulate.

In a visit to a native African prophetic ministry, I observed that people converted by remarkable miraculous healings, or deliverance from demonic power, or those who were set free simply by a prophetic word that highlighted issues that nobody else in the world knew about apart from the person who was the subject of the prophetic message, created a church group that were extremely strong in faith, and fervent in prayer and personal evangelism.

NO FAITH LIMITING TENETS TO RESTRICT PRACTICAL FAITH IN TISHBE.

My hope and prayer is, that once these pages are read, the contextual chapters will be seen as revelation on the chapters looking at the biblical text. My motivation is to encourage Christians to seek to prophesy, and to seek to move up the spectrum of prophecy with the appropriate weight of character, and to remain humble in the light of the weight of prophetic consciousness that people will be carrying as a result.

There is a spectrum in human accretions to prophecy as a whole, and to prophecy and prophets in particular. Many of those biblical so-called Hebrew "writing prophets" were working to reform the religious practices of the worshippers of Yahweh, attempting to free it from its historical heritage and misuse.

There is a spectrum in recipient nations and people. In the Book of Jeremiah, it is said that prophets, diviners, and soothsayers were in the neighbouring countries of Judah: in Edom, Moab, Ammon, Tyre, and Sidon (27:9). Since so little is known about those prophets, the question of the uniqueness of Hebrew prophecy is difficult to assess.

We need to get to grips with the dynamics and practice of the New Testaments definition of contemporary prophecy.

By examining the prophetic gift that carried Elijah, and was thereafter imparted to Elisha, we should have a chance to grapple with that which underlies all prophecy both Old and New Testament. We need to pursue Christ. In the pursuit of Christ, we need to pursue prophecy. In the pursuit of prophecy we need to emulate master prophets. To pursue them we need to scour the biblical scrolls.

EVERYTHING IN TISHBE IS UNCOMMON.

"And if you say in your heart, 'How may we know the word that the Lord has not spoken?'—when a prophet speaks in the name of the Lord, if the word does not come to pass or come true, that is a word that the Lord has not spoken."

Deuteronomy 18:21-22

"Remember the former things of old; for I am God, and there is no other; I am God, and there is none like me, declaring the end from the beginning and from ancient times things not yet done."

Isaiah 46:9-10

"Before I formed you in the womb I knew you, and before you were born I consecrated you; I appointed you a prophet to the nations."

Jeremiah 1:5

"For the Lord God does nothing without revealing his secret to his servants the prophets."

Amos 3:7

"Do not think that I have come to abolish the Law or the Prophets; I have not come to abolish them but to fulfill them."

Matthew 5:17

"In the last days it shall be, God declares, that I will pour out my Spirit on all flesh, and your sons and your daughters shall prophesy..."

Acts 2:17-18

"Follow the way of love and eagerly desire gifts of the Spirit, especially prophecy."

1 Corinthians 14:1

"But the one who prophesies speaks to people for their upbuilding and encouragement and consolation."

1 Corinthians 14:3

"For the testimony of Jesus is the spirit of prophecy."

Revelation 19:10

These few verses collectively, skeletally, illustrate the nature of prophecy as a divine communication from God, its role in sometimes revealing future events, and its general purpose is guiding and encouraging people. They highlight the consistency of God's message throughout scripture and the fulfillment of prophecies in Christ.

PART A

GETTING TO GRIPS WITH THE NATURE OF THE PROPHETIC GIFT

1

AN INTRODUCTORY PORTRAIT OF THE MAN FROM TISHBE.

(AS FAR AS WE CAN DESCRIBE HIM.)

The prophet Elijah is a total mind-blower no matter from which category or perspective one looks. He's, first of all, a bombshell if we only imagine what he physically looked like from all the biblical data – and there isn't much of that. He's a disturbing tornado, historically, when one considers where he went, the places where he turned up and the activities he undertook. He seems almost surreal. However, he is not a fictional character at all. How can I be sure of that? On the grounds that he is an integral part and parcel of the Jewish, biblical history, the most significant belts and braces that nails his narrative as factual and historical is that he appeared with Christ and Moses when the Master was transfigured (Matthew 17) and that he is highlighted in Luke 4:26 when Messiah Himself refers to the fact that Elijah was sent to a gentile widow in Zarapheth. Jesus didn't ever make tangible historical references to empty legends. Abraham Heschel thoroughly explains how all the biblical prophets were "some of the most disturbing people who have ever lived". Of all the prophetic disturbances and the disturbing personalities, Elijah takes the cake. He was wild. He was giant, and he was dangerous.

Elijah is the only man we know of that came from a place called Tishbe. In fact, nobody is 100% sure where Tishbe is. Scholars and archaeologists do not have a definitive pin on their biblical maps defining the site of Tishbe. Several distant, local-to-Gilead legends have it nailed, of course. "He lived here in our village!" I would not dare to call them dreamers. I would like to stand in the marketplace of anywhere that claimed to be Elijah's earthly domicile. The clearest historical geographic reference is in the Old Testament apocryphal scrolls: *"Tishbe, which is to the south of Kadesh Naphtali in Galilee above Asher" (Tobit 1:2 RSV)*. If this statement is true, it would suggest that sometime in Elijah's life, being born on the northwest banks of Jordan and the sea of Galilee, he must have at some time moved to Gilead on the east of Jordan precincts of the Promised Land. It is, however, widely asserted by theologians and archaeologists that Tishbe was in Gilead. It is probably because the rough, wild, lapidarian terrain of Gilead matches Elijah's character as biblically portrayed. Gilead is situated in modern-day Jordan and means "rocky". It is also contemporarily referred to by the Aramaic name Yegar-Sahadutha, which carries the same meaning as the Hebrew "Gilead," namely "a heap of stones as a testimony" (Genesis 31:47–48). There is a minority of scholars who suggest that "Elijah the Tishbite" should be translated as "Elijah the stranger". I refuse to play with that toy of a thought. Who in the Bible is known by such an epithet? Elijah was a prince among prophets, not a stranger.

All that we know of, concerning this man's activities, his appearance, his lifestyle, and especially his departing from this life, is extraordinary, if not bizarre. The man is a colossus of the faith as taught in the scripture, even with his flaws and weaknesses. Yes! He had a bag full of them too. I use the present tense "is" when referring to him simply because his presence in the biblical narrative in both biblical testaments brings him to life – life that impacts the serious reader when seeking after an ever-deepening relationship with God.

These pages are being written to "home-in" on this man. Hopefully, when negotiated with, both the writer and reader of these pages will see some stuff that we have never engaged with before. Elijah is a man who, once one can see the whites of his eyes and hear the timbre of his voice, will undoubtedly become a modelled harbour and a safe house for the recovery of one's meditative soul and the long-term sustenance of faith. God, assist me to tread where Elijah trod.

I have read many volumes biographing both Elijah as well as the history and development of prophecy. However, I have never read a book about Elijah that satisfies me. I have never read a book about prophecy that satisfies me. I am not a prophet, and I am not writing these pages because I think I know more than anybody else on the subject, far from it. In fact, it is my thirst to understand the dynamics of prophets and prophecy that have me spending long days (and even nights on occasions) scraping for understanding and vision about this divinely supernatural man and subject. Call it a "thinking aloud" book. Call it a "cry of my heart." Call it "Lannon's research notes," rather than a volume by "a man that knows". Because I don't know and am straining myself about it, I am seeking as I write, holding on to the principle that if I talk (write) as I think, my mind and spirit will be illuminated a little further to arrest the truth that emerges from my exploration. To meditate is to chew and to mutter to one's self. To chew and mutter my thoughts on paper is to write. May the thoughts of my soul and the meditations of my heart be acceptable to you, oh God, and be imbibed by my readers.

I am well aware that there are certain sections of the church of Christ around the world that believe anything supernatural is a "no-go-area" of thought and practice. They are referred to as "cessationists." They refer to *themselves* as "cessationists". If you have never heard that term utilised before about people who have faith in Christ, may I suggest that you pause for a moment or two to grasp why that word is used. I am very much ***not*** a cessationist. My own personal critique of myself is that I believe very much in the miraculous, but I sink into disappointment because I see very little of it in the lives of others, and most especially in myself. I see less of the miraculous that reading the Bible suggests I should be seeing. Why should the Bible feed us with "All things are possible to him that believes" if it isn't prompting us to expect miraculous things. That is another ingredient in the soup that feeds my motivation for the exploration that has created these pages. Why would the Person who declares to us that He is "The way, the truth and the life", tell us that if we meet certain prefatory conditions, we can tell mountains to move and call the dead to life and as we say it we shall see it. How can the cessationist declare that "the age of the miraculous" has ceased and then talk of inerrant scrolls of divine writ?

I have always been astounded reading books about Elijah. The reason why I have never been satisfied when reading tomes about him, is simply because writers hold him in such deep awe (especially the cessationists) that the lessons and spiritual applications are somewhat reduced, censored and expurgated to encouragements for us all to be strong, to follow Christ in hard situations and to be unafraid to stand alone. And there is nothing at all wrong or insipid about such exhortations. But …

But to learn such a lesson from such a man is like asking NASA's astronauts to encourage 4-year-olds to play spaceships. Nothing wrong or immoral about such a trite illustration, but the image of moon-visiting astronauts in such a simple toddlers class seems to have a ton of knowledge and understanding going to waste. Elijah clearly lived in a deep and heavenly well of the world of the Spirit (a well that has permanent vacancies for anybody who has faith in Christ) and gaining faith to "walk strong in God" is of course, always a sound exhortation for any human being. However, I have never read a book that says, "Strive to live, walk, and talk like Elijah in the realm of the supernatural." I have never read a volume that taught, "Learn to prophesy at Elijah's depth." "Learn to speak the words that God gives you as God gave Elijah, no matter how far-fetched they sound to the outsider". "Prophesy in a manner that impacts the world for good and solid transformation". Elijah trod - in reality - "giant steps|" for mankind, with small steps for the concept and reality of prophecy.

"But that was Elijah's call to move in those dimensions". Oh yes. There are several "spiritual benzodiazepines" that are prescribed by cessationists (as well as charismatics and Pentecostals) that are dosed as believers with the intention of calming down the zeal and spiritual ambition for exploring in realms where we haven't been before. But we should never forget that the drugs that are prescribed to remove anxiety also induce Drowsiness, sedation, dizziness and loss of balance. In fact, heavy doses of pacifiers can feed confusion, disorientation, depression, and amnesia. To declare, "But Elijah was a chosen vessel. I am just little me!" is a cop-out. It is true that "many are called, but few are chosen." I remember hearing a weighty Bible teacher say, "One has to agree with God and choose to be chosen". (I think it was Paul Yonggi Cho who said it).

Christ spent three years showing the twelve how to live and what to say and do to lift mankind to where God wants them to live. Even the likes of Judas Iscariot must have also healed the sick, cleansed the lepers, and raised the dead. Elijah went to those places before Jesus did it or taught it. What clearly was the common "day-at-the-office" for prophets and Godly people in Elijah's day was NOT anything like Elijah's routine. One can excuse oneself by saying, "I am not doing what Elijah did because 'that's not my calling," and go on with a clear conscience. (Remember, there were hundreds of prophets secretly hiding in caves. That should pacify your reasoning.) Or we can own up and confess that we don't know how, or at what stage of life Elijah arrived at the place where he could cancel nature's agenda and cancel rain for three and a half years.

"But that is God's decision – not Elijah's". Again an easy theology that excuses the believer from struggling, stressing – nay – downright fighting with biblical statements and concepts and seeking and searching for faith's ownership of what Yahweh has said to one's mind and heart.

Elijah mastered the mental and spiritual dogfight between what is God's sole responsibility, and what is the believer's imperative obligation. Healing the sick and casting out demons – in order to obey the injunction demands that we learn how to identify demons when we see them.

The triple X horror biblical truth is that Elijah simply read a few statements out of the books of Moses, and then instigated a system of logic that deduced and concluded that, as Yahweh told Moses to write it down that if Israel ever turned their back on Him, He would make the heavens like iron and rain would cease. From that scripture, Elijah chose to believe that, by owning his personal belief system, it was his responsibility to do all he knew to bring that scripture to pass.

That is how he set off to achieve the impossible. To swim up the Niagara. To go where no one has ever gone before.

So, I am herewith wanting to write the book, that I shall afterwards read with the intense prayer that it shall take me further than I have ever been before, adventuring into Christ Himself. Just a deeper meditation into the scriptures we already have will take us further and further into practical experiences with the Master. The challenge is to read the scriptures with an ever developing mindset that holds the conviction that in the scriptures God is attempting to teach us the conceptually practical ideas of the biblical narrative. We do not go looking for experiences, but every adventure of faith recorded in the Bible that took place because of somebody's faith resulted in experiences that were so exciting, that they had to be told, and told they were, by writing the scrolls. I believe Elijah's life is revealed in the Bible to draw us to live in a similar manner to him. Now, that is a scary prospect. It shakes the very foundations of the peace and quiet of 21st-century Christian lives. Let the foundations of your faith rumble as we fight, struggle and argue with unbelief in order to get us moving organically towards the Elijah model, which is only a limited, partial model of Him who lifted the limits off and said, "You shall do greater things than I"

Elijah adventured and progressed by hearing radical stuff from heaven concerning matters that were written by Moses and what God said to him through Moses' writings. So, let's start with what the Americans refer to as a 101 lesson. It means a complete beginner's talk, assuming the class knows absolutely nothing.

God relates to all people in the same way He did with Elijah. He talks to them. In order to fulfil His desire to relate, God speaks. He always has done, He always does, and He always will. In fact, it is intrinsic to His nature to speak to people. Creation is here because He spoke it into being. Since the creation of mankind, He has always shared His purposes with people, as well as angelic beings. Short-term, mid-term, and long-term (long-term meaning to the end of time and beyond), throughout and within all generations, God, even though He speaks to all of humanity, talks to a certain collection of persons about what He has done, what He is doing, and what He will do in the future. Those that receive such data are impelled to share that data with as many as can be reached. Amos 3:7 wonderfully and informatively declares:

"Surely, indeed it is certain that Sovereign Yahweh never does anything without revealing his secret plans and counsels to His servants the prophets. He will do nothing unless He tells His secrets to them first. He does not perform his word until He has told at least one prophet, or sometimes many prophets." (My own version with paraphrased addenda)

In other words, whatever He plans to do, He tells people, whom He refers to as His "servants". Elijah was a prophet and a servant of God.

Does that mean that He tells everything to every prophet with the same words and timbre of voice? As if it was discovering how to tune in to a heavenly news reader? Like a published statement for all the prophets to stand up and say the same thing? Definitely not! If that were true, the seventeen books of the major and minor prophets would be boring and repetitive of each other. One would only need one prophetic book. But Yahweh speaks to different generations in singular ages and diverse circumstances, to heterogeneous personalities even if it be a similar message. He relates to all, but he is intensely personal. Hebrew prophets who were peers were simultaneously told in different ways and different degrees.

Nobody acted the same as Elijah or Elisha – but the goals of all the prophets were the same.

The Old Testament tells us that before prophets were universally referred to as "prophets", they were referred to as "Seers." This suggests that the message of seers/prophets was not necessarily, or always, about what they heard God say, but also what they saw when God showed them His heart towards the world. One doesn't have to inform the reader that if 100 people saw some catastrophic occurrence on the news, when interviewed by reporters, they would gather 100 different stories of the same occurrence. 100 truthful explanations of a narrative can all sound different. Some see more detail – some see less. It's the same with the prophets. There is a spectrum of spiritual sight, knowledge and perception. It would seem Elijah saw deeper, further and more colourfully than anybody of his generation. He saw fire and death, food provision and divine government in heaven and brought those things down to earth's tangibility. I need to know how did he do this?

Elijah lived with the clear concept in his mind and the clear visual potential in his perception that "all things are possible to him that believes"- and he lived circa 800 years before Jesus spoke those words. It was this awesome cogitation that dominated his worldview and his image of God that has caused the world ever since to drop their jaws when studying the man from Tishbe.

Without any doubt, Elijah had fully understood and mastered in practice the contents of Mark 11:22-25, Mark 9:23 and even Matthew 17:20. In fact, I would say that the floor, the walls and the ceiling of Elijah's worldview were all plastered, covered and absorbed by the thought that "All things are possible." To him the impossible was the norm, or so it seems as one reads his narrative.

We have no formal statement from Elijah concerning his belief structure, just a demonstration. Without a doubt, if Elijah attended any cessationist church, he would be asked to reassemble his beliefs. He would be conceivably removed from a cessationist group as a wild, dangerous extremist, leading members astray. Elijah was very much attuned to the miraculous being a "normal day at the office". Not that there is any biblical text that suggests he saw a miracle every day, but he definitely carried the constant air of the miraculous. Elijah was a faithful Jew and a radical subculturalist. A scary gigantic disciple of Yahweh.

Elijah had to have absorbed the scrolls that were accessible in his day, and the absorption of all Pentateuchal scriptures were the meat that Yahweh presented to Elijah to feed and act on.

God's speech has, obviously, weight in it. From the opening chapter of Genesis, He speaks with purpose. When He speaks, the substance of whatever He says takes place. Yes! Prophecy is an event – especially at the higher end of the spectrum. God said, "Light be!" And light was. Throughout the days of creation, whether you accept seven twenty-four-hour days or otherwise, one cannot escape the fact that God spoke, and what He said impacted the entire cosmos. Moses' writings of those first seven days are referred to as prophetic writings. God, having invented time, prophesied and promised before time (Titus 1:2). He spoke to Adam and Eve. He spoke to killer Cain. He spoke to Noah. He spoke to Enoch, Melchizedek, and the king of Gerar. He spoke to Abraham, then Isaac and Jacob, amid His world directing dialogue with those people. People who don't look for what He is saying miss the boat of life and eternity. Miserably despised by his generation, Jeremiah heard Him and then said to the world, "You will seek Me and find Me when you search for Me with all your heart." Meaning that we need to get looking for what He is saying – and then act. This perspective of life centred around God, is the zone where Elijah was epically and extra-ordinarily accurate and diligent. The man from Tishbe needs to be emulated in the twenty-first century A.D.

When Christ came, God spoke in an entirely different fashion. God was speaking in and through the person of Christ. When Christ was silent – God was still speaking. Christ was God incarnate. His words were inspired and cosmos creating, moving, and directing. Christ was (and still is) God's Word incarnate. When the letter to the Hebrews says, as in most English translations, "in these last days He has spoken to us by His Son", we need to note that the Greek has no definite article. God has spoken to us in "Son". Meaning. You speak German, French, or Chinese. I speak in English. God speaks in "Son". Here in "times past and in diverse manners, God spoke by the prophets. And no prophet was as diverse as Elijah, the man from Tishbe.

The Gospel message that was delivered by the New Testament apostles was and still is a prophecy. The Gospel message predicts your future. Take Christ as your Saviour and grow and develop in Christ's teaching and you will enjoy the life of Christ within you in this existence of life, and you will also be ushered into the presence of God on the other side of the grave. That is a Divine promise. It is a Divine prophecy. It is unbreakably true. Reject Christ and refuse to listen to Him and not follow His teachings, and you will not experience the presence of God after death. That also is a promise. That also is prophecy. So, to a degree every witness to Christ, every preacher, if they are true to Christ, has a handle on prophecy. The importance of prophecy lies not only in the message, but in the role of the prophet as a witness.

Prophecy given to mankind is the bread and butter of the kingdom of heaven. It is not only a life of, "what God has said", but it is also all about what He is saying at this moment. What is He saying to other people? What is he saying to you, personally? God is always speaking. Are you hearing His voice? Have you heard His voice?

Every true, believing Christian has heard God's voice. They would not have been converted to Christ if they had not heard God speak. And just as a person hears the call of God to repent and be converted in whatever terminology and defining words that were used to bring them to Christ, it is the call of God that they continue in and develop in their understanding in defining their new relationship with Christ and the Father. So, to a degree (and there are always degrees to what I am saying), witnessing for Christ preaching the gospel is a prophetic action.

"But hold on!" you say. "You can't be serious, hinting that all Christians are prophets!" To a very simple, low degree; preaching is prophetic! But this is only my starting point. Not all who prophesy are prophets.

God still speaks today. If a person seeks to hear what God is saying, they can become prophetic. Many Christians around the world prophesy today. That doesn't mean that every one of them is a prophet. There are degrees of prophetic inspiration. There is a spectrum of the depth and influence of prophecies and, indeed, differences of the prophetic people that deliver prophecies. It is the gift of the Holy Spirit in the church of Christ worldwide. Some are, indeed, called to be prophets. They are a gift of Christ. Prophets have a prophetic air about them. Things they say and do speak to people. They have a gift for hearing God's voice and perceiving the divine purpose for individuals, families, churches, and nations even.

All this is meant to drill it into our minds that we need to emulate this man from Tishbe.

2

DEFINING THE SPIRITUAL PACKAGE THAT CONSTITUTES THE PROPHETIC GIFT.

(What is different in Old Testament prophecy, and what's the same.)

I was, around 2003-6, mixing with and working for one of the most powerful prophets on the planet in Nigeria. I was present at one "normal" Sunday service (Not that most "normal" routine church meetings would be anything like what was normal to this particular man) when he stopped in his tracks in the midst of a prayer line of several hundred people and grabbed a microphone. I do not have the transcript of what I heard and witnessed, but my memory is vivid as I recall the moment in order to make my point. The prophet concerned had freely imparted a healing gift to many pastors but often said in my hearing that he had not had any divine release to impart "the prophetic gift to anybody- yet." However, on this particular day, at that moment he stopped all movement in a congregation of thousands to say that he had just that moment received the liberty to release "prophecy" to one of his workers. The man stood next to him was a young fellow whose name was Benson who was a member of the ministry team working with the huge number of church membership. Benson was not clear in speech or diligent in debate and was not, to my observation sharp in leadership skills. The prophet took Benson's hand and maintained a grip on his wrist while the young man fell to the floor and wriggled for some thirty seconds or so. Moments later he arose to his feet while the senior and very influential prophet announced that he was going in to eat his lunch while Benson would take care of the rest of the prayer line.

The prophet's modus operandi was to bring healing and deliverance to the entire prayer line one by one, and stop every few minutes to prophesy over his "patients," revealing the depths of people's past and present and refer to their conduct for the future. As

I remember, Benson commenced to pray for the vast line of people that were still waiting for succour. The next 20 minutes had him prophesying over folks in desperate need, revealing ailments and flaws in people's lives that had precipitated maladies, infirmities and brokenness of bodies, souls and spirits. I was astounded. The simple Nigerian brother in Christ was never the same again. He was prophesying with total accuracy what were the backstories of a large number of God-seeking people.

In one brief exchange a few days afterwards, Benson explained to me that his perceptions about people when meeting them, and his internal responses to people coming to him with problems of many dimensions was utterly transformed and far-seeing, and I, personally, had never heard anybody say he was wrong or inaccurate with his recently received prophetic gift. His mind and heart were totally governed by the prophetic insight and wisdom that the entire ministry team were desperate to enter into, including myself. Benson still mumbled a little with his uneducated pronunciations, but explained that "the prophetic gift", the "Spirit of Prophecy" had enveloped him, and he was aware that from "elsewhere" he had a voice telling him, or a vision showing him all sorts of things about the world and the people he met and ministered to.

I have, through the years that have passed, since that exchange with Benson, in my life of meditation concerning his "immersion" into prophecy, likened what took place within his person to an "App" being downloaded to a computer. (The word "app", of course, is an abbreviation of the word "application")

For those unfamiliar with computer terminology, please allow me to explain.

One can discern what kind of activity your friends enjoy on their computer by asking them, "What apps they use?" In the realm of modern computing (I am writing mid 2024), applications (APPS) play a pivotal role in enabling users to perform a wide array of tasks efficiently and effectively. Applications are software programs designed to help users accomplish specific tasks or solve particular problems on their computers or mobile devices. The necessity for applications in computing arises from various factors that highlight their importance in enhancing productivity, facilitating communication, enabling entertainment, and streamlining daily activities.

One of the primary reasons for the indispensability of applications in computing is their ability to streamline complex tasks and to automate processes. Applications are designed to perform specific functions, ranging from word processing and spreadsheet management to graphic design, video editing and Banking. By using specialized applications, users can accomplish tasks much more quickly and with greater precision than they could manually. For instance, a word-processing application like Microsoft Word enables users to create, edit, and format documents efficiently, saving time and effort in the process.

Furthermore, applications are instrumental in facilitating communication and collaboration among individuals in today's interconnected Internet world. Communication applications such as email clients, messaging platforms, and video conferencing tools enable users to connect with others in real time, regardless of their physical location. These applications have revolutionized the way people communicate, making it easier to share information, ideas, and resources with colleagues, friends, and family members.

In addition to the aforementioned reasons, the continuous evolution of technology and the increasing complexity of computing tasks further underscore the importance of applications in modern computing environments. As new technologies emerge and user needs evolve, developers create innovative applications that give leverage to the latest advancements to deliver enhanced functionality and user experiences. Whether it's artificial intelligence, machine learning, augmented reality, or blockchain technology, applications play a crucial role in harnessing these advancements to address diverse needs and challenges.

My point is this:

In the realm of technology and spirituality, intriguing parallels can be drawn between the concept of applications (APPS) in computing and the gift of prophecy operating within the context of believers exercising faith. (Every spiritual gift can be paralleled as a spiritual app). Both phenomena involve the activation of specific functionalities or capabilities to achieve desired outcomes, albeit in distinct domains. By exploring these parallels, we can gain insights into the transformative power of the prophetic gift, revealing purpose-driven actions and the manifestation of divine guidance in the lives of believers.

One parallel between applications in computing and, specifically, the gift of prophecy lies in their purpose-driven nature in the field of their specificity. Just as applications are developed with specific objectives in mind, the gift of prophecy operates amongst believers to fulfil a higher purpose or calling in alignment with God's will. Both computer applications and prophecy serve as instruments through which individuals can access guidance, inspiration, and solutions to navigate the complexities of life and achieve their intended outcomes. Furthermore, both applications and the gift of prophecy require activation and utilisation to realize their full potential. In the realm of computing, applications must be installed, opened, and used by users to give leverage to their functionalities and capabilities effectively. Similarly, the gift of prophecy necessitates believers to step out in faith, exercise discernment, and communicate the messages received from God with humility and obedience. Just as an application remains dormant until activated by the user, the gift of prophecy lies dormant until believers choose to operate in faith and exercise it for the benefit of others. The apostle Paul encourages us all to stir up the gift of God that is within us.

Moreover, both applications and the gift of prophecy exhibit a transformative impact in their respective domains. Applications have revolutionized the way people work, communicate, learn, and entertain themselves, enhancing productivity, efficiency, and convenience in numerous aspects of daily life. Likewise, the gift of prophecy has the power to transform lives, bring clarity, provide direction, and offer hope to individuals and communities seeking divine guidance and intervention in times of need or uncertainty.

The parallels between applications in computing and the gift of prophecy operating within believers in the context of faith reveal profound insights into the transformative nature of purpose-driven actions and divine manifestations. Both phenomena involve the activation of specific functionalities or abilities to address needs, fulfil purposes, and bring about desired outcomes in their respective spheres. By recognizing and embracing these parallels, believers can gain a deeper understanding of the ways in which they can give leverage to their spiritual gifts, exercise faith, and impact the world around them for the glory of God and the benefit of humanity.

I do need to add to my story concerning Benson. Benson received the entire package of the "prophetic gift" in one momentary "ZAP!" He fell to the ground as a "no prophetic gifted" person and got back on his feet with what looked like to me and the thousands present who were watching as a fully equipped and prophetically astute prophet. Most prophets that I have talked to over the years (and that is not a huge number - perhaps half a dozen) explain how their journey into the prophetic started slowly and lowly. Their first dipping of their toes into prophecy were slight, non-dramatic, non-dangerous, slightly directive statements that were confirmed by those prophesied to as intensely relevant to their lives and helpful to folks grasping and running with their dreams and visions for life. The "prophetic gift" *per se* was never a Zap but more like a very slow, inch-by-inch growth of understanding and awareness. Yes! Some seem to have been born with the gift. However, we have to refer to 1 Corinthians 14:1, which in no way suggests the lack of a conscious gift of prophecy should never inhibit a person to jump into the waters. How deep should you go? How far should you leap? Your faith and courage writes the cheque.

3

AN AERIAL VIEW DEFINING THE WILD ANIMAL THAT IS THE PROPHETIC GIFT. (FROM A PROPHET'S PERSPECTIVE.)

Prepare yourself for dizziness on a Helter Skelter bringing you down to ground level, concerning a heavenly grasp of things. Hold on to your tummy for a Roller Coaster ride, revealing more ups and downs than you ever thought the Bible could reveal to you. We are about to engage with some of the hardest truths that some of the most dangerous men took hold of in the biblical narrative revealed to us.

You want to prophesy and/or you want to be a prophet? OK! The scriptures, however, tell us some terrifying facts about the gift of prophecy. No matter how zealous and hungry you are to move in the prophetic, take a pacifying drink of Cocoa before you read on.

The Old Testament prophets are the most varied selection of humanity types in a single genre. Christ Himself informs us that they all unjustly died for loving their own people and explaining God's purpose to straighten their faith, their lifestyle and their destiny. All the prophets in the Old Testament brought something enormous to the planet. And those people that they all loved, without reason hated them enough to kill them. All these men had a God given agitation called "the gift of prophecy".

The gift of prophecy can be likened to a wild vicious beast unleashed in the heart and blood system of the men we refer to as the prophets. I am referring to the Old Testament prophets more than those in the New Testament, though, make no mistake, New Testament prophets were commonly killed also. And I am thinking of Elijah, and his successor Elisha, as opposed to all the writing prophets, neither of whom were killed. But the activity of the bestial, untamed, ever-active gift of prophecy simultaneously blesses and torments all those appointed and anointed by God to be a prophet. This beast is wild, giant and dangerous. It eats away at its keeper yet increases their strength and character. Its carrier feels compelled to release the animal for a run and reveal, wherever and whenever it wants and wishes. The gift of prophecy has a life of its own. The beast is so precious to God, and desired to be understood by all and sundry engaged with the verbose beast, released in and through the prophet, Yahweh implants great aspects of His own flawless character into each of the characteristics of these prophetic persons. It rendered all the Hebrew prophets uniquely vulnerable, as well as uniquely majestic and divinely protected and watched over until there time came. How's that for a candidate for the "greatest paradox of all time?"

The man from Tishbe we are prodding and discussing "set the bar high" as a prophet. A prophet is a deeply burdened person - dare we say traumatised, by the weight of God-given factual insights that are, like magma, red and sometimes white hot, jumping and spraying in a volcano, where the volcano in this instance is the mountain of the human heart and mind of a human being, and the magma is the word concerning the insights divinely imparted to them. All of the prophets in the Old Testament carried a commission that was engrafted into their psyche by an unbreakable attachment that, no matter how intense the opposition was against them, they persisted in promulgating the contents of their burden. They all risked their lives because of their consistent repetition of what God had whispered in their ears and was thereafter burning in their hearts. Make no mistake, the gift of prophecy is an undomestic beast that we attempt to domesticate.

It seems by reading the scrolls that reveal Elijah to us and the writings of the other prophets that their very existence and raison d'etre was conjoined inescapably to what they were proclaiming and/or standing for. The insightful message they had been given was as a living roaring beast within their bones. Yet they concurrently possessed the ability to discern the unspoken sorrows of humanity alongside their own heavenly receipts. They were conjoined vertically to Yahweh, the Lord of all, while horizontally being passionately relating, pleading with their fellow human beings to submit to the divine correction. Could any story writer create a plot line of persons more conflicted than the prophets? The words of Elijah carried the DNA of the fervour, intensity and gravity of Yahweh Himself. While ordinary people may critique societal injustices and failures from a distance - to Elijah, these wrongs took on a monumental scale and a mountainous weight that he, like all the Hebrew prophets, found impossible to live with and let live. Iniquities that had settled as everyday cultural behaviour simply had to be confronted. The likes of Jeremiah, Amos, and Isaiah, made theft, unjust trading at the grocers, and the like - into major crimes that were crippling the entire economy of life.

The weight that some of the prophets carried had them complaining to God about things being "beyond their capability" to manage, and some even submitted their "resignation-from-post" application, including Elijah, and also much later Jeremiah. But all persevered to their end. Wanting "out" Jeremiah, after the huge humiliation with Passhur the false prophet, accused God of rape, having been seduced into a situation that was not originally on Jeremiah's agenda at all (Jeremiah 20:7-8). However when attempting to keep shtumm and back out, disowning the wild beast of the gift of prophecy, he claimed he had fire in his bones that would not allow him to stay silent (Jeremiah 20:9). Such is the beast of the prophetic call. It was something similar to Job who screamed wanting God to leave him alone (Job 7:19), yet yearned to find Him calling out, "If only I knew where I could find God! I would go where he lives. I would present my case to him." (Job 23:3-4). The light of God's word is to be declared and presented in a world of darkness to introduce the prophets to internal conflicts that are hard to handle, and almost impossible to experientially understand.

What Elijah carried was a huge unseen encumbrance on his spiritual shoulders. It impacted his mental health. It prevented him from relating to people in a social manner. It precipitated his social withdrawal and yet in the midst of his internal conflicts he revealed familial love, tender affection, gentleness and care to a gentile widow and her son in a place called Zarapheth. Those days of Elijah's journey, as a family-caring "uncle," were conducted with the weight of Israel's ungodly conduct gnawing at his heart. His prophetic pronouncement that actually altered the climate of the age must have been weighing him down severely. People were starving, children must have been dying and the responsibility was fully, under God, heavily crushing on his shoulders. And note this: His spoken prophetic word given to the king impacted *beyond* the borders of Israel. Zarapheth is not in Israel but was still ravaged by the 42-month drought. Oh, the agony of the prophet!

The significance of prophecy extends beyond the conveyed message. It encompasses the prophet's role as a witness to God's conversation. According to the German theologian Gustav Hölscher, prophets do not merely deliver divine messages; they speak as if they are God, merging their identity with the divine perspective. Their connection to God involves sharing divine emotions and a profound care for all of humanity. Worshipping and emulating Yahweh is utterly incompatible with looking down on others with pride. Every human is of divine concern. The concept of "divine pathos" highlights God's deep emotional involvement in human affairs. The beast that abode within the prophet's soul required daily feeding and exercise. No such thing as a part-time prophet.

I had never conceived of God's heart ever feeling pathos until I read Abraham Heschel's "The Prophets". I initially discovered the word "pathos" studying English Literature at school in my teens when pawing over Shakespeare and getting to grips with Othello, Romeo and Juliet, and even in the ravings of King Lear. I learnt that pathos is the quality that evokes pity and sadness towards another. It rises when engaging with distressing narratives of another's misfortune and adversity. It extracted from my heart exaggerated and even self-indulgent tenderness and desolation just running through Hamlet's grief over his murdered father. And to pair God Almighty with the characteristic of pathos took much bible reading and meditation before I could willingly acquiesce. Now I, myself, am occasionally brought to tears as I see it in many passages of scripture, especially reading the Old Testament prophets. Jeremiah's narrative is a major contributor to such emotional collapses while in prayer.

Prophets are not just conveyors of messages but are witnesses to divine compassion. They haven't received a cold, posted, registered letter from heaven to blandly recite to the people. They have entered the heart, mind, emotions and conflicts of Almighty God and are struggling beyond their natural sensibilities to handle both the wonderful futuristic vision of God's ultimate destiny for Israel, together with all of mankind, and the sickening horrors that immediately drew close to them in the generation in which they stood. They are touched by the same anguish that God feels in response to human suffering and their ignoring of the covenant historically made betwixt Israel and Yahweh in the days of Moses. That is why in several volumes on my shelf, the statement is made in a multitude of works, "Being a prophet is a deep honour as well as a horrific affliction". I have never read a book where that phrase is attributed to its original author. They all claim it was first spoken or written by that strange man named "Anon". Receiving their burden from heaven drives all prophets to prayer and stress. Not recited or written prayers, but "agonising, gut-wrenching screams of the spirit" kind of prayer. Prayers of the prophets are disturbing. They utter the kind of prayer that challenges our comfort rather than validating our beliefs, confronting our conscience and urging us to embrace responsibility for things that many would say is not at all their - our - culpability.

Systematic and dry theology, by emphasizing the completely objective and supernatural nature of prophecy, has historically overlooked the active role of the prophet in the prophetic process. It has focused on the concept of revelation, wonderful as that is, while neglecting the element of the human response – the response of the prophets themselves. Who need to process the word received in a struggle to find their own verbal presentation.

In contrast, theological psychologists (remember the great John Hercus and his writings?) have attempted to explain prophecy based on the mental, spiritual and intellectual inner experiences of the prophets. However, this reductionist approach treats prophecy as an objective and divine phenomenon only, disregarding the prophet's own consciousness and awareness of God's speech to them and their relationship with Him. There are lengthy, deeply moving prayers in scripture from Daniel, Ezra and Nehemiah where all three men of godly stature owned up to catastrophic destiny destroying conduct that none of them ever committed. Proving how the man of God can be totally responsible for an occurrence, without actually being at all guilty.

A thorough examination rustling through and meditating on the prophetic texts and the life of Elijah reveals the obvious truth that prophecy involves both personal revelation as well as personal analytical responses, blending receptivity from God together with their own human agency. The prophet is entrusted with a divine mission, wielding a transcendent message that surpasses his individual everyday capabilities, yet the prophetic word is also influenced by his temperament and emotional maturity.

The prophet's roll and call is to communicate the divine perspective as exactly as received. It is essential to explore not only the doctrines the prophets held to, but also the personal qualities they embodied: their perspectives, emotions, reactions—not just their words but their lived experiences; the hidden, the personal and the intimate.

The prophet's words carry a deep sense of disturbance bordering on excruciation, reflecting a deep concern for the moral fabric of the Jewish society. Unlike a mere observer of nature and current affairs, the prophet is primarily concerned with the tumultuous course of history that he is part of and the tsunami of the future repercussions, which lacks stability and is shaped by the urgent and weighty themes that God engrafted to the prophet's being. In plain language, loving the people and loving Yahweh was a cruel agonising state, especially when the people the prophet is addressing are physically and emotionally abusing the prophet in the midst of his delivery.

The core of a prophet's message is rooted in the prophet's commitment to share it fully and accurately. Their words reflect their very essence and the serious consequences of not delivering what God has entrusted to them. If they fail to communicate this message, their life, sanity, and mental well-being are all at risk. Instead of using vague or unclear language, the prophet speaks directly and passionately, infused with the urgency and authority of divine revelation. Their declarations are powerful and immediate, designed to inspire, alarm, and motivate listeners to take action. Unlike storytelling or poetic expressions, the prophet's speech serves as a warning, critique, and encouragement, illuminating reality through a moral and spiritual perspective and urging ethical reflection and change.

What distinguishes Elijah? What makes him more extraordinary than all the other prophets that are all extraordinary in themselves? He is like a lyricist, sermoniser, statesman, speaker, social commentator, and moral and spiritual authority. My aim is to delve into the mind of the man from Tishbe and grasp the pivotal moments of his life with this author's personal conscious desire to emulate him. My objective is to comprehend what it entails to think, feel, respond, and behave as Elijah did throughout his entire biblical narrative – and then strike myself with as much spiritual submission as I can, in order to emulate him. I am compelled to speculate about what lies beyond and beneath Elijah's conscious awareness. I desire to hold his heart and mind and – no matter how pathetically – pattern myself after him. This endeavour demands substantial mental and spiritual effort to acquire. I am painfully aware of being the mouse wanting to emulate the elephant, the gentle grassy knoll thinking he can copy Everest. The experience of being overwhelmed and tormented by the anguish felt by God Himself in response to human suffering is a central theme that deeply affects all the Hebrew prophets and particularly Elijah.

In the face of Elijah's encounters with apathy and indifference, the perception of Yahweh is not one of solace and comfort, but rather of an unrelenting call to action. While the world remains somnambulating, willfully blind, Elijah experiences the divine impact of the worlds apathy and hebetude. The desire for Justice, far from being a mere concept or standard, is portrayed as a divine fervour that drives Elijah's mission. The act of prayer is depicted as a deep subversive act that challenges our sense of satisfaction in status quo's, prompting us to confront our responsibilities head-on, rather than merely reaffirming our existing values. To Elijah, and indeed all the writing prophets, a conscience at peace is simply cowardice in the face of the enemy and AWOL from Yahweh's precious presence.

I read somewhere that it is arguably true that in the context of biblical logistics, the antithesis of goodness is not evil, but indifference. Our very essence as humans is said to be hinged on our capacity for empathy and compassion. The eternal cry of the blood of innocents (with men like Naboth in Elijah's encounter) is highlighted as a reminder that humanity's purposeful existence is contingent upon acknowledging and addressing injustice. That injustice seems to have greatly chewed on Elijah's thoughts. The notion of personal responsibility beyond one's own actions, terrifying notion that it is, underscores the collective duty we bear toward one another as fellow human beings. This insight drove Elijah almost constantly. The importance of revering both knowledge of the world and the act of reverence towards God, is emphasized, contrasting against the modern societal trend of demanding, "live and let live," to all evils we see in the world.

Drawing inspiration from Elijah, I can clearly see that he never viewed evil as the ultimate fate of humanity, but as a challenge that holds the promise of redemption and renewal. A complete resurrection of human awe and wonder towards God is high on the heavenly priority list, mixed with a resurgence of reverence towards God's word as well as Yahweh. In many ways Old Testament Elijah has the ethos of a New Testament evangelist.

The aspiration to revive the prophetic ethos, characterized by a stark acknowledgment of the world's chaotic defiance of its Creator, teetering on the edge of calamity, with the divine call imploring humanity to seek redemption, is a prevailing theme in all of the prophetic writings and narratives. Prophecy is defined as "an interpretation of existence from a transcendent vantage point", offering insights that surpass conventional knowledge.

Prophecy is divine inspiration that makes other people's catastrophes the personal responsibility of the man chosen to prophesy. The speaker and actors express deep concern, like Asterix and Obelix living in constant fear that the sky is about to collapse on the world. But there is nothing humourous or fictional about what the prophets see is about to collapse on both Hebrew nation-states. And that is a consequence of Israel's betrayal of God and their covenant with Him. The destruction of the glorious city of Jerusalem and the exile of the entire two nations are due to both major and minor injustices against the insignificant and powerless poor, as well as their crashing of the Mosaic covenant. Even though the never-ending list of seemingly "trivial" social misdemeanours seems paradoxical and absurd when seen in the light of their final retribution, the prophet emphasizes the gravity of these transgressions, highlighting the profound impact of human action against all of humanity and the covenant with Yahweh. This is true in Elijah as well as all the writing prophets.

The text delves into the emotional intensity of the prophet's convictions. Driven by a profound sense of empathy and moral responsibility, the prophet is deeply troubled by humanity's insatiable greed for all things unrighteous. Central to the prophet's message is the profound significance of human suffering and moral choices in the eyes of God.

New Testament prophets, though not caught in such potentially catastrophic collapses of nation-states, still need to experience the divine emotional intimacies with the Almighty for the delivery of clean water.

We call out for purity of heart. This insight into the heart of the Old Testament clearly separates "the men from the boys". Are you willing to allow the scriptures to impact you in the same way they impacted Elijah?

4

A GROUND LEVEL VIEW DEFINING THE HARASSING PEST THAT IS PROPHECY.

(THE GENERAL PUBLIC'S PERSPECTIVE.)

Those that love the darkness resist the light. As the apostle John made remarks of how dark powers and sin operates in the lives of people, what was true in the days of John's writing, so was it true in the Old Testament days of the Hebrew prophets. Darkness has its own hellish flow, which, once settled into the lives of any community becomes the social-cultural status quo that has a life of its own which clings to its own existence until human hearts resolve and repent to turn to the light.

In the days concurrent with Elijah the Tishbite, the common idolatrous population of Israel had mixed and varied reactions to all the prophets, including Elijah. The prophets were often seen through non-repentant eyes as disruptors of the status quo, challenging the people to turn away from idolatry and to return to the worship of the one true God. All true Prophets of God condemned the people for engaging in idol worship, offering sacrifices insincerely, and following rituals without true devotion, as well as conjoining Yahweh with idolatrous gods. This challenged the religious practices of the time and would have angered the wealthy religious establishment.

As in hideous mockery, Baal worship had their own hordes of prophetic voices. The prophets of Yahweh often clashed with false prophets who delivered messages that pleased the people rather than speaking the truth. Some were prophets of Baal, and some were even falsely prophetic "in the name of Yahweh. "This conflict would have led to animosity and hostility towards the true prophets of Yahweh. These reasons, among others, contributed to the hostility and persecution that many of the true prophets faced from the people of

Judah and Israel. They made big issues out of, what the masses considered little things. The false prophets were the "feel good" prophets and were motivational and contradictory when the true prophets predicted exile and destruction. The message of the prophets in the southern kingdom, post 722 B.C., was, "Don't worry about the Northern Kingdom being exiled. We of Judah and Jerusalem are still here, showing us all that we have nothing to bother about. The fall of Samaria and the Northern kingdom is proof that we are better than they and that God is on our side." Isaiah had things to say about that monstrosity of a wrong interpretation of facts.

All the prophets, both true and false, played a crucial role in the religious and social landscape of ancient Israel and Judah. These true prophets were seen by believers as messengers of God, tasked with calling the people back to the worship of the one true God and away from the temptation of idolatry. Among these prophets, Elijah stands out as a powerful and influential figure whose actions and words left a lasting impact on the people of Israel. The trail of the divinely miraculous activities of Elijah clothed the man from Tishbe with the aroma of Yahweh.

The common idolatrous population of the two Hebrew nation states had a complex relationship with the prophets. They were considered as activists interfering with the cultural lifestyle of the people. The prophets claimed to have heard voices in the night as well as the day, telling folks that their normal lifestyle of cheating, immorality, and their comfortable bit of "religion" as a part-time recreational hobby was wrong and eternally destructive. Telling the people that their comfortable lifelong habits were evil was not conducive to a social warm welcome. Telling the people that their casual and happy lifestyles of theft, adultery, and breaking all of the Mosaic Decalogue was evil and wrong was not received lightly by the masses.

So, on one hand, these prophets were often viewed with suspicion and hostility by those who were deeply entrenched in idolatrous and/or malpractice of many descriptions. The prophets' messages of repentance and calls for social justice were often seen as threats to the existing power structures and religious hierarchy of the time. The idolatrous and religious population in particular, saw the true prophets as troublemakers who sought to disrupt the status quo and undermine their routine way of life.

Elijah, in particular, was a prophet who faced significant opposition. His confrontation with the prophets of Baal on Mount Carmel is the ultimate and most vivid example of this conflict. Perceive and understand that the vast crowd that were audiential to Elijah calling down the fire at Carmel were mostly neutral or, if anything, more favourable to Baal. "Yahweh supporters" would have been rare. Elijah challenged the people of Israel to choose between the worship of Baal and the worship of the true God, Yahweh. The idolatrous population, who had long been swayed by the allure of foreign gods, viewed Elijah's actions as provocative and incendiary.

Despite the resistance and hostility he faced, Elijah's message resonated with some within the population. His miracles and demonstrations of God's power garnered him a following among those who were searching for spiritual truth and longing for a deeper connection with the divine. Elijah's unwavering faith and boldness in the face of opposition inspired awe and admiration in those who were open to his message.

The prophets often rebuked the people for their sins, idolatry, injustice, and moral corruption in economic transactions and legal matters, where the rich got richer, and the poor were pushed to absolute poverty. This message would have been unwelcome to many who preferred to continue in their sinful ways. The prophetic messages were the source of the people's guilt and condemnation. Prophets frequently spoke out against the rulers and leaders of the day, challenging their authority and calling them to account for their actions – from the king downwards throughout the ruling classes. This would have made the prophets a threat to the established power structures. The common idolatrous population of Israel and Judah held a range of opinions and attitudes towards the prophets, including Elijah. While some viewed the prophets as threats to their way of life and resisted their messages, others were drawn to their powerful demonstrations of God's presence and authority. Elijah, with his boldness and unwavering commitment to Yahweh, stood as a powerful symbol of prophetic truth in a time of spiritual crisis and moral decay. The prophets were rejected by the majority. They were seen as pests and social irritants. They constantly reminded the people of the Mosaic covenant and how their conduct, lifestyle and their total absorption of idolatry was an affront to God.

The prophets only warned them of the repercussions of the Mosaic covenant being imminent. Exile was promised clearly and repetitively. The messages of the prophets often included warnings of impending disaster, exile, or judgment if the people did not repent. Such messages were hideously unpopular and not well-received by those who preferred to hear comforting words. The idolatrous social and religious leaders told the prophets that they were irrelevant, except when they spoke positive things over the population. Many prophets spoke out against social injustices such as oppression of the poor, widows, and orphans. Their calls for justice would have been threatening to those who benefited from the evil status quo.

Sickness and poverty were promised as a result of the social evils. And the people were so ignorant of the ancient covenant that they just responded as if the prophets were strange mystics from "an evil elsewhere". Prophecy was seen by the religious and political leaders as a nuisance. The presence of the prophets was an affliction. To many, they were just awkward riot mongers. However, once heard, the prophets could not be unheard. Time could not be reversed to when they had not been known. To the unrepentant, the memory of the voices and the words of the prophets were an absolute nightmare.

As with modern anti-religionists, the people claimed that the anointed persistent prophets were to be ignored at first, but as time passed on, the people turned irritated and ultimately were violent towards the men of God. Like today, people were accused and despised simply because of what they thought and spoke of.

Prophets often used vivid and harsh language to denounce the sins of the people and their leaders. This could have been perceived as a personal attack and would have provoked anger and resentment.

The unflinching determination to stand in the midst of threats of violence and even murder seems to have been part of the average contract of divine employment for the prophets of Yahweh. Are you ready to sign on?

5

THE DIVINE ENCOURAGEMENT FOR ALL CHRISTIANS TO SEEK TO PROPHESY

"Follow the way of love and eagerly desire gifts of the Spirit, especially prophecy."

(1 Corinthians 14:1).

This verse of scripture is the initiating thought that validates the project that holds that seeking to emulate Elijah is a feasible, though distant, project of possibility. This startling revelation balances our goal as to how God wants prophecy prioritised in the Body of Christ:

EVERY CHRISTIAN IS A CANDIDATE FOR PROPHECY AND PROPHESYING.

I find this classic line from one of the greatest builders of the church of Christ that has ever lived utterly exhilarating. Every single person who owns Christ as Saviour can aspire and learn to prophesy. In fact, because of the way Christians worldwide preach about "love" – that is, "if we want to be like Christ, 'love' is a compulsory attribute that must be sought after and desired" - this opening verse of 1 Corinthians 14 suggests seeking to prophesy is equally as plenary.

So, why aren't more Christians seeking to obey this apostolic injunction? Good question!

It is a bit of a killer line for cessationists. I mean, love is required before all things, and rightly so. But here, the manifestation that they declare has "ceased" and is "no longer relevant for today"- i.e. prophecy - is partnered with the desire for "love". They try to tell us that the call to love was, is and forever will be, in this life and the next, a correct emulation of Christ. I completely agree. Prophecy, however, as they see it, is presently an irrelevant line of scripture since the biblical apostolic twelve died. A pox on that thought!

It is irrational and unintelligent to contemplate that the Apostle Paul could say such a thing without the self-evident presupposition that every Christian is a candidate for the exercise of prophecy. He does *not* say that everyone can be a "prophet". Every prophet prophesies. Not everybody who prophesies is a prophet – in fact, very few are called to the prophetic office. Because one prophesies – even often, it does not mean that that person, male or female, is a prophet. Prophecy throughout the church of Christ, springing up from a worshipping body of followers of the living Lord, is referred to as a "gift of the Holy Spirit." The same apostle, referring to a full-blown prophet, teaches that such a person is, "a gift of Christ." If the reader does not understand the two concepts, hang on to your safety belt as we will explore that statement later in these pages.

It is my opinion that by insistence on the absolutely objective and supernatural nature of prophecy, and there is no intrinsic error in that, the Christ-followers of all flavours and colours are qualified to learn and be taught how to prophesy. Dogmatic, cold theology has ignored (or even denied) the prophet's role in the prophetic act. Prophecy is the intelligent response to the inspiration of the Holy Spirit (a thing that even cessationists exhort to be a lifestyle) that must peak somewhere at the extreme stretches of prophecy. In emphasizing revelation from God to man, much reformed theology has ignored the response of man to God. In reducing the discussion purely to the activity of the Spirit of God towards the human perception and inspiration, it has lost sight of the dynamics of the human response.

The questions and queries that have well-nigh kept me awake over many nights throughout the last 50-plus years are:

1. If Peter quoted Joel, that along with the outpouring of the Holy Spirit, as in Acts 2, there would be people prophesying and dreaming, male and female, old and young – how come 2,000

years after Acts 2, prophecy is still a comparative rarity throughout God's kingdom around the globe? Peter said, "This is that," meaning the fulfilment of Joel's words had descended in Peter's day.

2. Why is prophecy in the church still a rarity?

3. Why are people like me still asking and not teaching? Why am I, personally, so desperate to move in the deep waters of the prophetic yet have hardly got my feet wet?

4. Why am I still asking and not yet telling?

EVERY CHRIST SEEKER IS SITUATED FOR DIVINE INSPIRATION.

No matter what level of prophecy a person moves in, divine inspiration is the common denominator, whether your name is Isaiah Ben Amoz or Joe Bloggs, who was converted to Christ last Wednesday night at the local church. The apostle Paul says that to be able to genuinely prophesy. There must be a basic desire to do so. I hunger for such alignment with God's purpose. Biblical prophecy is never an involuntary action that results in an "Oh! Did I just speak? I didn't know I was doing that!" However, it may have an "I didn't know what I was referring to," about it. Scholars reckon the Old Testament prophets spoke not knowing at all what they were talking about. I reject that hypothesis. Yes, it may have been that they didn't fully understand the full depth of what they were saying (I have shared with and or listened to contemporary prophets who saw something, heard something, or sensed something that they verbally expressed, not fully understanding the physical reality of what they had stated.) To prophesy, from level 1 to the highest peak of the spectrum, inspiration of the Spirit of God is a non-negotiable attribute of the whole gradation and continuum. And every seeker after Christ reaching for more of the Holy Spirit in their life is a candidate for prophetic inspiration.

EVERY BELIEVER WHO SUBJECTS THEM SELF TO THE AUTHORITY OF CHRIST AND OF SCRIPTURE IS ENCOURAGED, IF NOT INSTRUCTED, TO SEEK TO PROPHESY.

I researched 50 different English translations of the New Testament. I gleaned the following facts from high-profile and widely esteemed scholars of New Testament Greek as well as Christian Theology to ascertain the most accurate exegetical English that would impact readers with the exact nuance of the original Greek and Aramaic scripture in 1 Corinthians 14:1. This is what I found:

"…desire spiritual gifts, but rather that ye may prophesy." (AV, NKJV, KJ2000 Bible, American King James Bible, Webster's Bible Translation)

"…seek the spiritual things, and rather that you may prophesy" (Literal Standard Version)

"…eagerly desire gifts of the spirit, especially prophecy" (NIV)

"…earnestly desire spiritual gifts, but especially that you may prophesy." (NASB, NASB1995, NASB1977, WEB, A Faithful Version.)

"…earnestly desire spiritual things, and especially that you may prophesy." (New Heart English Bible, Berean Literal Bible.)

"…seek earnestly the spiritual things, and rather that ye may prophesy," (YLT)

"…be emulous of spiritual things, and rather that ye might prophesy." (Smith's Literal Translation.)

"…be zealously earnest of the spiritual things, especially that you may prophesy." (Literal Emphasis Bible.)

"…be zealous for spiritual gifts; but rather that you may prophesy." (Douay-Rheims Bible – Catholic Translation.)

"Be zealous for spiritual things, but only so that you may prophesy." (Catholic Public Domain Version.)

"…eagerly desire spiritual gifts, especially the gift of prophecy." (Berean Study Bible)

"…desire spiritual gifts, and above all that you may prophesy." (HCSB)

"Be eager to have the gifts that come from the Holy Spirit, especially the gift of prophecy." (CEV)

"…keep on desiring spiritual gifts, especially the ability to prophesy." (ISV)

"…be eager for the spiritual gifts, especially that you may prophesy." (NET Bible)

"…yet desire earnestly spiritual gifts, but rather that ye may prophesy." (ASV, ERV)

"But you should also desire the special abilities the Spirit gives—especially the ability to prophesy." (NLT)

"…earnestly desire the spiritual gifts, especially that you may prophesy." (ESV)

"…yet earnestly desire and cultivate the spiritual gifts [to be used by believers for the benefit of the church], but especially that you may prophesy [to foretell the future, to speak a new message from God to the people]" (Amplified Bible)

"…desire spiritual gifts, and especially that you may prophesy." (CSB)

"…be emulous of spiritual [manifestations], but rather that ye may prophesy." (Darby Bible Translation).

"…earnestly desire spiritual gifts, but rather that you may prophesy." (Anderson New Testament.)

"…seek the spiritual gifts, but rather that you may prophesy." (Goodbey New Testament.)

"…zealously seek spiritual gifts, but rather that ye may prophesy." (Haweis New Testament.)

"…be earnestly ambitious for spiritual gifts, but let it be chiefly so in order that you may prophesy." (Weymouth New Testament.)

"…earnestly desire the spiritual gifts, but rather that ye may prophesy." (Worrell New Testament)

"…be desirous of spiritual gifts: but especially that ye may prophesy." (Worsley New Testament.)

"Make love your aim, and then set your heart on the spiritual gifts-especially upon prophecy." (Moffett Translation)

"…And the gift you should want most is to be able to prophesy" (Easy-to-Read Version)

Some translations are based on the Aramaic New Testament. The Aramaic-translated versions I can find say:

"…be zealous for the gifts of The Spirit, but especially that you may prophesy." (Aramaic Bible in Plain English.)

"…desire spiritual gifts, above all that you may prophesy." Lamsa Bible.

The first translations of the Bible into English were before a standardised written English language had been achieved. Even the random spellings (and probably the pronunciations) lead us to a solid conclusion. They read as follows:

"…covet spretuall giftes: and most chefly forto prophesye." (Tyndale Bible 1526)

"…covet spirituall giftes, but specially that ye maye prophecye. (Coverdale Bible 1535)

"… covet spirituall giftes but most chiefelie that ye may prophesie." (Bishop's Bible 1568.)

"…covet spirituall giftes, and rather that ye may prophecie." (Geneva Bible 1587)

"Follow ye charity, love ye spiritual things, but more that ye prophesy" (Wycliffe Bible)

For reasons of all round integrity, we include these last translations. Scholars who translated scripture with the presupposed belief that prophecy is "not for today" have an obvious problem with the New Testament call to "προφητεύω" (pronounced "prophéteuó"). The original Greek word was anglicised with the exact same pronunciation and meaning from Greek to English. Even to the most cursory Bible reader, these 7 translations below have deliberately mistranslated the inspired scrolls – not through skulduggery or dishonesty, but because a presupposed conviction that requires certain manipulation of the meaning of the text:

"Set your hearts on spiritual gifts, especially the gift of proclaiming God's message." (GNT)

"…desire spiritual gifts, but especially the gift of speaking what God has revealed." (GOD'S WORD Translation)

"Cultivate social virtue; then desire spiritual gifts, but chiefly that of explaining the prophetical writings." (Mace New Testament.)

"...Follow after friendship, but earnestly desire mental powers, and especially those enabling you to instruct." (Revised Ferrar Fenton Translation)

"...You must pursue love while you are cultivating the spiritual endowments, and especially inspired preaching." (Goodspeed Translation)

"Let love be your greatest aim; nevertheless, ask also for the special abilities the Holy Spirit gives, and especially the gift of prophecy, being able to preach the messages of God." (The Living Bible - paraphrase)

"Go after a life of love as if your life depended on it—because it does. Give yourselves to the gifts God gives you. Most of all, try to proclaim his truth." (The Message)

We are all children of the culture we were and are immersed in, especially Christians and the differing cultures within Christianity across the entire English-speaking world. However, I cannot grasp how anybody can translate "that you may prophesy" into anything else than in the same manner that the rest of the 66 books of the bible define the word to mean.

Using the NIV and searching for the four words, prophet, prophets, prophecy, and prophesy, I discovered that one or all of those words appear in 48 of the 66 books of Holy Scripture 630 times. Nowhere can "that you may prophesy" refer to "explaining the prophetical writings", "while you are cultivating ... inspired preaching", and "the gift of proclaiming God's message" (even though prophesying is indeed proclaiming God's message.).

I am left without the slightest doubt that the apostle writes inculcating a personal desire in anybody who reads his letter to prophesy, i.e., to present a statement from your own spirit while under the inspiration of the Holy Spirit.

THERE IS A SPECTRUM OF DEGREES AND GRADATION OF DIVINE INSPIRATION.

There must be a spectrum of degrees of prophetic inspiration. This is seen throughout scripture. There were seventy elders of Israel who prophesied in the days of Moses. Some of the anointing on Moses was placed on them, yet not one of them said anything that was important enough to be referred to in the texts of scripture. It simply says, "they prophesied", without note of the content of their prophecies. The same applies, of course to whoever was prophesying in the Corinthian church in Paul's day.

Two of the main errors concerning New Testament prophecy that cessationists carry as grounds for rejecting contemporary prophecy are (i) that the scriptural canon is complete and the doctrinal body of revelation must not be added to. For these reasons, they say, prophecy is unnecessary. To most people who are active in those churches where prophecy is exercised, that response is received as a pathetic and bigoted refusal to understand scripture. I have never heard a prophecy in 50 years that has added or subtracted the slightest doctrinal element. The truth is that every prophecy I have heard has been spoken without even touching the subject of doctrine yet has always been in line with accepted biblical truth. In the book of Acts the prophet Agabus predicted (a) a coming famine, and (b) the owner of a certain belt who was going to have hardship in Jerusalem. Hardly doctrinal theses. And those statements could only be weighed by the discernment of those that received the prophecy. Preparation to raise funds to help the victims of the predicted famine had to be commenced before the famine started. The discernment of the church was the issue of acceptance or rejection, not consistency or otherwise, with the scriptures. How could such a prophetic prediction be assessed through scripture? A second reason for prophecy rejection is that (ii) when Pentecostal and Charismatic churches release members to prophecy, they are releasing untutored and uncredentialed individuals to say things that may be deficient in expertise or finesse.

One of the most influential and powerful prophets that I personally have encountered and shared with was neither polished nor educated in school beyond 11 or twelve years of age. In the Old Testament, the prophet Samuel was educated in God and by God, while the educated experts were bypassed. There are prophecies collated and revered from the eighth century BC written by men of various classes and backgrounds. The heart is the essence of a prophet, not education nor social standing in the context of the church membership – and that is in no way to look down on highly educated people or socially accepted folks. Man looks on the outside. God looks at the heart.

Throughout scripture a lesser anointing of prophecy is never belittled. Only false prophecy or prophetic words spoken under a different power than the Holy Spirit are to be rejected. Contemporarily, the body of believers are expected to be able to discern the spirit that a message is spoken with (1 John 4:1-5). Prophets in the Bible who spoke without their content being biblically recorded (and there are quite a lot of them) are merely stated to have been prophets. (See the appendices at the end of this book).

THE PRINCIPLES AND DYNAMICS OF THE PROCESS OF PROPHECY AND DIVINE INSPIRATION ARE THE SAME IN BOTH TESTAMENTS.

The role of prophecy in the Old Testament is radically different from prophecy in the New Testament, but the dynamics of hearing from God and delivering God's contemporary word for the peer population of the active prophet is the same. The person who is to prophesy must hear what God has initiated and spoken, and then the person who is to prophesy must deliver it with as much accuracy and Divine love as there would be as if God Himself were speaking.

PROPHETIC NARRATIVES AND BIOGRAPHIES THROUGHOUT SCRIPTURE ARE RARELY TAUGHT TODAY, IF EVER, ON A "HOW TO DO IT" BASIS.

One of the reasons I am writing these pages is because I find frustration in being taught of love and devotion to Christ as exemplified by the prophets, yet rarely, if ever, have I ever been taught how to prophesy. Elijah and Elisha are used in lots of books. Sermons and Bible studies are used solely as prime examples of how to follow Christ. Not that there is the slightest fault in such an exposition, but my gripe is that it is only half the story. Elijah and Elisha both carried the word of God for their generation. I have never heard or read Elijah's and/or Elisha's biblical biography to be used as an exhortation to learn how to prophesy.

ELIJAH AND ELISHA ARE THE EXTREME EXAMPLES OF THE WHAT, HOW AND WHERE OF PROPHECY.

The mystery of Elijah and Elisha is the mystery of every biblical prophet. I scream to know the answer to questions like:

1. How did this person hear from God? I was in the same room at the same moment when a prophetic person says, "God just said to me ..." Why didn't I hear the same words?

2. Is there any routine of commitment or frame of mind or heart that precipitates prophetic communications from heaven coming to a hungry soul like you or I?

3. Based on 1 Corinthians 14:1, can I be justified to say to myself, "Ah well, the other person is called to prophesy but not me. Perhaps it is not the will of God for me to prophesy." So does the scripture in 1 Corinthians 14:1 have exceptions to its addressees. And if the call to seek to prophesy is limited, is it also limited when he calls us to walk in *agape* love? Love and prophecy seem of similar priority in 1 Corinthians 14:1.

4. How does the confident conviction come that faces incredibly violent opposition and still stands strong to make prophetic pronouncements that contradict the external circumstances? This is exactly what Elijah and Elisha both did all their lives as we know them. They invariably spoke ridiculous impossibilities that were almost always immediately validated by coming to pass.

5. What are the itemised secrets of the life of the prophet that sustain the faculty of hearing God, seeing inspired visions, and knowing what is happening to people and circumstances beyond their natural knowledge and way beyond their locale?

Whatever the answers are to these questions, Elijah and Elisha seemed to have mastered the whole dynamic and atmosphere of the prophetic Spirit of God to a degree that is not seen with others.

In Paul exhorting believers to seek to prophesy, we must negotiate the associated issues no matter how daunting they may seem to be. We must start somewhere and not be afraid of being corrected or counselled in our conceptual understanding of the agency of God in this life. Let us encourage each other to desire to prophesy. That is what the New Testament is all about and what these pages are all about. And this author is no prophet.

You and I certainly qualify in being in line to capacitate prophecy. The apostle Paul said so.

6

THE DIFFERING FRAMES OF REFERENCE OF PROPHETS HAS ALWAYS BEEN.

Prophets exist today despite the scepticism and dismissal they often face from evangelicals who cling to traditional theological frameworks that overlook ongoing prophetic voices. I am referring to the narrow perspectives of cessationists. The reality is that prophets have been present throughout biblical history, from the Hebrew Bible to the New Testament, and continue to emerge in contemporary contexts. I will explore the concept of "non-canonical" prophecies and address the mindset that insists the "canon is complete, so we don't need prophecy" syndrome. Rest assured; this discussion will be looked into later on in these pages.

While it is true that some individuals may incorrectly or even falsely pose as prophets, we do not discard all fifty-pound notes simply because counterfeits exist. The existence of fakes highlights the genuine article's value. Why would anyone counterfeit a masterpiece from centuries ago if the original did not hold immense worth? Consider Leonardo da Vinci's Salvatore Mundi (Saviour of the World), which sold for an astounding $450 million in November 2017. Initially misattributed and once sold for a mere $60, its value skyrocketed upon authentication as a genuine da Vinci work. The owner, fearing theft, has reportedly hidden it, leading to speculation about its true whereabouts.

The presence of fraudulent prophets should not deter the Church from recognizing the authentic prophetic gifts that continue to thrive.

Throughout all the books of the Hebrew Bible and the New Testament, we find a mixture of born and made prophets, alongside many whose stories remain obscure and names are plainly omitted. These unnamed prophets, with their fleeting mentions, invite us to piece together what we do know while remaining open to the mysteries of divine communication throughout the Old Testament.

In today's world, some claim prophetic status based on sporadic, perhaps sensational, predictions that garner them acclaim within their denominational groups. It is crucial to differentiate between those who prophesy and those who are called prophets. While all prophets will exhibit a prophetic gift, not everyone who prophesies holds the title of prophet. The distinction lies between the gift of prophecy—a spiritual gift bestowed upon many—and the gift of Christ to the church – the prophets. This difference between a gift of the spirit and a gift of Christ is to be noted and understood. This nuanced discussion warrants further exploration later on.

Take Elijah, for instance. We cannot neatly categorize him as a "born" or "made" prophet, nor can we pinpoint his educational or spiritual background. Our understanding is limited to scriptural accounts. Prophets have existed since the dawn of creation, beginning with figures like Enoch in Genesis 5. When referring to prophets, I mean those divinely appointed to serve as God's mouthpieces. It is important to recognize that alongside genuine prophets, there have always been false ones. Various religious groups define their prophets through differing lenses. A charismatic leader or a progressive thinker may not necessarily be a prophet in the biblical sense. The Church must critically assess these figures, maintaining its convictions without casting aspersions on differing interpretations of faith.

The critical question is not whether prophets are born or made, whether they are male or female, or whether they come from privilege or obscurity. Rather, it is about whether they carry the living word of God. As we delve into the nature of prophets and prophecy, I hope to provide insights that will illuminate this topic. Many non-Pentecostal evangelicals may scoff at the notion of "prophets today," making it imperative to build a compelling argument.

A. BORN PROPHETS

1. THOSE WHO HIT THE GROUND RUNNING FROM BIRTH

The Bible presents John the Baptist as an extraordinary example of a prophet whose calling was evident even in the womb. When Mary, pregnant with Jesus, visited Elizabeth, John leapt in his mother's womb, demonstrating an innate spiritual sensitivity. This signifies that the prophetic anointing can manifest with some, even before birth.

In more recent church history, figures like William Branham, Paul Cain, and John Paul Jackson recount early experiences of prophetic insight, often sharing profound revelations before they fully understood their significance. It appears that their prophetic gifts were active long before they identified themselves as ministers of the Gospel, and even in early childhood.

2. THOSE BORN WITH THE PROPHETIC GIFT YET UNRELEASED

Jeremiah serves as another compelling case. God informed him, "Before I formed you in the womb, I knew you; before you were born, I set you apart" (Jeremiah 1:5). This suggests that Jeremiah's prophetic potential was concealed within him until the appointed time. His struggle to accept this divine calling illustrates a common theme among prophets: the revelation of their gifts often unfolds gradually.

Similarly, Jesus, the ultimate prophet and source of all prophecy, did not begin His public ministry until the age of thirty, following His baptism by John and the anointing of the Holy Spirit. This does not imply that His gifts were dormant; rather, He awaited the moment that fulfilled all righteousness.

Abraham was the first human being in the Bible that God Himself verbally owned as His prophet. But this gets a little more complex with the father of the faithful because we have no particular textual account where Abraham prophesied in the stereotypical manner of the later prophets – that is – declaring some message or insight as a word from God. I have always understood this as simply revealing that, uniquely, Abraham was himself the message by nature of the new name God gave to him, changing it from Abram to Abraham. Although he did make some startling statements that preachers have always presented as prophetic statements, i.e. things like building altars and instead of making sacrifices on the altar he simply called on the Name of the Lord. Wow! Swallow that if you can dear reader. And then there is the answer to his son Isaac who asked where the lamb was for sacrifice as he ascended Mount Moriah. The earth-shaking reply, seen by many as a prophecy with universal application was, "God will Himself provide a lamb." Prophecy? Yes! But those throw away lines and moments that are scattered through Abraham's 175 years on the planet do not exactly qualify him as "a prophet" of any particular degree. But Yahweh Himself revealed to Pharaoh and Abimelech that they should be afraid to mess around with Abraham or his wife because, said Yahweh, "He is my prophet." Strange, eh?!

3. THOSE WHO WERE MADE PROPHETS BY THE IMPARTATION OF AN EXISTING PROPHET.

There are prophets who are made prophets by the ministry and impartation of other prophets.

God sent Aaron to Moses to be his (i.e: Moses's) prophet. Aaron was thereby an illustration of what a prophet is prophet. We have no evidence that God spoke directly to Aaron, in fact, it is emphasized – especially in Leviticus, many times – that Yahweh told Moses what to say and do with Aaron. The call to Aaron was enacted and empowered by Moses who was the prophet who had a partner who would do the speaking.

Then there is Elijah and Elisha. Elijah cast his mantel over farmer Elisha. And after some years of being Elijah's valet, butler and hand washer, the invisible spiritual prophetic mantel of the Holy Spirit that was symbolically cast over him by prophet Elijah, fell upon him from above as Elijah ascended into heaven. The reality was wrapped up in the symbol. The anointing of God was so heavy that the substance was equivalent to and imparted immediately by the symbol of Elijah's mantel. Elisha, after Elijah's ascension and departing, lived in double the anointing that had rested on Elijah. It would seem logical to state that a candidate for prophetic ministry enters into the depth and breadth of the prophetic gift that is at least equal to the man who ministers the imparting – unless one asks for more, of course. As with Samuel to Saul, Elijah to Elisha, and Paul to Timothy and the "about twelve" in Acts 19, the principle of the prophetic gift being given by the ministry of another "man of the Spirit" is clearly exemplified in scripture enough times to be understood.

The spirit of Elijah did **_REST_** upon Elisha. Elijah cast his mantel originally at the instructions of Yahweh. The size of Elisha's farming operation suggests that at the time Elijah found him, Elisha had no plans at all to take holy orders. He was a secure, wealthy, firmly entrenched farmer.

B. UNKOWN FACTORS OF PROPHETS.

1. THOSE WHO APPEAR FULL GROWN AND EMPOWERED WITHOUT ANY CREDENTIAL OR HUMAN VERIFICATION OF THEIR SPIRITUAL DERIVATION.

Compare John the Baptist and Elijah. Who tutored Elijah? Who taught John? Was there any human connection to Elijah's call? Was John walking as a prophet from childhood? That is not inconceivable. Elijah appears fully grown and mature as a prophet in 1 Kings 17:1. However, who taught him? Who baptised John the Baptist? Both of these men were pursued by Godless women into doubt and depression. Both of them lived in the wilderness. But in a more physically determined profile … where and how did the two of them fill their spiritual armoury.

Where did the prophet Obadiah come from, and how did he assert his prophetic authority? How did Hosea maintain his authority and kudos among his people being married to a prostitute? How did Joel rise? And from where and how did his anointing fall upon him? Nobody knows when he lived or where he came from. All we have is the book that is verified as inspired by the way Christ and the apostles utilise its contents.

There are several prophets that appear momentarily in the pages of biblical history only to disappear as quickly as they appeared, leaving nothing behind them but the trail of inspired utterances that changed the course of the Middle Eastern world in biblical days.

Some of these men seem to be utterly unqualified by worldly standards. Like Elijah and John, the Baptist, there was absolutely nothing to cause a following, apart from the fact that they had heard from God and were speaking on His behalf. Somehow, despite the strange, distant profile and lifestyle of Elijah and John, the masses gathered around them, and they fully served and impacted their generation. Did you know that John the Baptist is surmised as having ministered to the public in the desert places for no more than three months? Even Christ Himself stated that amongst the prophets of men, there was none greater than John the Baptist. That is one remarkable eulogy for a prophet who was only known as such for a ninety-day ministry.

The landscape of prophecy is complex and multifaceted. Recognizing the various dimensions of prophetic ministry—whether through born or made prophets, and regardless of their societal status—enriches our understanding of God's communication with humanity. The ongoing dialogues about prophets today should be approached with an open mind, allowing for the possibility that God continues to speak through His chosen vessels in our contemporary world.

Following the deep encouragement for Christians who seek to follow the injunction to prophesy, we conclude that one's roots in or out of prophetic tutorship, in or out of prophetic fellowships, every believer can step into the experience and ministry of sharing God-given prophecies to the body of Christ.

7

THE OVERARCHING EXPERIENTIAL TRUTHS MARINATING EVERY PROPHETIC ACTIVITY OF ELIJAH.

The man from Tishbe stands as a towering figure in the annals of biblical history and prophetic portraits. His life and ministry present a vivid masterpiece of engaging with divine encounters, unwavering urgent obedience, and fervent repetitive prayer. The essence of Elijah's prophetic acts is deeply rooted in what I believe are four overarching experiential truths. I do not say that these four aspects of his life are the only aspects ubiquitous to all we read of him, but these four grab my attention each time I read through the relevant narrative, together with the New Testament commentary statements about the man.

1. His intimate dialogical relationship with Yahweh. There was dialogue both ways.

2. His unwavering adherence to the Word of the Lord what he had read from the Pentateuch. He undoubtedly had a simplistic attitude to the statements written in Deuteronomy as to God's response to idolatry amongst the chosen people.

3. The continuous communication from God, including that wonderful repetitive statement: "The word of the Lord came to him" six times, and "The Angel of the Lord came to him" twice.

4. His persistent, fervent prayer life. Even after having acted on the word of God, having obeyed Him, having called down fire at Carmel, and slain 450 prophets of Baal, he still had to petition Yahweh seven times before the rain cloud finally showed itself. These four ubiquitous elements of his life coalesce to reveal not only the character of Elijah but also the profound nature of prophetic ministry *en bloc*.

1. WE CANNOT BUT CONCLUDE THAT HE QUITE LITERALLY LIVED IN THE PRESENCE OF YAHWEH 24/7.

Elijah the Tishbite, as far as his biblical narrative is concerned, appears fully grown and developed as a prophet. We have not the slightest clue as to his age, his prophetic experience or his standing amongst the prophets or in the eyes of the nation. He appears with one of the heaviest assignments anybody ever negotiated apart from Moses or Samuel.

It is parr for the course to assume from human experience in almost every strata that mega "world impacting" performances are the result of some considerable time of gaining skill, knowledge and understanding in whatever skillset one is referring to. Even David learned his giant-killing skills by slaying Lions and bears in his childhood. We abandon any imaginations of biblical silence and have to launch into our appraisal of the man from Tishbe from the point of him clearly being an active, fully mature and experienced prophet of God.

The storyline begins with the outrageously enormous declaration in 1 Kings 17:1, where he incredibly proclaims, "As the Lord, the God of Israel lives, *in whose presence I serve.*" This assertion is not merely a statement of faith; it encapsulates the reality that defines his existence. He was facing the King of the northern kingdom of Israel fully endorsing his wife's zeal to abolish Yahweh worship and to fully install Baal into the national psyche. Elijah is not a prophet who dabbles in spirituality from a distance; he lives in the very presence of Yahweh. He is declaring that as he stood before Ahab visibly and geographically, he was concurrently standing in the throne room of Almighty God. This profound relationship shapes every aspect of his ministry. I believe I am on safe ground in saying that most believers who are sensitive enough to know and experience the tangible presence of God in prayer leave their prayer time hoping and believing that the consciousness of being in His very presence will sustain them as they leave their prayer room to get on with life. *Elijah never left the conscience presence of Yahweh wherever he went.* That 24/7 experience of the touch and the presence of the Almighty was his daily staple.

To understand the significance of Elijah's proximity to God, one must consider the cultural context of his time. The ancient Near Eastern milieu was rife with polytheism and spiritual confusion, yet Elijah stood as a solitary beacon of Yahweh's truth, rooted in an experiential knowledge of God. His connection with Yahweh is characterized by intimacy and immediacy – alignment and oneness, allowing himself to confront the idolatrous practices of Israel with divine authority. This closeness with God provides Elijah with a unique insight into God's will, enabling him to act decisively and fearlessly, whether challenging King Ahab, calling down fire from heaven, telling a poor widow to feed him before she fed herself and her son, or calling her son back from death.

2. INCREDIBLY SENSITIVE SPIRITUAL EARS TO THE WORD OF YAHWEH.

Elijah's life is a testament to his remarkable sensitivity to the arrival of the Word of Yahweh and then his immediate obedience to whatever the directives were. In 1 Kings 18:36, during the climactic showdown on Mount Carmel, Elijah prays, "Lord, the God of Abraham, Isaac and Israel, let it be known today that you are God in Israel and that I am your servant *and have done all these things according to your word."* This statement underscores a critical observation: Elijah never acted on his own initiative but was a vessel for God's Word to be heard and brought to reality. His language suggests to the cursory or secular reader of the scripture that Elijah was making up the plot guide and storyline of his activity by his own spontaneous thoughts and intentions. And that would be a logical conclusion if it wasn't for the statement, *"and have done all these things according to your word."* If his conduct for cancelling rain and do, calling down fire, and ordering the execution of 450 people fell under that blanket word from God, we are logically concluding that his other tasks fell into the same criteria.

This consistent practice of utter obedience reflects not only a sensitive spirit that hears God's faintest whisper but it also reveals a profound trust in God's wisdom and timing. In a world that often prioritises personal ambition and self-serving motives, Elijah's example challenges us to consider the depth (or otherwise) of our own obedience. He models a life that is responsive to divine revelation and instruction, demonstrating that true prophetic ministry flows from a posture of complete submission to God's voice, having mastered the art of tuning in his spirit to the mind and heart of Yahweh Himself. Each prophetic act Elijah engages in is not simply an expression of his personal enduement of power but a fulfilment of God's purpose in the world. This alignment with divine intent becomes crucial in understanding the efficacy of his ministry.

3. CONTINUOUS COMMUNICATION FROM GOD

I separate this gift of hearing from his characteristic obedience deliberately. We really need to home in on the aspect of Elijah's prophetic experience in the continual communication he receives from the Lord, as noted in numerous passages (1 Kings 18:15, 19:9, 21:17, 21:28; 2 Kings 1:3, 1:15). By this list of texts, we meet the repetitive phrase of the truly awe-inspiring statement, *"The word of the Lord came to Elijah"*. This ongoing recurrent – almost habitual habit of Yahweh in the person of Christ dialoguing signifies a deep relational dynamic that is the essential "bread and butter" for prophetic insight and action. The prophet has a word, a burden, a message to give to people and circumstances only because he first heard God speak. My experience of sitting under the influence of prophets and prophetic men of God through the years leads me to dogmatically declare that there is a spectrum in the realm of the prophetic. Elijah moved in the peak of that spectrum. God's word comes to Elijah not sporadically but rather as a steady stream of revelation that guides him through adversities and challenges. By studying the prophetic ministries that have touched my life through the years, the more a prophet flows towards groups of people, the more tiredness overpowers them after an hour or two of ministry.

This continuous flow of divine communication highlights the nature of prophetic ministry as inherently relational. Elijah is not merely a spokesperson for God; he embodies a life of communion with the Divine. His emotions and timbre of voice organically rise and fall inherently with the tone of the words they receive. There is nothing robotic about true prophetic impartation. This aspect of a prophet ministry serves as a powerful reminder that prophecy is not just about foretelling the future but much more about participating in the unfolding story of God's redemptive work in a person's history. The frequency of God's communication with Elijah indicates a God who desires to engage intimately with His people, ensuring that His plans are made known and that His servants are equipped for the tasks ahead.

4. PERSISTENT REPETITIVE PRAYER LIFE

Elijah's prayer life is undoubtedly one of the most striking dimensions of any ministry revealed in both the Hebrew Bible and the New Testament. In 1 Kings 18:42-48, we witness a remarkable scene where Elijah prays quite literally seven times for rain to fall after a prolonged drought and the climactic spiritual battle on the heights of Carmel. His persistence in prayer is not a display of desperation – far from it - but a demonstration of faith and commitment to God's promise. Each repetition is an act of trust, reflecting the belief that God hears and responds. He was not in any way afraid of praying for a miracle *publicly*. Note that even though he had seen the fire fall on his sacrifice, and even though there was a turning of the masses from Baal to Yahweh, he did not consider sitting back as if, "Job done" was in his mentality. The battle had cleared the way for the prophet to confidently ask for the rain to now fall after the 42-month drought. Praying for an out-and-out miracle before an audience was no problem to him.

His fervent prayer culminates in the manifestation of God's power as "the hand of the Lord came upon him" (1 Kings 18:46) as he ran the entire journey from Carmel to Jezreel, which is anything between 15 to 30 miles, depending on what location in Jezreel Ahab's palace was. Not only did he gird up his garb to run the whole distance, but we are told that he ran in front of Ahab who was following in a horse and chariot. Such moments accentuate the interplay between human agency and divine action. Elijah's relentless intercession reveals the importance of perseverance in prayer—an invitation for believers to engage in spiritual warfare through communication with God. His example challenges us to reconsider our own prayer life. Are we persistent in seeking God's will? Are we willing to wait for His answers, even when the skies seem barren?

Beyond these core truths, Elijah's life invites us to explore other striking observations. One such element is the duality of his experience—moments of triumph juxtaposed later with profound discouragement. After the victory at Carmel, Elijah fled in fear of Jezebel, revealing the human vulnerability behind the seeming ever-successful prophetic mantle. This tension illustrates that even the most anointed servants of God can experience doubt and despair, yes – and even negativity, yet it is precisely in those moments that God's grace and provision is manifested in profound ways.

Elijah's encounters with God often come through seemingly unexpected means. In 1 Kings 19, after his flight from Jezebel, Elijah finds himself in a cave, where he hears God not in the wind, earthquake, or fire but in a "still small voice" these days commonly translated as a "gentle whisper." One volume I have read demanded that the phrase *"still small voice"* should be properly translated as *"divine silence"*. This serves as a reminder that divine communication often occurs in the quiet, subtle moments of life, urging us to cultivate attentiveness to God's voice amid the clamour of the surroundings of life.

The biblical scrolls that reveal the life and ministry of Elijah offer rich and chasmic insights into the nature of prophetic acts and the experiential truths that undergird them. His unwavering existence in the presence of Yahweh, his obedience to divine instruction after hearing and listening to the continuous stream of communications from God, and his persistent prayer life all coalesce to form a paradigm of faithful living in the Spirit. Elijah's legacy challenges us to embrace a holistic understanding of prophetic ministry—one that is deeply relational, obedient, characterized and punctuated by fervent intercession.

In a world yearning for truth and divine intervention, Elijah's example stands as a clarion call for believers to engage boldly and faithfully in their own prophetic journeys, ever attuned to the voice of God.

These four experiential truths are dimensions of the human spirit that myself and all my readers can enter into. To emulate Elijah, it is not optional.

PART B

THE DYNAMICS OF PROPHECY

8

DEFINING THE DYNAMICS OF THE "PROPHETIC SPIRIT".

(HOW DID ELIJAH PROPHETICALLY RECEIVE THE MESSAGE THAT WAS TO CHANGE ISRAEL'S HISTORY?)

We are hereby exploring an area where no book, sermon or research paper has ever gone, as far as I know. Yes, F.B. Meyer talks about, "The secret of Elijah's power." Yes, Stephen Kaung states, "We know that Elijah was a man of prayer," and then jumps a little later to "If God said go, he went," without explaining any practicalities of joining the dots of those two statements. Prayer that achieves things on earth does not just happen. The practicality of such prayer is built as a regular exercise and practice – and tenaciously built with firm foundations. Stendal observes, "The fact is that Scripture says a true prophet of God must be one hundred per cent accurate." Now, that may or may not be true in the Old Testament (I am not going to be blustered into stating an unnecessary certitude as Stendal does. The fact that all the Old Testament prophets were accurate does not logically demand that all true prophets had to be true 100%..0but cannot be blanketed as true in the New Testament because we have the injunction to "test the spirits". A false claim like Stendal's kills any desire to aspire to prophesy in those who are fearful of being referred to as a "false prophet" (1 Corinthians 14:1). However, he holds such a high status of prophets and prophecy without explaining how to climb that ladder that men like Elijah have climbed and to stand with them on the peak of hearing God and delivering "load bearing" truths. He clearly has some kind of romantic concept of Old Testament prophetic accuracy, and with that red line clearly drawn, refuses to explore any deeper. He writes a fabulous volume that has omitted any attempt at an explanation of how Elijah arrived at such a mountaintop of prophetic clarity. MacIntyre and Davidson's "Study the Prophets: Elijah and Elisha" is an intriguing volume examining the two great men. However, as non-charismatics, they have even less insight into the hows and wherefores' of issues and influences that bring a man to full prophethood than I do. After all, to the uninitiated cessationists, "true prophecy is a thing of history only", so there is no practical purpose in explaining how one can emulate somebody like Elijah because, as far as they see it – prophecy isn't possible in our day.

Shawn Bolz, an outstanding contemporary prophet, referring to the development of prophets and prophetic people in general, wisely explains, "The reality, however, is that if you want a person to be successful, then you must define the identity, responsibility, administration, and role of what you are inviting them to do, or they have to help define it to you. So much of the prophetic has been undefined or defined by needs that are not sustainable. Or even worse, the wrong types of people are placed into the wrong roles." Alph Lukau, a weathered and far-seeing contemporary prophet and pastor, minimally explains, "To be prophetic is to be in the atmosphere of the prophetic and to flow in accordance with where the Spirit of God is leading … in this season." I receive Lukau's words as a cry to hang out with prophets and prophetic people. One has to find such groups in order to hang out with them.

We can all turn into sermonic mode and explain insights. We can analyse and declare that a prophet is biblically portrayed as a man of affliction and heartbreak (remembering there were prophetesses also), whose personage in whose entire heart and soul is stanchioned in what he says, yet who is also gifted to discern and be aware of the exhaled wheeze of human desolation. We can all read the scrolls and behold that even as we may all deprecate unjust sustained iniquities in our civilisation, we mentally are intolerable of ingrafted societal evils, yet we tolerate those laws and practises that affront God Himself. The Old Testament prophets found it impossible to live with inaccurate scales in shops and financial greed in political leaders. Such parallels filled Israel and Judah in the days of the prophets, tolerable to society in general, yet to the prophets, all injustice is dark and carries almost astronomical proportions of engrafted darkness. Shopkeepers with false weights selling vegetables to people at exorbitant prices are addressed in the same breath as murder and idolatry. The late Abraham Heschel wrote that "the importance of prophecy lies not only in the message, but in the role of the prophet as a witness". "To be a prophet," he writes, "is to be in fellowship with the feelings of God, to experience communion with the divine consciousness."

However, I want to ask: How did Elijah come to possess such remarkable conviction and receive such a prophetic spirit in a manner never seen before in his lifetime, and possibly not since? Where did he go in his thoughts and spirit? Who did he meet in the invisible world as well as other people? How was he taught? How does the authority of Almighty God activate itself when Elijah speaks? "When did it start? To my mind, answering these questions is vital for facilitating a valid discovery of the activation button needed to begin to fulfil 1 Corinthians 14:1. Sadly, the Hebrew texts do not give us a specific plain answer to these multiplied questions. One has to dig, meditate, chew, and ask for insight from Yahweh's created "elsewhere."

So, after absorbing scripture enquiring from contemporary prophets, here are my thoughts on what catapulted the man from Tishbe into an all-time mountainous high of prophetic possibilities. None of the following are in any way prioritised. This is stuff that I hear from contemporary prophets, and can validate each point by biblical examples.

A. IMBIBE AND ACCEPT BIBLICAL STATEMENTS – EVEN THE UNPLEASANT ONES.

Not to be too simplistic, my first offered suggestion is that Elijah simply read or was told what the Bible stated about God's retribution towards idolatrous practices and Godlessness in Israel. I see Elijah being familiar with the following titbits from the Hebrew scrolls. These lines carried a vertiginous (dizziness-creating) implication and relevance for the generation in which he lived. Sometime in his life, as a child, or possibly recent to his confrontation with earthly and demonic powers, he was challenged by these sections of the Torah and was impacted by them. This is where Yahweh Himself is quoted in Leviticus 26:14-21 as saying:

"But if you will not listen to me and carry out all these commands, and if you reject my decrees and abhor my laws and fail to carry out all my commands, and so violate my covenant, then I will do this to you: I will bring on you sudden terror, wasting diseases and fever that will destroy your sight and sap your strength. You will plant seed in vain because your enemies will eat it. I will set my face against you so that you will be defeated by your enemies; those who hate you will rule over you, and you will flee even when no one is pursuing you.

If after all this you will not listen to me, I will punish you for your sins seven times over. I will break down your stubborn pride and make the sky above you like iron and the ground beneath you like bronze. Your strength will be spent in vain because your soil will not yield its crops, nor will the trees of your land yield their fruit. If you remain hostile toward me and refuse to listen to me, I will multiply your afflictions seven times over, as your sins deserve."

Then there was Deuteronomy 11:16-17.

"Be careful, or you will be enticed to turn away and worship other gods and bow down to them. Then the LORD's anger will burn against you, and he will shut up the heavens so that it will not rain, and the ground will yield no produce, and you will soon perish from the good land the LORD is giving you."

The above needs to be also thought of when reading Solomon's prayer at the opening of the first temple.

1 Kings 8:35-36.

> *"When the heavens are shut up, and there is no rain because your people have sinned against you, and when they pray toward this place and give praise to your name and turn from their sin because you have afflicted them, then hear from heaven and forgive the sin of your servants, your people Israel. Teach them the right way to live and send rain on the land you gave your people for an inheritance."*

My first suggestion is that having read or been informed of these scriptures, Elijah absorbed the significance of these words.

B. BELIEVE THE VERACITY OF THE SCRIPTURES.

At the risk of being acutely sermonic, I see that Elijah's roadway took the ensuing process:

a. Elijah had a fundamental acceptance that the scriptures were truly words from the ever-living Yahweh. The text was dependable. He believed the scripture as, today, a so-called "fundamentalist" would. No redaction! No dilution! No "God must have been using analogies or euphemisms"! There was no submission to the priestly professional theologians who asked for "balance" and/or "plain reasonableness". If Elijah read the above scriptures, the narrative suggests that he processed it as a literal threat of divine judgement, with the goal of restoration, on the other side of the judgement, if repentance was rampant..

b. The man from Tishbe would have entered lengthy and deep absorption of the text. Because of his conduct in addressing Ahab, it cannot be denied that he was immersed with the concept of a heaven-sent drought and famine. It wasn't a bad mood that descended upon himself or Yahweh. It was a correction of the invisible evil forces that are existent in the world. Elijah had deep, life-changing convictions. Reading the story from the viewpoint of the twenty-first century, knowing how the story ends, we may think, "No problem! Elijah was not in danger! He was safe in God's arms". We can all say that when we are out of the far end of a predicament. Yet Elijah's life was continually threatened throughout all his days. Jezebel's threats were not the only ones.

c. But the text does not actually say that Elijah read the books of Moses. If he did not read the text, did he talk to people who knew the text and shared what they knew with him? And if not that, we would ask if the Word of God (i.e. The very person of Christ) came to Him and instructed him? If that was how he received the news of the required judgement, it still led to the same understanding on Elijah's mindset and worldview.

Whatever the means, something was imparted to the man that substituted cast iron for a moral backbone and immovable rock for spiritual insight. Elijah was possessed of a comfortable yet unbreakable faith that had a firm hold on the very substance of what he hoped for, standing on the evidence of something he had not seen before. And that is the New Testament statement of Hebrews 11. That means that the faith that Elijah was fuelled with is accessible to every believer. The placing of that statement in Hebrews 11:1 is not only accessible to New Testament believers but is clearly exemplified by a "believers hall of fame" from the Hebrew bible. What am I saying? I am saying that the sort of faith that Elijah carried is equally valid and accessible to you and me today in the twenty-first century.

C. CARRY THE IMPARTED BURDEN AND THE ENGRAFTED WORD AS A MATTER OF LIFE OR DEATH.

a. Next, presupposing a., b., and c. above, we can safely and definitively conclude that, with these words filling and influencing his mind, the man from Tishbe prayed over what he saw in his imagination – an imagination fed by the Hebrew scriptures, quoting them back to Yahweh. How do we know this? "Elijah was a human being, even as we are. He prayed earnestly that it would not rain, and it did not rain on the land for three and a half years." (James 5:17).

The point being that it is legitimate to quote God-given-promises back to Him when praying.

    b. Having addressed God in deep prayer (i.e., praying as opposed to "saying prayers") there was a responsive dialogue with Yahweh. The dialogue may have indeed been audible. The Theophany may indeed have been visible. This writer believes it is necessary to presume that dialogue with God in the scriptures, where a human is recorded as speaking to Him, God replies, and conversation thereafter ensues, cannot consist of any human being talking to an invisible Yahweh with a voice speaking from heaven without a tangible, visible Theophany.

This is the crunch element. What we say, believe, understand and hear while we are praying, and whether we stay long enough to hear an answer. There are no instructions or set rules how to hear from god. The demand is to simply persevere until the answer lands in your consciousness, i.e. your spirit.

D. **TAKING THE WHOLE PACKAGE INTO GOD'S PRESENCE TO GET HIS RESPONSE.**

The huge galactic-sized issue is: What did Elijah say or think, and/or what did Yahweh impart to him that was valid enough, strong enough and clear enough to motivate a man to walk mile upon mile to the likes of Samaria, risking his life and telling the very King of Israel such a "sci-fi" type remark that would either make him the funniest comedian in Israel's history, or the greatest form of prophet ever experienced in Israel. And goodness knows the Bible tells us of some eye-watering, jaw-dropping giant prophets prior to Elijah's lifetime.

The prophetic impartation may have been wordless, as when best friends or husbands and wives communicate questions and answers without any audible words being uttered. We can only deduce that Elijah's initial prayer went along the line of, "Yahweh, this is what you have said in your book. Neglect of your word, your worship and You yourself is causing your name to be spoken against and even pilloried amongst your people in your Land. So; fulfill what you have promised!" Oh, to get my hands on Elijah's script – or even his prayer points that precipitated the heavenly response that led to the moment of 1 Kings 17:1.

And if he had not seen a copy of the scriptures, possibly the impartation was an engagement with "the God of glory" in the same way He appeared to Abraham, as explained in the first verses of Acts 7.

Elijah owned what he had read or heard. Through whatever means heaven chose, something was imparted to Elijah that resulted in the offering of this prayer referred to in James 5:17. Something huge was divulged to him from the elsewhere of God's throne room. An extremely heavy load-bearing divine intention was delivered into the arms and heart of the man from Tishbe. God does nothing but that he reveals it to His prophets. (Amos 3:7) It was a mutual embrace of Elijah wilfully engrafting the array of a prophet's responsibilities as part of his own being, and the suite of purposes of Almighty Yahweh being imbedded into his soul. It was a two-way exchange (That is the presuppositional meaning of the English word, dialogue.)

1. TAKING FULL AND TOTAL RESPONSIBILITY FOR WHAT HIS SPIRIT OWNED.

Methinks such a heavy and momentous prayer took some considerable length of time and exertion of physical as well as spiritual effort. Whether the word, the message, or the responsibility came to Elijah little by little or in one flash of a moment, we can only ponder. All we can honestly conclude is that somehow, someway, Yahweh laid it on Elijah that he was carrying a message and, therefore, responsible for its delivery. Added to that responsibility was given the means to carry out the full required act, Elijah wilfully accepting and owning the responsibility of the whole mission. Elijah had been the recipient of a "prophetic spirit". Elijah had a connection and a kind of "mind-meld" with the Almighty. (Apologies for the Star

Trek connection – but complete alignment with the almighty needs to be, indeed, a melding of minds.) As a result of this prayer, Elijah left Gilead, crossed the Jordan, marched over to wherever Ahab was and delivered one line to the idolatrous king – a line that was never to be forgotten or ignored again.

Without any doubt whatsoever, we can confidently assert that both Yahweh and Elijah assumed mutual responsibility for the entire mission of confronting Baalism in Israel. But for human eyes, ears and understanding Elijah was in charge of the providential climate over all the Levant.

Simply because 1 Kings 17:1 is the initial moment in the chronology of First Kings, where we see Elijah in prophetic action, it does not necessarily demand that this was the first prophetic mission of the Tishbite. The pleasure of pondering and seeking the whys and wherefores of biblical history by squeezing the juice out of the scriptural fruit can lead us into many flavours of conclusions.

9

INSPIRATION IS AN EVENT, NOT A SLOW GROWING AWARENESS.

To the consciousness of the prophet, the prophetic downloading from heaven is more than a subjective experience; it is an objective event. This is its essential form. Whatever be the motive or content, contrary to how many Pentecostal/Charismatic "prophecy-accepting-churches" in this generation, "I feel God is saying…" or "I feel the Spirit would have me say …." is not to be found in the 66 volume Bible. Words received by characters in the biblical narrative is consistently received as an event that occurs in our time-space world, not merely an internal process. What is the difference between process and event? A process happens regularly or gradually, following a relatively permanent pattern; an event is extraordinary, irregular, and might even be just a single event. A process may be continuous, steady, or uniform; events happen suddenly, intermittently, or occasionally. Processes are typical; events are unique. A process follows a law, events create a precedent. The term "continuous revelation" when talking of the Old Testament Hebrew prophets receipts from heaven, is, therefore, as proper as a "square circle." "The word of the LORD came to …" reveals a literal event in the experiential life of the prophets.

We must admit that revelation is remote from "the daily experience of modern man today"; even the thought of it is intellectually embarrassing in common secular circles and even some Christian circles. Yet, to identify it with our own intellectual preference is to distort it before we explore it and is to abuse what we are supposed to understand. We must be ready to go beyond the categories of our own experience, even though such a procedure may upset our own mental routine and ease, not to mention turning a lifetime's habit that has been warmly accepted by many totally upside down.

Inspiration, then, is not a process that goes on all the time but an event that lasts, possibly a mere moment. We are talking biblically. The term used in the Bible to describe general events in history - "it happened" - is employed to describe prophetic inspiration, particularly in Jeremiah and Ezekiel. The Lord appears, and/or "The word of the Lord came". Christ is the Word. God is not simply available once and for all, to be found whenever man so desires. God will be found by those who seek Him. There is an alternative to God's presence, namely, His absence. God may withdraw and detach Himself from history or from individuals. While exposed to Yahweh's overwhelming presence, the prophets predict even His absence.

"With their flocks and their herds, they shall go to seek the Lord, But they will not find Him; He has withdrawn from them." Hosea 5:6

"Then they will cry to the Lord, But He will not answer them; He will hide his face from them at that time, Because they have made their deeds evil." Micah 3:4

"I will wait for the Lord, who is hiding His face from the house of Jacob; and I will hope in Him." Isaiah 8:17

"Behold, I go forward, but He is not there; And backwards, but I cannot perceive Him; Bending to the left, I cannot take hold of Him; Turning to the right, I cannot see Him." Job 23:8–9

It takes great inner power to address a nation. It takes divine strength to address heaven and earth. The prophets do not speak in the name of a personal experience or an inner illumination. They speak in the name of a divine experience, of a divine event – they actually met with God in this time, space world and received information that burdened them along with an internal need to pass on whatever they receive. Inspiration is more than an act that happens within the prophet. Inspiration is a particular moment of the prophet's life, being present at a divine event, just as one would have an event as meeting a friend out on the streets.

"The mouth of the Lord has spoken" (Isa. 1:20; 40:5; Mic. 4:4).

"The Lord has spoken this word" (Isa. 24:3; Jer. 46:13),

"has sworn in my hearing" (Isa. 5:9),

"has revealed Himself in my ears" (Isa. 22:14).

Inspiration involves two key participants: the One who reveals and the one who receives.

To fully understand the nature of inspiration while investigating Elijah's inspiration, we must explore its significance for both parties. A crucial item to see clearly is how the prophet interprets the importance of the revelatory experience in relation to the divine. "The Word of the Lord came to Elijah".

Before we delve into this, we need to clarify the concept of Yahweh in prophetic thought and experience. As previously discussed, prophets typically do not describe God as He exists in His essence or as the ultimate Being. Moses talked to a man stood in the fire of the bush. Samuel dialogued with a man stood near his own bed. Isaiah saw the gory of Christ in the Temple in heaven. Jeremiah saw God in human frame reach out and touch his mouth. In sort, their focus was on God's relationship with humanity and the world. The term "Divine self-revelation" is misleading when discussing biblical prophecy. God does not make Himself known in a direct manner as eternal, all-powerful, all-knowing and all seeing. He transcends all forms of revelation and communicates solely through His words, and more commonly in the Old Testament than in the New, revealing in human or angelic form (was that still in human form?) sharing His emotions and intentions without unveiling His true essence. Hearing the Word spoken to the prophet would impart the emotion and "mood" of God as He spoke, with whatever facial expression he revealed. Thus, we must reframe our inquiry: What does the act of revelation signify and impart in terms of emotion and expression? What was the body language of Yahweh when he appeared to Adam, Eve, Cain, Noah, Abraham, Isaac, Moses and the long list of others.

The scrolls says quite clearly that Yahweh appeared to some. Where no physical appearance is stated, are we to conclude he didn't appear. If we do that we are being influenced by our common experiences. Christ appearing to people is hardly common in the west, though testimonies tell us sometimes He does. Anecdotally, it seems Christophanies are more common the middle and Far East. We seriously need to understand from the texts how the visible manifestations of Christ speak and impart whatever communication He brought.

When face to face with a Theophany, which I believe is always a Christophany, discussion of the being of God, and His attributes are rarely brought to the table. Job perhaps had god pose questions concerning his eternal activity. We are so thankful for Isaiah's verbal revelatory wanderings concerning Yahweh's plans, purposes, and attributes of infinity. Yet combining Genesis 12:1-3 and Acts 7:3, when Yahweh appeared to Abraham and instructed him to go on his world changing destiny, we have no record of Abraham asking, "Who are you?" The visible sight of God in His glory is more than enough. The visible glory seems to tell the whole story of who the biblical characters are meeting.

We have no prophets or prophetess in the Bible saying things like, "I see a picture!" or, "I think God is saying," or, "I have been reading the Bible and have come to a revelation". And let me say that in no way am I deprecating such practices. What I am saying is that the biblical prophets experienced an event. God came. God spoke. God receded out of view again. What was spoken was delivered. Yes, there was human subjective responses, but the revelation was clearly objective and seen with the eyes and/or heard by the ears. An event.

Every event can be understood as comprising two distinct phases. Since an event occurs within a finite timeframe, it must begin at a certain point and unfold in a particular manner. These two components, the initial moment and the subsequent progression developed in the prophet's decision-making and choices, define the event's structure from beginning to end. The first phase marks a departure from the previous understanding status quo. The second phase reflects a tendency toward development and continuity. We refer to the first as the turning point or revelation and the second as the preparation for the despatch of the revelation.

Each event originates from a change, representing a pivotal moment where a stable, understood truth is disrupted. This transition marks the shift from routine motivations of life to action on the word received, birthing the final action of the event itself. The turning point is intimately linked to what precedes it, representing the source from which the event emerges. Although we have to say that what precedes many of the biblical revelatory events is either not mentioned or explained in the process of the revelation. We have absolutely no clue as to what Abraham was doing when his revelatory event in Genesis 12:1-3 took place, nor any light on Mary's preparation for her pregnancy of Christ, apart from Gabriel's explanation of her purity and faith.

There is always a scene set, and at this stage, on the cusp of the event about to take place, it is filled with potential yet lacks tangible manifestation. The event cannot be guessed or even suspected. Humanly speaking, it is always a surprise. The critical turning point reveals the driving force behind the event, highlighting its dynamic nature and the impulse toward a new path, vision, or change in a society.

The occurrence of revelation signifies a shift from silence to a word of disclosure, marking a break from a seemingly eternal state of concealment. This shift transforms an abstract, timeless condition into a unique moment in time, where eternity intersects with the present, where the revelation intersects with the unknown. This moment disrupts the perception of uninterrupted continuity amongst mankind.

Revelation starts a whole new "taken-for-granted" facts that changes life. Like the discovery of the germ. The discovery of DNA. The technology of the technology that brought to birth the internet. We are talking of the revelation of Christ and the continuous revelation brought to earth through ever-broadening revelations of Christ Himself. Heschel talks of how, outside divine revelation, "We can only envision timeless silence as an impersonal state—an order that obscures what would otherwise remain hidden."

In this context, revelation is an act within Yahweh's own life. Man was ignorant of something. God comes and reveals it. Man carries on with the Divinely imparted knowledge. It transcends mere miraculous occurrences or influences on the prophet. Unlike the creation of the world, where God commanded, "Let there be" and it came into existence, revelation emerges from God's own essence, choice and activity.

The prophetic experience is perceived by the prophet as an event exclusively stemming from God's will and initiative. The prophet cannot summon inspiration. It must arise solely from God. It is entirely dependent on His desire. This independence from the prophet's will underscores the transcendent nature of inspiration and highlights that the moment of turning signifies God's intention to communicate. The biblical assertion that "Surely the Lord does nothing without revealing His secret to His servants, the prophets" (Amos 3:7) encapsulates a fundamental tenet of biblical faith. The decision to reveal is an event intrinsic to God's life, stemming from His motivation to share His thoughts with the prophets and thus to all mankind.

A personal event is inherently an act of communication, conveying intention from one individual to another. This act has a clear direction. The arrival of the communication initiates the event, while the direction of the recipient represents its culmination. It signifies a moment where the inner working of one person translates into an outward act for another. The inner workings and thoughts of

Yahweh translate into the mind and burden of the prophet. This establishes a very special relationship, culminating in the prophecy being delivered and giving what is prophesied its form, representing the peak of its realization.

It's necessary to differentiate between a divine manifestation and divine communication. A divine manifestation can be directly observable (as in Exodus 24:9–11) or sensed through its impact on nature and history (such as in Judges 5:4 and Habakkuk 3:3); however, it does not engage the prophet directly.

A vital aspect of prophecy is the directionality. For instance, when Amos proclaims, "The Lord roars from Zion, and utters His voice from Jerusalem," it exemplifies this direct communication.

10

A CONSCIOUS AWARENESS OF HEAVENLY AUTHORITY.

PROPHETS CARRY A MESSAGE FROM ELSEWHERE

What few expositors take stock of is Elijah's assured knowledge and his tangible air of authority that seeps out of the text on the scrolls. His words had an absoluteness about them, which is staggering. There was no, "I feel the Lord is saying ..." There was not a hint of, "Eh! I have a picture ..." There was no caveat that even hinted that, "At least that is what I *think* God is saying!" The man appeared as if from "elsewhere". The Tishbite approached the king of Israel as if from another world. He made a decree of an absolute statement that, until that moment, nobody would have believed that any human being could seriously utter. Elijah carried a "This is how it will be. It cannot be anything else apart from what I say," faculty and facility. He was a man who was conscious and aware of the authority that had been imparted to him and was energetically exercising that authority in true humility. His awareness and consciousness of the power and authority that he carried is, until he fled from Jezebel, highly tangible and real.

THE PROPHET WITH A MESSAGE BASED ON WHAT GOD HAD ENSHRINED IN SCRIPTURE.

He must have learned from heaven about what would happen if Israel turned to false gods and/or idolatry. Then he must have inwardly demanded that the scripture be fulfilled irrespective of the human authority in the land, the misled masses that followed the direction Jezebel and Ahab had taken them, and the hundreds of prophets that had stayed silent in fear of their lives. He understood the realm of the Spirit elucidated by Moses, even though he obviously knew nothing of or grasped any importance about the Levitical laws. He was, humanly speaking, a total individualist. He was an individualist who was totally aligned with and submissive to Yahweh, His Word, and His Spirit. He ignored the reality of the culture of the society of Israel and Judah at that time and was completely overwhelmed with the statements of scripture and had a greater knowledge of the Spirit of God who had inspired that scripture. We have no line of scripture that tells us that Elijah read the books of Moses. Scholars waffle on about how difficult it is for them to presuppose that there were copies of the Pentateuch in Elijah's day, especially in Transjordan Gilead. Non-academic writers, like me, have a rationale as to why I believe he would have access to the first five books of the Bible. However, irrespective of whether he did or did not, the motivation and the stated goal of his prophetic word to Ahab is thoroughly biblical and utterly coherent from what Moses predicted in his writings.

THE PROPHET WHO WAS STANDING IN THE HEAVENLY COURTS OF YAHWEH.

My point is that the contents of the prophetic forecasts of Moses were clearly more concrete to Elijah than the reality of the evil that what was happening around him. The present tense used when he refers to the "Lord God of Israel before whom I am standing" needs to be seen for what it is. It is the reverse of what happens to millions of Christian believers. We ask God for "His continued presence" and then refer to our daily interactions as separate from the time we have spent in His presence. Such practice has to be crass error.

And not only that. Elijah's words tell us that he is more aware of the presence of Yahweh than the oppressive atmosphere of the idolatrous culture and the reigning earthly monarch of his contemporary Israeli customs whom he was looking at face to face. The heavenly and spiritual realities of God, His presence, and His Word were all more concrete to Elijah than the flesh and blood, time-space world of matter and physical substance. The prophet's words defied the realities of this world and forcefully imposed the realities of God and His word here on planet Earth.

THE PROPHET WHO KNEW HIS MESSAGE WAS TO STAND FOR YEARS.

He was aware that the authority over the climate that had been given him, would not be utilised for "these years." The man was here to stay. He was no "fly by night" big mouth who would disappear never to be seen again. His words let it be known that even though he physically would not be seen for "these years" (a period that turned out to be three and a half years), his words would hang over the ground, the heavens, the clouds, the laws of precipitation from the Mediterranean Sea or the Sea of Galilee, and the physical universe as it existed in Elijah's generation. He was to be physically absent for "these years" nevertheless present by the word he had left sustainably living and hanging over Israel and its people – and beyond.

The rain would not have stopped if he had not said so. God does nothing without revealing His plans and intentions to His prophets. The prophetic word does not take place until and unless it is spoken. The drought would not have started had Elijah not issued 1 Kings 17:1 into the cosmos. The drought would not cease until he was to give the word. The prophetic word has the full and active drive of the Spirit of God behind it. It is not merely speaking biblical promises out loud. That is good. But that is not necessarily prophecy. It is all a matter of the human spirit and the Holy Spirit. How many take hold of the scriptural promises and speak the promise, "In the name of Jesus Christ – be healed!" – and yet nothing happens? It is the same principle. If the Spirit of God is not energising the words spoken, nothing happens. Lord, take us there.

THE PROPHET WITH A TINY DROPLET OF DIVINE OMNISCIENCE.

Elijah was given a tiny droplet out of the infinite ocean of God's omniscience, omnipresence, and omnipotence. Books and professors talk of the communicable attributes of God and how they are clearly differentiated from the non-communicable attributes. But what is

Elijah's prophecy if it is not a tiny sliver of God's "omni attributes." Elijah was privy to the future. It was, as it were, in his hand. The power to stop rain and to grant rain was in his mouth. Elijah was to travel out of Ahab and Jezebel's kingdom to Zarapheth, and yet he carried this tiny morsel of God's omnipotence by holding the rain back from the land and conceivably from millions of people down south in Judah as well as the northern kingdom of Israel, including also the ten surrounding kingdoms of Israel and Judah and possibly even further.

THE PROPHET WHO STOOD AT THE EXTREME PEAK OF THE PROPHETIC SPECTRUM.

We learn that there are different depths of prophetic gifting. While hundreds of prophets were hiding in caves and staying silent with their prophetic calling and gifting, what they had been given from God was neglected, yet in no way compromised. Some prophets see further than others. Some prophets see deeper than others. Some prophets are bolder than others. Some prophets say things that can be ignored without loss. Some prophets shake the world by what God has made them privy to. There is a gradient of prophetic power. Elijah and Elisha were at the peak of that gradient.

Elijah walked with divine authority. It was authority so much higher than the king as not to be even compared. Years in the future of the real-time of 1 Kings 17:1 a king wrote to one of Ahab's royal successors saying, "Heal my most loved servant of his leprosy." The king of Israel at this time was in despair when he saw the servant with his leprosy and read out loud the royal missive from the enemy kingdom. But the king, with all his authority and knowledge and courtiers, was utterly ignorant that there was a prophet in Israel who carried authority that the king knew nothing of. His lowly servants told him of a man called "Elisha". It is difficult to conceive that he had not encountered Elisha prior to that time. But the servant Naaman was directed to the kingly prophet Elisha and was healed. That story is for another time, but the principal was current and present here with

Elijah. Divinely imparted authority was seen, known, sensed and experienced wherever Elijah went.

"No rain till I say so." It was as hard to calmly believe and accept them as it would be if such a thing happened today.

The foundation of the New Testament church is built on the foundation of apostles and prophets. May we taste the sweet authority and direction of the prophets of God in this day and generation.

11

"MAN SHALL NOT LIVE BY BREAD ALONE, BUT BY EVERY WORD THAT PROCEEDS FROM THE MOUTH OF GOD."
(Matthew 4:3. Deuteronomy 8:3)

Give us the raw, undiluted, unsanitized word.

1 Corinthians 14:1 has earlier already been processed into our thinking concerning who are candidates for exercising prophecy. Opposite to what we have just previously stated concerning prophetic inspiration, the renewed mind in Christ must be an ever-expanding vision that is stretching for things we have not yet seen. Christ's promises are beyond what we have seen or done. It is to my mind a sin to teach people not to expect healing or blessing or improvement from the hand of the love of Christ and His heavenly Father. Do not back out, but hold tightly to yearned for goals, even if it is against the cultural flow that one is part of in a fellowship or church of friends and other Christ-followers. Whether it is the Christians's cultural flow or the culture of the secular stream, the man or woman of God, prophet or not, achieves one's own cultural life without necessarily agreeing what others say is the priority of the moment. The battle in the mind that has to be fought for and clarified (mostly alone) with God is not to be feared when being alone with one's personal revelations. Not that we should ever have to walk alone when discovering the sort of revelation and blessing we are discussing in these pages. Sound out your biblical discoveries and spiritual insights with trusted mentors and pastoral leaders. Robustly test what you learn and air it with those who have journeyed beyond you. Pray for people to be healed until they *are* healed. John Wimber prayed for hundreds and hundreds of people who were sick, and for years, he saw absolutely nothing. He was shocked when, finally, one day, a woman was instantly healed. He didn't know what to say at that moment. But from then on, the healing never stopped. There is an interplay and a conjoining requirement of

persistent human faith, extreme biblical promises of healing (that only seem extreme because of our cynical unbelief) and problematic resolutions in the midst of desperate human predicaments. A major need is to keep on being *unreasonably* persistent with Heavenly Father concerning what the praying person believes of God's known will from scripture.

All these faculties are never seen as clearly as they are in Elijah's battle as a sole prophet attacking the gates of hell.

Refuse to allow scripture to restrict your vision, your beliefs, your hunger for seeing the Kingdom come, and your desire to be like Christ - and here in our biblical cogitations - to be like the man from Tishbe. Having said all that. we have no insight as to how Elijah turned up as an experienced veteran prophet to announce a single sentence from the King of all kings to the king of ungodly Israel which, under a totalitarian reign of cruelty and evil, had wilfully dug deep potholes on the straight road that God had laid out for the Jewish people.

The biblical narrative surrounding Elijah, particularly in 1 Kings 17:1, offers a bottomless abyss of truth and grace, leading us to enter into explorations of the dynamics and the clashes between human agency, divine prophecy contained in the Hebrew scrolls, and the consequences of Israeli societal submission to the evil regime that was holding the masses under their thumb. My assertion that Elijah's personal engagement with the Mosaic writings, characterized by unmoving faith and deeply persistent and repetitive prayer, directly precipitating the drought, underscores a pivotal theological concept: the intersection of prayer from a biblical faith and divine intervention can move the universe. The two must meet somewhere, and they do not meet by accident or chance. The person of faith and the promises that declare the kingdom must stand in the midst of the dark, broken world and clash into an explosion of life, health and healing. The Kingdom of God does not just happen - it is built. Kingdoms are fought for as a matter of life and death. I want, here, to briefly delve into the intricacies of this relationship, examining the themes of idolatry, prophetic responsibility, and the transformative power of prayer mixed, mingled and ground finely with the promises of God.

At the heart of Elijah's story is the rampant idolatry that plagued Israel during the reign of Tyranny. The worship of Baal and Asherah symbolised a profound, ridiculously acute departure from the covenantal faith established by Moses, leading to societal decay and spiritual desolation. Jezebel entered into a political marriage with Ahab and was violently evangelical with her demon Baal and the Asherah, the false god of Sidon, from where Jezebel originated. To put it clearly, Baal worship and the practices associated with Asherah represent significant cultic and moral issues. Baal was a Canaanite demonic deity worshipped primarily as the god of storms, rain, and fertility. Its worship was prevalent in several ancient Near Eastern cultures, particularly among the Canaanites, which later influenced Israel. Baal worship constituted hideous Canaanite religious practices that was hastily gradually into Israelite worship, leading to syncretism with the worship of Yahweh. This was condemned, to express it gently by the biblical prophets (e.g., Hosea 4:12).

Worship of Baal directly violated the First Commandment (Exodus 20:3), which called for exclusive devotion to Yahweh. Some practices included the sacrifice of children to Baal, particularly in the form of passing children through the fire (Jeremiah 7:31; 2 Kings 23:10). This act represented the ultimate betrayal of the covenant community's values. The act of sacrificing children reflects a profound moral depravity and devaluation of human life, which stood in stark contrast to the teachings of Yahweh and the Mosaic scrolls.

Baal worship often involved ritual prostitution, where cultic practices included sexual acts as offerings to promote fertility (Numbers 25:1-3; 1 Kings 14:24). This practice violated the sanctity of marriage and family. Such practices contributed to a culture of promiscuity, undermining societal values and leading to further moral decay throughout the Israelite culture. Baal was primarily worshipped for agricultural fertility. Farmers would engage in rituals believing

Baal would ensure a bountiful harvest, leading to economic dependency on false gods rather than on Yahweh (Deuteronomy 11:16-17). This reliance on Baal undermined the cultural and spiritual identity of Israel, as the community began to attribute their prosperity to Baal rather than to Yahweh's provision.

Asherah was often viewed as a consort to Baal, representing a goddess of fertility and motherhood. Worship of Asherah frequently accompanied Baal worship. Wooden poles or trees, known as Asherah poles, were erected in high places as symbols of worship (Judges 6:25-30; 1 Kings 14:23). These poles were often associated with sexual rites and fertility practices. Asherah was worshipped in sacred groves, which were often sites of immoral practices. The destruction of these poles was commanded by Yahweh (Deuteronomy 12:3). Worship of Asherah included sexual rites performed by cultic prostitutes, reflecting the belief that such acts would ensure fertility for the land and people (Ezekiel 16:17-18).

The bottom line of all this demonisation as that these acts were normalized within society, leading to widespread moral corruption and a departure from the ethical mandates established by Yahweh. The evils associated with Baal and Asherah worship highlight an abyss-sized conflict between the worship of Yahweh and Canaanite religious practices. The idolatry, moral depravity, and societal consequences of these practices serve as a constant prophetic denunciation within the biblical narrative. The consistent prophetic call to return to Yahweh emphasizes the importance of fidelity to God and the consequences of straying into idolatry. But from the Mosaic statements of such a situation, Elijah's message embodied the tension between God's justice and mercy that was still extended to Israel. Make no mistake reader, the battle at hand was to be raw, bloody and brutal.

Elijah's prophetic identity is crucial to understanding the significance of the drought. He serves not only as a verbal manifestation of God's intentions but also as an active participant in the covenantal dialogue. His reading of and faith in the Mosaic texts highlight the importance of scripture in shaping the prophetic manifestations of the day. The act of prayer—intensely personal yet profoundly communal—positions Elijah as an intercessor like no other, bridging the gap between the divine and the human, between the promised land of peace and joy and the demonic-infested rat hole of Baal and Asherah.

The drought can thus be viewed as both a divine judgment as well as a Divine response to Elijah's fervent prayer (as explained in James 5:17). By believing in the possibility of such a drastic event as a cessation of rain, Elijah exemplifies a unique facet of faith: the conviction that the divine will can manifest through being precipitated by intense prayer and courageous action. His understanding of the Mosaic writings impelled him to act, illustrating that faith is not merely a passive acceptance of religious tenets, important as they may be, but an active engagement with God's promises and warnings and an assumption of complete personal responsibility of what the statements meant.

The assertion that the drought would not have occurred had Elijah not read, believed, and prayed over the Mosaic scrolls raises critical questions and debates about human agency in the divine narrative. It suggests that prophetic action, informed by scriptural understanding, can strongly influence the course of human history. Elijah's prayer, motivated by the recognition of Israel's idolatry, becomes a catalyst for change, underscoring the belief that human beings can invoke divine responses through sincere prayer and repentance.

The consequences of this clash and interplay are manifold. The drought serves as a wake-up call for Israel, a painful yet necessary measure to bring the people back to repentance and Yahweh. It invites a collective introspection regarding the nature of their Mosaic covenant with God and their commitment to forsaking idols. The severity of the drought mirrors the depth of the spiritual crisis, emphasizing that the severity of divine judgment often correlates with the gravity of human sin.

Elijah's prayer, as reported in James 5:17 is a poignant reminder of the transformative power inherent in sincere supplication. Prayer is not merely a ritualistic act but a profound expression of faith that can alter any circumstance. Elijah invoked a tangible spiritual reality that transcended the physical realm, illustrating that prayer can be both a declaration of faith and a powerful tool for bringing about divine action. Faith's warm finger goes through the veil and touches the hem of the Master's garment.

The notion that prayer can influence the natural order of the cosmos challenges contemporary understandings of initiating causality and the effect of divine sovereignty. It raises theological inquiries about the raw nature of prayer. The major question is: does it change God's mind, or does it align human will with divine purpose? In Elijah's case, his prayer reflects a deep understanding of Israel's moral and spiritual state, suggesting that true prayer arises from a place of prophetic insight supplied from the biblical text and compassion imparted from Christ Himself into an extended delving into the human situation.

I repeat my assertion that Elijah's reading of and faith in the scrolls, as well as his prayer that aligned with the statements of the scrolls, were all instrumental in the occurrence of the drought in 1 Kings 17, encapsulating a rich theological dialogue about faith, scripture, and the will of God. It highlights the profound responsibility of the prophet to engage with the inspired writings and act in accordance with divine principles, and also to be seen and perceived by the masses to be doing so. It's called leadership.

This narrative invites believers to reflect on their own roles within the tapestry of faith in their own lives, challenging us all to recognize the power of prayer and the importance of aligning our lives with the values espoused in the sacred texts.

The entire narrative of the man from Tishbe serves as an ever-present reminder that the chemistry of the mix between human agency and divine action is a dynamic process that encapsulates the entire Christian life, one that calls for both introspection and active engagement simultaneously. In a modern world still, in the twenty-first century, rife with idolatry and spiritual apathy, the lessons we are gleaning from Elijah's experience remain as relevant today as they were in ancient Israel, urging a return to the foundational truths of faith and a commitment to living in accordance with the will of the Living God.

Yet again, while meditating on as many aspects of the biblical teaching that we can squeeze from the scrolls that surround Elijah's story, we conclude that there is not a single constructive statement that dissuades us to cease from seeking to emulate the man of God from Tishbe. There is nothing at all that excuses or denies us from stretching our spirits to live in the same realms that he did. "Elijah status" is our aim. The saying goes that, "If one aims for the moon, one may hit the top of the trees. But we still need to aim for the moon. However, if one aims for the common height of the average trees, we will get next to nothing."

Yes! We want sensible rationale when handling people in grief or sickness. Yes! Poverty, sickness physical, mental, emotional and spiritual, is more rampant around the planet than it ever has been. The sick man healed in Acts 3 must have been passed many times by the Lord Christ Himself. There must have been thousands that died during the days Jesus walked the land of Israel. But this teaches us that even Jesus could only bring his influence and power to those situations that were brought to Him. And it's the same with us. Matthew 4:23-25 tells us that *all* the sick people from Syria, with every conceivable sickness one can think of, were brought into His immediate presence, and Jesus healed them all. But there were still sick people everywhere he went, and who knows how many were still sick after he walked past them. The message from that is that we are called to minister Christ to those we meet and not to have sleepless nights over those we never touch or never have a chance to influence. But it is essential we use the biblical teachings and examples to govern our attitudes and behaviour.

Church leaders in the western world who have never seen a miracle justify their cessationist error from their own experiences and not from scripture. When I hear of a man or woman moving in the miraculous, I strive to go and see what's going on. We all thank God for the experiences that life has taught us. But we should always remember that any experience we have learnt from is drastically limited. There are those in the West who move in the power of God, and there are many more who have healing ministries and have even raised the dead in Africa, India and further beyond. We conclude that even the manifestations of the power of God are seen as a spectrum. Some see the miraculous almost daily. These are those that we need to emulate and not cynically criticise as "fakes" without having even met them.

Why did Jesus Himself encourage us all to speak to mountains and tell them to move? Why did Jesus say to the disciples that they would do greater works than even He did? Why did He say, "All things are possible if you believe," if we are not expected to put his words to the test? I was told by one person several years ago, "You don't understand! Jesus was speaking to the disciples, not the masses?" My answer was, "But Jesus told the disciples to teach the world everything He had taught them!" Stephen was conducting his own ministry of the miraculous, and not only was he not one of the apostles, his job in church was to serve food to the widows. The slightly restrictive teachings of cessationists, suggesting that the odd line of scripture here and there is not relevant for us today, finishes up with us ignoring or denying some of the greatest inspirational and faith-building statements Christ ever uttered. It also causes us to leave the broken world with the status quo and say, "We are so sorry, but we Christians cannot help you". Agh! A pox on that thought.

12

THE AGENCY OF GOD IN THE EARTH AS SEEN IN ELIJAH'S PROPHETIC MINISTRY.

The God of the Bible is a vital, tangible and visible agent in this time-space world. That truth is simply not up for negotiation. In the Pentecostal circles where I was converted and developed in, this subject is the clearest and easiest to grasp presupposition from Sunday School lessons from the nursery age, and because of this basic presupposition to the entire biblical faith, I feel this delivery is hardly needed. It is only the modernistic sort of "Christians" that doubt the validity of the scriptures, as well as the resurrection, holding to the belief that God is not at all interventionist to anything on earth, that needs this issue to be discussed.

The gift of prophecy will not be tolerated or accepted as a normal practice at all if one doesn't believe God speaks at all. However, we make the push of a truth that has to be held firmly to the wallpaper of the house of prophecy. I declare loudly and boldly that I believe God is always active and always speaking. The only problematic challenge is to learn how to listen to the sound of His voice. The logic and theory of this issue goes as follows:

THE BLUEPRINT OF DIVINE AGENCY IN CREATION.

The narrative of creation, as described in the book of Genesis, illustrates God's 100% activity, being agent as the ultimate creator. "In the beginning, God created the heavens and the earth". And referring to Christ, the Bible states in John's gospel that, "By Him were all things made, and without Him was not Anything made that was made "(Genesis 1:1. John 1:1-4). These classic verses of biblical text establishes that God in Christ is the originator of everything that exists, intricately designing the universe with intentionality and purpose. The physical world, from the vast galaxies to the minutiae of cellular structures, reflects God's creativity and wisdom.

God's agency in creation is not merely a one-time act; it is ongoing forever. Colossians 1:16-17 states that "all things were created through him and for him... and in him, all things consist and hold together." This indicates that God's sustaining power is actively involved in the maintenance of creation. The laws of nature, the cycles of life, and the intricate balance of ecosystems all testify to God's ongoing involvement. As Christians, we are called to recognize and celebrate this divine handiwork, acknowledging that every aspect of the physical world is under God's sovereign rule and governmental activity.

THE DIVINE AGENCY IN UNIVERSAL PROVIDENCE.

Beyond creation, God's agency is evident in His providence, i.e., the way He governs and sustains His creation. Providence encompasses God's involvement in the unfolding of history and the lives of individuals. It assures believers that God is not removed from the daily realities of life but is intricately involved in every circumstance. In the book of Romans, Paul writes, "And we know that in all things God works for the good of those who love him" (Romans 8:28). This verse encapsulates the essence of divine providence, suggesting that God's agency operates even in the midst of suffering and chaos. "... God works ..." For evangelical Christians, this provides spiritual backbone, affirming that God is orchestrating events according to His will, often in ways that transcend human understanding.

Consider the story of Joseph in Genesis. Betrayed by his brothers, sold into slavery, and imprisoned unjustly, Joseph's life seemed to be governed by misfortune. Yet, through his trials, God was working behind the scenes to position Joseph as a leader in Egypt, ultimately saving many from famine. This narrative exemplifies how God's providence can transform adversity into opportunity, highlighting His agency in the physical world.

In the vast tapestry of human existence, the interchange and reciprocity between things spiritual and things physical, things invisible and visible, raises profound questions requiring and feeding a good understanding of God's agency in human existence. Pentecostal and all Evangelical Christians affirm their belief that God is not a distant observer "from a distance" but is ever actively involved in His creation, be it animal or abstract. God never slumbers nor sleeps and is and will be, forever, guiding and influencing the world according to His divine purpose. And no matter how things seem to be falling apart because of violence and hatred, we are assured that all things are working together to bring God's plan and purpose into being. We need to explore the manifold ways in which God's agency manifests in the physical world, encompassing creation, providence, and redemption. The biblical statements scattered through all its scrolls are to be immovably known and trusted and prayed over in order to see the divine plan manifested for us all.

THE ULTIMATE ACT OF DIVINE AGENCY - THE REDEMPTION OF MANKIND

The culmination of God's agency, of course, is found in the redemptive work of Jesus Christ. The incarnation, crucifixion, and resurrection of Christ are the apex of God's intervention in the physical world. This profound act of divine love demonstrates and underscores God's desire for a relationship with humanity and His commitment to redeeming a fallen world.

Through Christ, God not only addresses the spiritual needs of humanity but also engages with the physical realm. The miracles of Jesus - healing the sick, raising the dead, and calming storms - demonstrate His authority over the physical world. These acts reveal that God's agency extends to all aspects of life, affirming that He cares about our physical suffering and seeks to restore wholeness.

Elijah stands as one of the most significant figures in the Jewish prophetic narrative. His life and ministry vividly illustrate God's agency on earth through his prophetic work. Elijah's life's work occurs during a tumultuous period in Israel's history, marked by the reign of King Ahab, his evil wife Jezebel, and the institution of widespread shrines and the worship of Baal. This context of spiritual and moral decline sets the stage for Elijah's prophetic mission, where he becomes a voice of divine authority and power amidst rampant idolatry.

The legacy of Elijah extends beyond his immediate actions. He symbolizes the enduring struggle between faithfulness to God and the temptation of idolatry. His prophetic voice continues to resonate through subsequent generations, as well as in these pages, ultimately influencing the New Testament portrayal of John the Baptist and even aspects of Jesus' ministry. Elijah's agency as a prophet exemplifies God's ongoing work in human history, bridging the gap between the divine and the earthly realm.

Elijah, the man from Tishbe, epitomizes this divine agency, illustrating how a single human being can effectuate significant change within society. His life and ministry encapsulate the heart of prophetic work: a call to recognize God's sovereignty, respond to His guidance, and remain faithful amid adversity. Ultimately, prophecy and prophets like Elijah remind us of God's relentless pursuit of a relationship with humanity, underscoring His active role in the unfolding narrative of history.

God's agency in the world and non-acknowledgement by people is often a total mystery to me. Even though I disagree with people who argue that a person's lifestyle change after so called "conversion to Christ" is nought but a psychological phenomenon, I declare that I see the hand of God in all and everything I come across.

THE DIVINE AGENCY IN THE WORLD AS SEEN IN ELIJAH'S LIFE.

The biblical narrative of the prophet Elijah encapsulates a profound exploration of divine agency in the lives of individuals and communities. Elijah, the pivotal biblical figure we are staring at in these pages, serves as a pipeline for God's will, reflecting a dynamic interaction that transcends even the word communication. God's dealing with Elijah, and then Elijah's dealing with his public mass embodies and demonstrates a transformative relationship between the divine and humanity, between Yahweh and mankind. We must seek to unpack the multifaceted agency of God as manifested throughout all the biblical prophets, particularly through the life and mission of Elijah, while also considering the unconventional implications of this divine-human interplay.

Prophets in the biblical Old Testament are often perceived as mere mouthpieces for God, delivering messages that serve to guide, warn, or inspire. Elijah's narrative vividly illustrates this role. He confronts the idolatry of Israel, particularly the worship of Baal, and calls the people back to their covenantal God. This prophetic act is not merely an announcement of divine displeasure; it is an invitation to deep repentance and restoration. The agency of God is not solely about imposing authority over circumstances and people, but also about fostering a Father/son relationship grounded in covenantal love and responsibility.

Elijah's confrontation with the prophets of Baal on Mount Carmel (1 Kings 18) serves as a dramatic illustration of this interaction. The contest, where God answers Elijah's prayer, sending fire so much and so hot as to lick up Elijah's sacrifice that was lying on the altar, signifying that divine agency operates through extraordinary events that challenge the status quo. Yet, it is the aftermath of this demonstration that reveals a deeper layer of God's agency: the call for national repentance, the execution of 450 Baal priests and the re-establishment of proper worship.

Prophets function as catalysts for divine action, urging communities to reassess their allegiances to Yahweh and behaviour.

Prophecy, in its essence, is not merely predictive but is deeply relational and contextual. It emerges from the lived experiences of the prophet and reflects the socio-political realities of the time. Elijah's life is later marked by moments of despair and doubt, when his flight to Mount Horeb following the threat from Queen Jezebel (1 Kings 19). In Elijah's narrative, God's agency extends beyond the miraculous to include quiet, personal encounters with God's prophet. God does not respond to Elijah's despair with grand displays of power but with a gentle whisper, emphasizing that divine presence often manifests in discreet subtlety rather than bombastic spectacle.

This reveals an uncommon aspect of prophetic agency: while prophets are often seen as bold declarers of God's word, they are also vulnerable human beings navigating their own crises of faith. This duality invites a re-evaluation of how we perceive divine agency in the light of man's own failing. It suggests that God's interaction with humanity is not always through triumph or vindication but can also be experienced in moments of intimacy, reassurance, and personal renewal.

Elijah's narrative reveals God's agency as a call to action, not just for the prophet but for the entire community. The aftermath of Elijah's victory over the prophets of Baal leads to a significant moment of communal reflection and renewal. The people, witnessing the power of God, declare, "The Lord, he is God! The Lord He is God" (1 Kings 18:39). This collective acknowledgement signifies a pivotal shift, illustrating that prophetic agency can catalyse communal transformation. God's agency is inherently communal, relying on the active participation and response of the people.

Furthermore, the role of the prophet is not confined to the moment of revelation but extends into the realm of leadership and guidance. After the dramatic confrontation, Elijah's subsequent actions demonstrate the importance of sustained prophetic presence in guiding the people toward a renewed relationship with God. He anoints successors and mentors, like Elisha, ensuring the continuity of God's work among the people. This aspect underscores the notion that divine agency is often collaborative, involving multiple agents—both divine and human—in the unfolding narrative of faith.

The story of Elijah extends far beyond its historical context, inviting contemporary reflections on the nature of divine agency today. In a world marked by fragmentation and disillusionment, the prophetic call remains relevant. Prophets, whether formally recognized or emerging from within communities, challenge societal norms and beckon people toward deeper truths. This connection to Elijah's narrative encourages a re-engagement with the prophetic tradition, urging individuals to consider how they might embody prophetic agency in their own lives.

Moreover, the dynamic between God, prophets, and the people invites us to reflect on our own responsiveness to divine agency. It asks us to consider how we might act as channels of God's love and justice in a world yearning for meaning and connection. In this light, the agency of God through prophets is not a relic of the past but a living, breathing aspect of faith-today that calls for active participation in the divine narrative.

The agency of God in the lives of people, as seen here through the narrative of Elijah, reveals a complex interplay of communication, vulnerability, action, and communal transformation. Prophets serve as vital intermediaries, carrying messages that challenge and inspire while also embodying the struggles and triumphs of faith. By embracing the unconventional dimensions of prophetic agency, we uncover a deeper understanding of how God interacts with humanity—inviting us into a transformative relationship that is as relevant today as it was in ancient times.

THE ROLE OF HUMANITY IN GOD'S AGENCY

Understanding God's agency in the physical world also involves recognizing the role of humanity as agents of God's will. Created in the image of God, humans are given the responsibility to steward creation and participate in God's redemptive work. The Great Commission (Matthew 28:19-20) calls believers to actively engage in sharing the gospel, making disciples, and transforming society through Christ's teachings.

This partnership underscores that while God is sovereign, He invites us to be co-labourers in His mission. Our actions, choices, and prayers are significant; they reflect our engagement with God's agency. As we live out our faith, we become vessels through which God's purposes are fulfilled in the world.

The agency of God in the physical world is a multifaceted reality that encompasses creation, providence, and redemption. Evangelical Christians affirm that God is actively involved, guiding and sustaining His creation with purpose and love. As we navigate the complexities of life, we can find solace in the knowledge that God's hand is at work, orchestrating events for our good and His glory.

In light of this, we are called not only to recognize God's agency but to participate in it. By living out our faith, we contribute to the unfolding of God's kingdom on earth, bringing hope and light to a world in need. Ultimately, the agency of God reminds us that we are not alone; we are part of a divine narrative that is unfolding, one that assures us of God's unfailing presence and love in the physical world.

The concept of divine agency, particularly as it relates to God's interaction with humanity, is a profound theme in theological debates. This agency is often manifested through prophetic voices that convey divine will and guidance. I will explore the agency of God on earth through the tinted lens of prophecy in general and then particularly through the life and ministry of the man from Tishbe.

PROPHECY AS A MANIFESTATION OF DIVINE ACTIVITY/AGENCY.

Prophecy serves as a critical medium through which God communicates with humanity. In the biblical tradition, prophets are seen as intermediaries who convey God's messages, warnings, and promises. These communications underscore God's active involvement in human affairs, revealing His desire for a relationship with His creation.

Prophecy can be understood as both foretelling but mostly in our generation, forthtelling. Foretelling involves predicting future events, while forthtelling emphasizes the proclamation of God's truth and moral guidance. Prophets like Isaiah, Jeremiah, and Ezekiel exemplify this dual role, delivering messages that address immediate concerns and future hope.

Prophets are often called to speak against injustice, idolatry, and moral decay. Their messages are not merely predictions but are calls to repentance and transformation. For instance, the prophetic literature frequently emphasizes social justice, urging the people of Israel to align their actions with divine expectations. This highlights God's agency as He seeks to redirect humanity toward righteousness. The agency of God through prophecy necessitates a human response. The challenge posed by prophets is often met with resistance, as seen in the lives of figures like Jeremiah, who faced persecution for his messages. This tension illustrates the dynamic relationship between divine will and human agency, emphasizing that while God communicates His plans, He also allows individuals the freedom to accept or reject His guidance

13

TAKING AUTHENTIC RESPONSIBILITY FOR THE SINS OF THE NATION.

The Ultimate Example of Assuming Personal Responsibility for the Evil of His Own Nation

In the annals of biblical narratives, few figures embody the profound complexity of carrying personal responsibility as vividly as the prophet Elijah. I am convinced that this mindset is one of the major factors that precipitates the authority and power that Elijah carried. His life and ministry, woven intricately into the fabric of Israel's tumultuous history, present a compelling case study in the ethical dilemmas faced by leaders and individuals alike. Elijah carried the load of the nation's terrible series of choices as if nobody else was responsible but he. Elijah's actions and declarations resonate with a poignant urgency, echoing the perennial struggle between personal righteousness and the pervasive influence of societal corruption. Here we see Elijah's role as a prophet, his confrontations with power, and the striking implications of his assumption of responsibility for the evils of his entire nation.

Over five decades as a bible believing Christian I have always presented to audiences the absolute priority of taking personal responsibility for one's actions, and to carry also the culpability of secondary sins that occurred because of one's action – second level sins, if you will.

Carrying such responsibility before God in repentance is primary, reparations towards human beings is a secondary possibility also. But repentance for one's own nation state is taking this principle to its furthest level.

This is nowhere taught in the Bible as a precept to be added in the tenets of one's faith, but it is clearly exemplified in the Old Testament together with a hinted blurred example in the writings of the apostle Paul in the New Testament. There is of cause the death in the middle of three crucified men in the Gospels, who sinlessly carried the guilt of all of humanity when He that new no sin, became sin for us.

THE BURDEN OF INTERCESSION: DANIEL'S PRAYER (Daniel 9:3-20)

In Daniel 9, Daniel approaches God with a heart burdened by the sins of Israel. Because of the nation's sins, which was majorly instigated by generations of idolatry which slid to a darker and darker lifestyle, Daniel was born in the midst of the evils of Israel and removed to Babylon in captivity. From all we can see and read in the scrolls, Daniel was deeply spiritual and Godly all his days. His prayer from verses 3 to 20 is profound and powerful. Daniel has just noted that the 70-year exile prophesied by Jeremiah had now been fulfilled. So Daniel set himself with prayer and fasting, with the full battle dress of supplication, sackcloth and ashes – and a consciousness of full responsibility to clear the burden of national sin to bring about the Jews being released to return to the Promised Land. He begins with an acknowledgement of God's greatness and faithfulness, juxtaposed against the backdrop of Israel's failures. His confessional tone is striking and very obvious. The amazing aspect, as a prophet of God was that he did not distance himself from the sins of his people but instead embodied their collective guilt. He states, "We have sinned and done wrong; we have been wicked and have rebelled." This language of self-inclusion is critical: Daniel does not merely represent himself; he stands as a voice for the entire nation. When addressing the people he speaks for God, identifying himself with God alone. When addressing God, he identifies himself with the sins of the millions of individuals and speaks on their behalf.

This prayer offers several uncommon insights into the nature of repentance. First, it emphasizes the importance of recognizing one's role within a larger community. It wasn't a case of, "me praying for them", it was clearly leading the nation's requirement as if he was the leading sinner in the entire history. This is the greatest illustrative model of "prophetic prayer". By confessing on behalf of the nation, Daniel acknowledged that individual sins contributed to the collective moral situation. This observation raises pressing conceptual understanding concerning personal responsibility in the face of societal failures. Where are the verses that teach such an incredible thing. In today's context, it challenges us to consider how our actions and inactions impact the moral fabric of our communities. Daniel's recognition of shared guilt invites a deeper understanding of how societal issues—be it injustice, corruption, or apathy—can be traced back to individual choices.

After Daniel's prayer for national guilt and the release of Israel from the exile,

THE CRY OF A LEADER: NEHEMIAH'S SUPPLICATION (NEHEMIAH 1:4-11)

Similar to Daniel's intercession, Nehemiah's response to news of Jerusalem's desolation illustrates the profound effects of communal grief to be carried by one recorded prophetic man. Upon hearing about the plight of his homeland, Nehemiah is quite literally overwhelmed with sorrow, which drove him to prayer and fasting for several days, sitting and in tears (Nehemiah 1:4). His approach to God mirrors Daniel's, as he acknowledges both the greatness of Yahweh and the failures of the people: "We have acted very wickedly toward you."

Nehemiah's prayer is striking in its emotional intensity and the personal investment of himself with the broken, fallen, exiled people. He identifies with the plight of his nation, suggesting that true prophetic leadership requires a deep sense of empathy and responsibility. Nehemiah is nowhere labelled as a prophet *per se*, but the prayer is truly prophetic. His plea for forgiveness is not merely a ritualistic act; it is a heartfelt scream for restoration. Nehemiah's intercession underscores the idea that, prophetically, leaders bear a unique responsibility to advocate for their people, especially in times of crisis. This raises an essential observation: the power of a prophetic leader's repentance can catalyse collective change, highlighting the ripple effect that one individual's actions can have on an entire nation.

THE WEIGHT OF GUILT: EZRA'S CONFESSION (EZRA 9:3-15)

Ezra's narrative offers a complementary perspective on communal repentance. In Ezra 9, upon realizing the extent of the people's intermarriage with idolaters of their surrounding nations, Ezra was struck by the gravity of their sin. Ezra's shock was after repenting and asking for return to their land, idolatry had once again gained a foot in the door of the Israeli culture and the hearts of the masses. His reaction is one of immediate despair, leading him to tear his garments, pulling out his hair and beard and falling to his knees in prayer. Ezra's confession is laden with emotional depth, as he laments the shame faced by the people before God: "Our guilt has become great because of our sins."

What is particularly striking about Ezra's approach is his acute awareness of the consequences of sin—not just for individuals *but for the entire community*. He recognizes that their actions have resulted in spiritual and social ramifications, and his prayer reflects a profound understanding of the interconnectedness of individual and collective identity. Ezra's prayer is both a confession and a call to action, urging the people to return to their covenant with God. This duality of acknowledgement and commitment serves as a powerful reminder that repentance is not merely about regret; it is also about the intention to change and wilful restoration.

The prayers of these three men, all praying prophetically highlight the necessity of humility in leadership. In an age where leaders frequently deflect blame and seek to distance themselves from the consequences of systemic failures. The willingness of these biblical figures to confront their nation's sins offers a striking counter-narrative. They demonstrate that true leadership is rooted in vulnerability, empathy, and the courage to admit wrongdoing on their watch and even before their "watch" commenced.

The prayers of Daniel, Nehemiah, and Ezra serve as timeless examples of individuals who took on the mantle of intercession and repentance on behalf of their nation. Their heartfelt confessions illuminate the intricate relationship between personal responsibility and communal identity. As we grapple with the moral complexities of our own societies, their examples challenge us to embrace the weight of accountability, to recognize our shared guilt, and to engage in a transformative process of repentance. In doing so, we not only honour their legacy but also contribute to a more just and compassionate world.

ELIJAH'S PROPHETIC BURDEN

Elijah had emerged in a period marked by moral decay and idolatry under the reign of Ahab and Jezebel. The worship of Baal, a hideous foreign invented deity, permeated the societal landscape, oppressively leading to the systematic erasure of Yahwistic worship. In this context, Elijah's prophetic ministry becomes not just a voice of dissent but a clarion call to accountability. He does not merely observe the corruption; he internalises it. This is a profound observation: Elijah embodies the notion that a leader's moral fibre is inextricably linked to the state of their nation. His fierce denunciations of Ahab are not merely political; they are a personal indictment of the collective conscience of Israel.

Elijah's most notable confrontation occurs later on Mount Carmel, where he challenges the prophets of Baal in a dramatic display of divine power. This episode is not just a theological debate; it is a moment of existential reckoning for the Israelites. Elijah assumes a mantle of responsibility that transcends mere "prophetic duty". He stands in the breach, representing not only his own convictions but the weight of his nation's sins. His famous declaration, "How long will you waver between two opinions?" encapsulates the urgency of choosing between fidelity to God and the seductive allure of idolatry.

In this confrontation, Elijah's actions suggest a radical form of personal responsibility that invites reflection on the nature of leadership. He does not shy away from the consequences of his nation's choices; instead, he confronts them head-on. This confrontation becomes a microcosm of the larger societal struggle, illustrating that the moral failures of a nation are often shared by its leaders. Elijah, in his passionate advocacy for truth and justice, exemplifies the idea that the responsibility for societal evil does not rest solely on the shoulders of the corrupt; it implicates all who witness and remain silent, even the most Godly amongst the.

A MAN ALONE

Elijah's journey is also marked by profound isolation, a poignant reminder of the burdens borne by those who dare to challenge the status quo. After the victory on Mount Carmel, we find Elijah fleeing from Jezebel's wrath, consumed by despair and self-doubt. This moment reveals the psychological toll of personal responsibility. Elijah, despite his triumph, grapples with feelings of inadequacy and the belief that he is alone in his quest for righteousness. His plea to God, "I am no better than my ancestors," underscores a striking observation: the weight of responsibility can lead to a profound sense of alienation, even among the righteous.

This isolation serves as a cautionary tale for modern leaders and individuals. The path of integrity is often fraught with loneliness, as it requires standing against the tide of collective complacency, as well as deliberate acts of evil.. Elijah's experience highlights the importance of community and support for those who seek to bear the burdens of responsibility. It challenges us to reflect on how we can foster environments that empower individuals to act against societal evils without succumbing to despair.

A LEGACY OF ACCOUNTABILITY

As Elijah's narrative unfolds, his legacy becomes a testament to the enduring nature of personal responsibility. His ascension into heaven in a whirlwind signifies not just a prophetic departure but an enduring call to future generations. The mantle he leaves behind carries the weight of accountability, urging us to confront the evils within our own societies. In a world where moral relativism often reigns, Elijah's example serves as a beacon of hope and a reminder of our collective obligation to challenge injustice.

Elijah stands as the ultimate example of assuming personal responsibility for the evil of his own nation in totality. His life encapsulates the struggles of confronting societal corruption, the isolation that accompanies moral integrity, and the enduring call to accountability. In a contemporary context, where many grapple with the complexities of leadership and moral responsibility, Elijah's legacy invites us to reflect on our roles within our communities. It challenges us to recognize that the fight against evil is not merely a collective endeavour; it is an individual commitment to uphold truth, justice, and the well-being of our nations. In embracing this responsibility, we honour the profound lessons imparted by one of history's most striking prophetic figures, who set an example for Daniel, Nehemiah and Ezra some 250-300 years later.

14

ELIJAH ALIGNED HIMSELF TOTALLY WITH YAHWEH.

The Prophet who spoke as God, without saying, "Thus says Yahweh."

Elijah's life and mission, particularly his bold prophetic first mention in 1 Kings 17:1, challenges our common understanding of prophetic authority and the nature of divine agency. By taking command over elements that are typically forever reserved for God alone, Elijah not only identifies himself with the divine but also intimately connects with the sons of his nation. We need to explore how the man from Tishbe's remarkable actions and language demonstrate an uncommon fusion of divine authority and human responsibility, ultimately redefining the relationship between God, nature, and humanity all together.

Elijah's narrative is punctuated by his extraordinary, wilful, authoritative statement to influence the very climate. This act of withholding rain transcends mere prophecy; it is a direct assertion of omnipotent authority over creation itself. In the ancient Near Eastern context, where weather and agricultural fertility were closely tied to the understanding of divine favour, Elijah's proclamation carries the immense weight of God Himself. By wielding language typically reserved for God, Elijah steps into a role that blurs the lines between human and divine agency.

This striking observation raises critical questions about the nature of prophetic authority. Elijah's ability to command the climate signifies a profound identification with God's sovereignty. He does not merely serve as a mouthpiece for divine will; instead, he embodies that will, employing language that evokes the very voice of God. In doing so, Elijah becomes a conduit through which divine power and authority flows, allowing him to act as an agent of change in a society plagued by idolatry and moral decay.

IDENTIFICATION WITH THE NATION

Elijah's authority over even the climate is deeply intertwined with his total identification with the people of Israel. When he declares a drought, it is not merely an act of judgment against Baal worship; it is also an expression of solidarity with his own people, the nation of Israel, even when it brings as much hardship to Israeli people, as it does to the prophets of Baal and the Sidonians that had immigrated to Israel following Jezebel. The drought serves as a sudden shock wake of a wake-up-call, forcing the Israelites to confront the consequences of their actions. In this way, Elijah's pronouncement is both a divine judgment and, concurrently an act of intercession. He stands between God and the people, articulating a shared plight that compels them to return to their covenant with Yahweh. Jezebel and accompanying Sidonians had little or no understanding of the degree to which the mosaic covenant with Yahweh was hanging over and influencing the fortunes of Israel, as was Elijah's promise of, "No rain till I say so."

This duality of identification is striking and painful to empathise with. By taking authority over the elements, Elijah positions himself as both a representative of God and an advocate for his nation, as well as personally declaring war against Baal and Asherah worship and their followers from Sidon. He speaks the language of authority not only to invoke God's power but also to galvanize the Israeli people towards repentance – and perhaps, including a few Sidonian immigrants also. His actions serve to remind the Israelites that their relationship with God is not merely transactional; it demands active engagement and accountability. Yahweh was the God of Israel. In this context, Elijah embodies a prophetic model that is both relational and authoritative, empathetic and violent.

Elijah's boldness in addressing the climate and weather raises profound theological implications. By asserting control over nature, he challenges the notion of divine sovereignty in a way that invites deeper reflection. In traditional theology, of course, God is viewed as the sole architect of natural order, yet Elijah's actions suggest a collaborative relationship between the divine and the human. This interplay asserts that humanity possesses a unique role within creation, one that includes stewardship and responsibility for the world around us. God had never lost a millimetre of cosmic rule and responsibility. Elijah was solely under the authority and drive of the Word of God that had come to him in an event of imparting knowledge to Elijah, as well as authority and power.

Furthermore, Elijah's authority can be seen as a precursor to a broader understanding of prophetic agency. His ability to command the weather illustrates that prophetic voices can challenge and reshape the tangible, physical realities of their time. This observation invites contemporary readers to consider how they might assume authority, no matter how far on the prophetic spectrum, over the pressing issues of their own time— social injustice and moral decay. Just as Elijah wielded the language of divine authority, modern individuals are called to speak out and act decisively in the face of societal challenges, recognizing their role in the ongoing narrative of creation.

Ultimately, Elijah's proclamations over the climate serve as a catalyst for repentance and restoration. When the drought culminates in the dramatic confrontation on Mount Carmel, Elijah's invocation of fire from heaven signifies not only divine approval but also the possibility of renewal. The rains that follow symbolize hope and restoration for a nation that has strayed from its roots. This narrative arc underscores the power of language and authority to effect change, inviting the people of Israel to reclaim their identity as a nation chosen by, and living in the grace of Yahweh.

Elijah's actions remind us that true authority is rooted in love and a desire for restoration and alignment of Israel with Almighty Yahweh. His use of language typically reserved for God is not an act of arrogance but rather an expression of deep commitment to his people and their covenant with the divine. In this light, Elijah's authority becomes a model for contemporary leadership—one that balances strength with compassion and authority with responsibility.

Elijah's unique position as the prophet who takes authority over climate and weather, authority not previously known of, reveals striking insights into the furtherance of the nature of divine-human relationships. By employing language traditionally reserved for God alone, he identifies with both the divine and the sons of his nation, embodying a prophetic role that is both authoritative and relational. His actions challenge us to consider our own roles within the fabric of creation, reminding us that we, too, are called to speak boldly in the face of injustice and to assume responsibility for the world around us.

In a time when societal decay looms large, Elijah's example serves as an urgent call to action. It invites Christians to embrace our authority as children of God and to wield our voices in pursuit of justice, restoration, and hope. In doing so, we honour the legacy of a prophet who dared to speak the language of authority, bridging the divine and the human in a quest for a better world.

PART C

ELIJAH IN THE SACRED SCROLLS. REAL-TIME.

15

THE HISTORICAL SETTING OF ELIJAH'S ARRIVAL. (1 Kings 1-16)

I am very aware that some people do not appreciate history. Memories of school days I suppose. Too many dates to remember and too many detentions if those dates weren't remembered. It's a good job we are all wired differently.

I love history. When I say that, I am not wanting to delude myself or my readers that I know a lot of history, but I can confidently assert that you would be hard pushed to find anybody who has a deeper interest and fascination – nay - obsession – with history, dates, stories, and consequences that were future to what happened in historical narratives.

I also have engaged with Christians over the years who think that discussing biblical history demeans the scriptures and detracts from the Word of God embodied in the text. What silliness! I hold to Charles Haddon Spurgeon's remarkable quote i.e. "A text without a context is a pretext." It is a bit of a cliché these days but was revolutionary when first uttered back in the 1800's. History and geography is part and parcel of scripture's context.

I would suggest that if the reader has a particular phobia concerning some fairly detailed history account, you could if desired, skip this introductory chapter without losing the thread of the book.

The history that surrounds the days of Elijah highlights the depths of courage as well as the divine insight that motivated the prophet through his high-profile days. This is not an apology for recounting the 58 years of biblical history from Solomon's death to Elijah's appearance, but a rationale as to why I find it a little bit insipid to read Elijah's journal without having fully imbibed the nature of the thick dark, ugly context that this brightest of prophetic lights operated in.

So, for the sake of those who are uninitiated by the biblical and historical context of the mushroom-like explosion of divine mystery with which the man from Tishbe arrived on the radar, let me put you in the picture.

THE DEGENERATION OF ISRAEL'S UNIQUENESS.

Rightly or wrongly I always picture the days of Dickens as being a time when England was full of dirt, smoke, grime, evil, poverty, ignorance and just a terrible time for most people to live in lack. In my head, I picture the days that led up to Elijah's arrival in just the same motif. Things were dark – I mean seriously, morally, and spiritually smog-ridden and depraved.

The days of David and Solomon are hailed by all and sundry in the know as the brightest and most glorious days in Israel's history. Much of the wealth attained through David's reign was used by Solomon to affect a remarkable grandiose style of court and national life much more than the one his father created. Solomon built what can only be referred to as a "complex of structures" to enhance his image in the sight of his people and all the nations that surrounded Israel. He built his own royal palace, a palace for his Egyptian queen (whose name isn't even mentioned), suggesting that he built other grand homes for his other (many) wives. He built a "hall of pillars," a "throne room of justice," and a "house of the forest of Lebanon," which is assumed by scholars and Jewish historians to have been his treasury and/or his armoury. He had thousands of horses, hundreds of chariots and a population that served him in a manner that cannot be referred to as anything but slavery.

THE DETERIORATION OF SOLOMON'S INIMITABILITY.

Solomon's extravagance clearly brought him into national debt, forcing him to have to mortgage part of his territory to Hiram king of Tyre. F.F. Bruce memorably wrote something to the effect that: "the text of First Kings refers to the cities that Solomon built for his chariots and horsemen (1 Kings 9:19 and 10:26) and we may be sure that Solomon's horses were better housed than many of Solomon's subjects were." Solomon was obscenely rich. He spent his wealth obscenely freely. He was obscenely cruel to his people overall.

Solomon found it necessary to impose heavy taxes on his subjects and to exact forced labour from them. This sad situation was predicted, even before Saul was anointed King, by the great prophet Samuel. It was light years away from the freedom, joy and prosperity promised by Moses and the legacy of the Law he left with humanity.

These facts explain how the wine of prosperity and joy, which accompanied the peace that overwhelmed Israel at the start of Solomon's reign, decomposed into the horribly bitter vinegar of disillusionment towards the end of his reign.

Solomon left behind him a nation that was well departed from the ancient ideals that their scriptures inculcated. It meant that if or when the Pentateuch was ever read, it seemed like a dream and a fairy tale that simply was not evident after Solomon's demise. For all the above reasons, Solomon's death around 930 BC precipitated the collapse of what was David's empire and had become Solomon's inheritance. Solomon is the only Davidic king who had no prophetic voice in the circles of his court.

THE DEPRECIATION OF THE NORTHERN KINGDOM'S MONARCHY.

After the death of Solomon, the kingdom of Israel was immediately torn in two. Judah was the name of the nation-state of the southern two tribes, namely, Benjamin and Judah. By these days, strangely, the tribe of Simeon had been completely assimilated into Judah and was no longer referred to in the biblical history as an existent tribe apart from one single mention in the book of Revelation. Israel was the name of the nation-state of all the other Hebrew tribes.

As far as the Israeli public of the northern ten tribes were concerned, it was their deep-seated complaint that Solomon had abused them. It was the proverbial split that many nations suffer between their north and south. The southern section of Israel's torn real-estate had Jerusalem, the temple, the governmental establishment and, thus far up to the days of Ahab, the descendants of David and Solomon on their throne. This southern state, however, immediately after Solomon, was under the almost fascist-like reign of Rehoboam, Solomon's son. The northern "kingdom" was under the depraved hand of a man the Bible refers to as, "Jeroboam the son of Nebat." He was a man who had superintended the vast public works during the reign of Solomon. So, he was thoroughly au-fait as to how monarchs of his day kept a grip on power. He was shockingly told by a prophet during the reign of Solomon that he would rule over the ten northern tribes of Israel at a time when the very suggestion was an unspoken concept of rebellion and treason – but shown by history to have been a desire of the masses that lived in the governmentally "neglected" north of the land.

Jeroboam the son of Nebat, years before Solomon's death, for several reasons, fled to Egypt, where it seems he was further mentored and tutored into the protocols of contemporary kingship by Pharaoh Shishak, the first ruler of the 22nd dynasty of the double kingdom (i.e., North and South of Egypt in unification). We know that Shishak reigned from 945 BC through to 914 BC. So, Rehoboam was doubly acquainted with how the machinery of royalty worked in his day.

The southern Hebrew kingdom of the breach, even though within its borders were the much smaller numbers of Simeon (a people in a small circle of land in the midst of Judah, no longer acknowledged) and Benjamin, were virtually buried amongst the huge population of the tribe of Judah. The people of the northern kingdom began to think of Judah as almost alien and, at times, sadly, even enemy territory.

Signs of rivalry and envy between Ephraim and Judah (Isaiah 11:13) became increasingly evident during the reigns of Saul, David, and Solomon. There was also a tendency to reckon the two tribes and the ten tribes apart. Moreover, we see a readiness on the part of the latter to join rebellious movements (2 Samuel 15-20), which reached the culminating point in the breakaway under Jeroboam after Rehoboam's catastrophic succession to the Davidic throne on the death of his father, Solomon. In the prophet's writings, the northern kingdom of Israel is often referred to as, "the house of Joseph," or, "Ephraim," the name of the leading tribe representing the whole ten tribed nation.

Getting back to the sustained motivation of the national split, Jeroboam, up north, was desperately eager to keep his hold on the people of what was now the "Ten tribes of Israel". However, he lived with the fear that he could lose his kingdom if the masses were to go three times a year to the annual feasts in Jerusalem as ancient custom dictated. He thought that old associations with the established religious form, as well as the associations of old friends, might overpower their new-born loyalty to him as their king and ruler. For that sole reason, he decided to set up the worship of God (perhaps we should say, "god.") in his own kingdom and built two temple shrines - one at Dan, in the extreme north, the other at Bethel, in the extreme south of the Northern state. The Bethel shrine was something of a risk as Google Maps tell us that Bethel was only 4.8 miles from Jerusalem. That is a 1-hour 43-minute walk. It was just down the road from the centre and hub of Judah. (These days, one can ride betwixt the two in 18 minutes.) Playing on people's ignorance, as well as their vulnerability to religiosity, Jeroboam's cunning rule was done with pomp and ceremony. In both these shrines he had installed a golden calf, that "the God of Israel" might be worshipped under the form of a bull that eats hay. Don't laugh! This man Rehoboam was serious to the point of life or death.

To say it clearly and plainly, this sin, perpetrated by this rebel king, trod underfoot the second commandment of Moses - which forbade the children of Israel to make any graven image or to bow down before the likeness of anything in heaven above or in the earth beneath. Such weak and sinful bids for popularity are never forgotten throughout Holy Scripture, be it the Hebrew Bible or the New

Testament. The whole concept of Israeli idolatry in the worship of Yahweh seems to have been a 100% "no-no" to the nation of Israel until Solomon, in his "wisdom" (nudge, nudge, wink wink), married a series of foreign queens who all came to Jerusalem along with their various priests, shamans and whatever idols and god's they submitted to.

Reading through Israel's history in the generations that followed, like a demonic mantra from hell, we read of many kings and people who committed sins and crimes that followed, "the sins with which Jeroboam, the son of Nebat, made Israel to sin." The northern state of Israel lasted no longer than 208 years, and then almost the entire population of northern Israel was scattered around the Middle East – and some think even the Far East - and were never heard of again. Thus, we have the factual legend of "The Lost Tribes of Israel."

A man must reap what he sows. The revolution instigated by Jeroboam came back on his head and severely upon the heads of the northern Hebrew nation-state. Having sown to the wind, history shows how the North reaped the whirlwind. Revolutions in Israel occurred time and again and were all marinated in betrayal, murder, and bloodshed. It was dark.

So, stealing a pretentious throne in the year 930 BC, Jeroboam, the son of Nebat, reigned 21 years or so, and the scripture states that, "The Lord struck him, and he died". Piecing together the texts of 2 Chronicles 13 and 1 Kings 14, it seems his was a slow death. He was succeeded by Nadab his son. He lasted only a year. His soldiers did not approve of his battle strategy, and while besieging a Philistine fortress, a man named Baasha, one of his own people of the tribe of Issachar, killed him (1 Kings 15:25-28). So, it is still 908 BC – 22 years since Jeroboam's revolution, and three kings had ruled Ephraim already. Talk about instability!

Baasha lasted 23 years and built a city called Tirzah his capital. Baasha finally died, and his son Elah inherited the troublesome, idolatrous state. Elah had a serious drink problem. A problem that turned fatal. A legendary infamous traitor called Zimri killed Elah whilst the king was in a drunken stupor. Zimri lasted only seven days and then seemingly committed suicide by burning down a building while he was in it. There was certainly something rotten in the state of Israel. After Zimri's death, rebellious, divisive people throughout the northern kingdom had yet another divisive and rebellious split. If things weren't dark and confused enough at this time, the populace of the ten tribes were hideously divided into two factions. One half chose a mighty warrior called Omri. The other half wanted a man called Tibni to be king. Is this chaos, or what? It was probably some dispute over tribal pre-eminence. The truth is somewhat obscured in the biblical text. The two leaders and their forces fought each other for several years until Omri's forces prevailed and Tibni was killed. It, therefore, appears that Tibni was regent over half the kingdom of Israel for a period of four years. Tibni's death is written in the Hebrew Bible but not detailed nor explained. Omri's reign is recorded as having started in 881 BC. First, Kings 16:28 tells us that he died and was succeeded by his son Ahab.

Omri left Ahab a small empire that comprised Gilead (or part of it) East of the Jordan River and probably Bashan, as well as the land of Moab, whose king was tributary to Ahab as he had been to Omri. The southern kingdom of Judah is reckoned by leading historians to have been, if not actually subject to Omri, certainly a subordinate ally. Ahab's marriage to the infamous Jezebel, daughter of Ethbaal, king and High Priest of Sidon, revived an alliance with Phoenicia that had been in suspension since the time of Solomon.

Throughout Ahab's reign, a fierce border war was waged with Syria in which Israel, in spite of occasional victories, proved the weaker, and in the meantime, Mesha, king of Moab, successfully revolted and occupied the southern portions of the territory of Gad – one of the tribes of Israel. The forces of Israel retained enough strength to contribute the second-largest contingent of soldiers (and the largest force of chariots) to the combined armies that, under the leadership of Benhadad I of Damascus, checked the westward movement of Shalmaneser III of Assyria at the battle of Karkar. After the Assyrians were repulsed, however, the alliance broke up, and Ahab actually met his death through fighting the Syrians in a vain attempt to recover Ramoth-Gilead.

Domestically, contact with a wider world and, especially, the alliance with Phoenicia had far-reaching consequences for the kingdom of Israel itself. Jezebel attempted to establish Baal worship and governmental fascism that were common enough elsewhere throughout the ancient world but alien and despised by Israel. She tried to set up Baalistic worship to maintain the familiar oriental principle of the absolute despotic power and authority of the monarch. This roused the bitter anguish of that small conservative and loyal party, which clung to the sole worship of Yahweh and, at the same time, held to those vaguely democratic conceptions of society that the Hebrews had brought with them from the wilderness hundreds of years before Elijah's time and had consistently maintained. The spirit of this party found expression in the prophet Elijah, who protested against both the establishment of the Baal priests and Ahab's judicial murder of the man called Naboth (A story examined in this manuscript). Elijah and his successors seem to have been able to eliminate the foreign worship, though in the end, their purpose was achieved only by a bloody revolution. However, they were powerless to stem the tide of social and moral deterioration. To the reign of Ahab may be traced the beginning of that sapping of the national life, which led to the condemnations stormed by the 8th-century prophets and to the downfall of Samaria.

That was 873 BC. Ahab was married to Jezebel. Ahab reigned 21 years. His reign started a mere 57 years after Solomon's death and died 74 years after the northern kingdom of Israel had been created. This means that Elijah's sudden appearance in 1 Kings 17:1 took place, at the very least, 57 years after Solomon's death and at the very latest, something like 67 to 70 years after.

THE DIMINISHING OF ISRAEL'S NATIONHOOD.

Those 57-plus years were truly dark days becoming ever darker, especially as Jezebel settled in her new territory. After the fallouts, the splits and much murderous blood spilling, the kingdom passed into the hands of a cunning, idolatrous female witch. She was the strong one in the royal marriage. Ahab, the scripture declares, "did more to provoke the Lord God of Israel to anger, than all the kings of Israel that were before him" (1 Kings 16:33). Did I tell you how dark these days were?

I must expand and explain, however, that Ahab's actions that provoked Yahweh's anger came about not strictly because his character was more depraved and evilly motivated but much more because he was insipidly submissive and subjected to a crafty, unscrupulous, and cruel woman filled with hate and stinging selfishness. This woman was so bad that in modern Western society, her name is used as a synonym for any woman of bad character. We are talking of Jezebel. Digressing for a moment, I could write a lengthy tome showing how some of the worst crimes that have ever been committed have been wrought by weak men at the instigation of worse - but stronger – female spirits. However, we move on.

When youthful Jezebel left the extravagant palace of Tyre to become the consort of Ahab, the newly crowned king of Israel, it was no doubt regarded as a splendid match. The Royal wedding of the year. At this period and within the bookends of this generation, Tyre (where Jezebel came from) really was the queen of nations on the Mediterranean, in the zenith of her glory. Her colonies dotted the shores of the Great Sea as far as the Spanish harbours. Her trading vessels were seen on every known sea and even ventured to the coasts of Cornwall for tin. Marrying a princess of Tyre meant that Ahab was punching far above his own weight. Socially and royally, Jezebel was of a different class. As Jezebel left her home for Israel, she took with her a considerable number of Baal-worshipping priests who would have influenced her religious outlook strongly and who, therefore, would have exercised an irresistible spell over her - to do her utmost to introduce into Israel the hideous and cruel rites of her hereditary religion.

THE PATHOLOGICAL BASENESS OF JEZEBEL'S INFLUENCE.

Jezebel was a veritable apostle of Baal worship while married to Ahab. First, she seems to have erected a temple to Astarte in the neighbourhood of Jezreel. That old divine, FB Meyer, likens the people and social structure of Jezreel at the time to be paralleled with the image of classy Windsor in the UK. Jezebel financially supported her 450 priests. Ahab and Jezebel also built a temple for Baal in Samaria, the capital of the kingdom of Israel at that time. Shrines and temples then began to rise in all parts of the land in honour of these idolatrous false deities. The land literally swarmed with the priests of Baal and of the high-placed groves. The institution of the priestly hierarchy that came with Baal worship, revelling in their sudden rise to power, was ambitiously licentious and morally debased. The fires of persecution were lit and began to burn with furious intolerance towards anything or anybody that fell short of pure Baal worship. As one writer puts it: "The schools of the prophets were shut up, as grass grew in their courts." The prophets of the schools ran away into hiding. The darkness was that of a terrible midnight of terror to righteous-God-fearing people. The whole land seemed to be silently submitted to the apostasy instigated by Jezebel and weakly allowed by Ahab. Of all the population of Israel, only "seven thousand remained who had not bowed the knee to Baal". However, they were so paralysed with fear, they kept so still and quiet that their very existence was unknown- even to Elijah in the hour of his greatest loneliness.

And so, during this political and spiritual chaotic anarchy, we arrive at 1 Kings 17 and the first verse. One can easily perceive how it was that Elijah appeared in Israel at a most crucial time. Jezebel's influence was very great, not merely over her husband but throughout the kingdom, and as a result, the worship of Baal, the god of the Phoenicians, spread with ever greater force and was the cause of much trouble that befell the people of Israel.

It is important to note that Elijah, the man from Tishbe, appeared before Ahab the king – NOT Jezebel the queen and confronted him with an extremely brief, "state of the Nation" speech. And so it was, in the time when the sin of Ahab and his people had degenerated into an obscene abomination, Yahweh had, standing ready, out of view, poised to enter stage right, a man already trained and willing to assert the sovereignty of Yahweh to that crooked and perverse nation.

THE STRIKING PARALLEL OF THE CONTEMPORARY WESTERN CULTURE.

Multi-culturalism is an undoubtedly positive cultural phenomenon. However, it seems historically that multi culturalism cannot be properly integrated without multi-religiosity. That is what the planet is now experiencing everywhere. Elijah was a child of the God-given land. It was God's gift. This was Israel. God's own land. Multi-faith society was not acceptable as defined in the Torah of God.

This historical multi-cultural scenario in the state of Israel demonstrated a need for a wild, giant, dangerous prophet. Parallel symptoms in the twenty first century demand a similar cure for a similar sickness.

16

THE REAL-TIME DELIVERY OF ELIJAH'S REVOLUTIONARY PROPHETIC WORD.
(1 Kings 17:1)

One man declares war against demonic tyrants and all of hell.

"And Elijah the Tıshbite (the man from Tishbe) from the inhabitants of Gilead, proceeded to say to Ahab: "As Yahweh the elohe of Israel, lives, before whom I am standing - there will occur during these years neither dew nor rain, except at the order of my word!" (1 Kings 17:1) (My own translation/paraphrase of the Hebrew text)

ELIJAH'S AWARENESS OF THE DIVINE PRESENCE AND ITS WEIGHT UPON HIM.

Enough of all the introductory perspectives and thoughts about prophecy and characteristics of the biblical prophets while sharing my own convictions. Now, to run the opening reel that takes about 3 seconds to run and a lifetime, if not eternity, to fathom. We are discussing the curt, sharp, brief statement that changed the entire world of prophecy and spiritual authority forever. Snuggle down in your bomb shelter and, get ready for Tsunami Elijah and keep your head down. This is the prophetic atom bomb that I have been warning you of. Now to the opening moments of the narrative of the "days of Elijah". Get ready to be shocked and traumatised!

I want you to see the staggering, nay stupefying word image that we have here. A wealthy and accepted monarch of the Northern Kingdom of Israel in the 9th century B.C. was all about his kingly duties one day. In the midst of his regular routine (we suppose), a startling and shocking figure appears unannounced in the royal presence. "Enter stage left?" Or was it, "...stage, right?" It might well have even been "Enter stage from above!" Who knows? The man from Tishbe arrives before our view, and, most importantly, before the king's view. Drink in and absorb the startling choreography. His sense of dress is hardly fashionable or acceptable. It may have been 800 years before John the Dipper was born, yet he was dressed exactly as the Baptist is described. A camel skin girdle with a leather belt is how they are both pictured in the biblical text.

In 1 Kings 17, the scene often assumed and painted with the best attempts at graphic verbal illustration by preachers, writers, and teachers is the very moment when the prophet Elijah appears from nowhere and confronts Ahab regarding the rampant idolatry and the worship of Baal. This passage describes Elijah declaring briefly and directly - a drought as a judgment. It is shockingly sudden, out of the blue as it were (pardon the pun), illustrating the harsh and violent tension between the true God, Yahweh, and the false gods of Sidon, ignorantly immigrated into Israel by the king marrying the princess of Sidon. Many interpretations emphasize Elijah's boldness in delivering his message in such a hostile environment. The significance of drought in an agrarian society as Israel was, and the stark contrast between Elijah's straight faithfulness and Ahab's ignorance, is jaw-dropping. This scene is often depicted as a turning point that sets the stage for all of Elijah's subsequent miracles and confrontations with the prophets of Baal and Jezebel, highlighting themes of faith, redefining the boundaries of authority, and the degrees of divine intervention.

The entrance of the Tishbite was so shocking; no royal guard stopped him, nobody bid him remain silent, and nobody accosted him when he spoke clearly to the monarch without all the protocols, pomp and circumstance. It was a never-to-be-forgotten moment for all that were present. There was silence surrounding the king as all who were present momentarily stared in awe. The awe was grounded in shock.

In all the hundreds, if not thousands of biblical word pictures vividly painted in a thousand colours and shades, 1 Kings 17:1, and the following 2 verses is surely the most fascinating and outrageously brief narrative that produces books, essays, films and dissertations to make clear.

The weird, strange man had come with a mission. His Curriculum Vitae hitherto is totally non-existent. He has, however, hereafter, a historic track record of saying the unsayable; thinking the unthinkable; doing the undoable, and authentically going deep in the realm of the Spirit and into the mind of God where no man had ever gone before. He went into things that were not known to exist before he had gone there. This is why people of faith are utterly gripped by Elijah the Tishbite – the prophetic-contrarian, polarised against all things religious and orthodox, antipodal to all things ungodly and idolatrous. This is the giant of the faith, the human gargantuan who walked so intimately aligned with Yahweh that he never even had to say, what nearly all prophets felt required to say: "This is what Yahweh says," who defied naysayers, Baal-sellers, idol treasurers, and all deistic rationalists.

He followed Yahweh in a totally committed manner that would defy historical religious traditions and realise the imagined far-fetched dreams of many a godly-minded Israeli of his day. He spent his life's work ridding the world of idolatrous demon worship and introduced to humanity the heavenly concept of actually conquering death. OK! OK! OK! I see and hear you gesticulating and crying with bellied, high-pitched demands, "How does one set about killing death?" We shall set about trying to answer that question as we hack our way on through the sacred scrolls.

Truly, despite my attempts to make this scene as graphic as the scrolls suggest, we are not given the slightest clue as to the geographic scene of Elijah speaking to Ahab, and I am to some degree, conforming to the image most biblical expositors have painted through the centuries. We are talking of the wild man from Gilead. Let's not call it the realisation of a dream. Let's call it Yahweh's strategically mapped plan of action for planet earth. We need to always remember that what is surreal to lesser mortals is but a normal routine day-at-the-office for Almighty Yahweh, together with the man from Tishbe.

We seriously have to reset our worldview and paradigm to see 1 Kings 17:1 with a full understanding. It is a declaration of war. It is a prospective conflagration that threatened more violence than any of the temporary subjugations of the tribes and nations that the book of Judges records. But the violence here was not the violence with armies and swords on battlefields of flesh-inducing rivers of blood. The man from Tishbe fought in the reality of the spiritual world. He fought invisible powers that had impact in the visible realm.

Whatever your mental picture of a man of God is, bin it! Whatever preconception of the ultimate man of God you carry in your heart, throw it on the fire. Gentle appearance, social graces in abundance, befriending folks with a handshake, and a "Good morning, brother and sister!" niceness - put it in the shredder immediately. Get used to the fact that the man from Tishbe is clearly one of the greatest men of God that trod on Israel's dust. Western cultural and religious norms are not to be even considered. Live with it! The entire issue for the man from Tishbe is what should be the main issue for every Christ seeker, Holy Spirit chaser and God follower. That is, to relate completely and openly with Yahweh Himself through the person of Jesus Christ.

"As I stand in the presence of the Ever-Living God - there will occur during these years neither dew nor rain, except at the order of my word!" He doesn't even hint that God has told him what to say. His claim is that he was at that very moment standing in the imminent actual presence of God Himself. On the grounds of which, he boldly asserted something that was fully endorsed in the writings of Moses, which was indeed validated by the text so highly treasured by the nation of Israel.

The statement was released. The invisible world, the angels and demons, the circumstances and facts that run the universe all pulled themselves in, and the cosmos was not about to argue. The man from

Tishbe had just spoken. King Ahab and Queen Jezebel and all the priests and Baal worshippers may not have given a fig what this unknown "weirdo" had just announced. They were utterly unable to recognise the authority of Almighty God that had just been unleashed upon them all. Was he a madman? Was he a jester? Was he attempting to make people smile?

And then...

...Where did he go?

Humanity's dream of the future is the practical strategy God has planned since before time and the foundations of the world. Billions of people scream with a spiritual top "C" for a better world. In so doing, they are globally, perennially unknowingly, crying out for a wild, giant, dangerous prophet to speak out and bring about the change. We are looking at such a one here, now – in the real-time of 1 Kings 17:1.

In a parallel type of explanation to another "weirdo", the man named Melchizedek, the opening and closing of the Tishbites' temporal chronicle is blanketed with enigmatic queries. Just as the absence of any mention of Melchizedek's birth and death was designed by Yahweh to prefigure the eternal Priesthood and Kingship of Christ, so too, the absence of similar datum concerning Elijah's parentage and his temporal departure leads us to the astounding fact that he was supernaturally translated from this world without passing "through the valley of death". This all marks him a typical forerunner of the Everlasting Prophet, the Messiah and Saviour – Christ Himself. The church of Christ is indeed, as Luther taught, "a kingdom of priests and kings", but let all Christians take note: we are a kingdom of prospective prophets, too. The only three offices that required anointing for service in the Old Testament are similarly for the church today. The agelessness of biblical prophecy is a striking witness to its divine origin. We are not discussing some improvised quixotic theology, impractical and dream-like, encouraging mindless extroverts to steal platforms with pseudo-religio-exhibitionism. We are talking of the meat of life and the reality of God's agency amongst men. Peter quoted Joel as having stated something that was current to the church age – namely and mainly that God will pour out of His Spirit upon all flesh: and your sons and your daughters shall prophesy, and your young men shall see visions, and your old men shall dream dreams, and on my servants and on my handmaidens I will pour out in those days of my spirit; and they shall prophesy."

Never was a carrier of Christ more dangerous than this man from Tishbe. Never was one so gigantic. Never was seen such a wild, untethered God-sourced messenger. God is wild. How on earth can we conceive of Him as anything less.

It may have been some 800 years before Christ humbled Himself to become man, not thinking it robbery to be equal with God, but this person, this man from Gilead, this man of like passions such as we, as a member of the fallen race, aspired to and so ascended into, a state of grace and power - and ultimately glory - that causes us, even in New Testament times, to see him as the very peak of an example to follow in striving to be like the Master. "He flamed like a lightning flash upon the prevailing darkness," said Campbell Morgan. That flash still impacts today. The 17th century Bishop Hall wrote, "He comes in like a tempest and goes out in a whirlwind." The first that we hear from the man from Tishbe is an oath, a threat and a promise. His words, like lightning, seem to slice into the firmament of Israel, locking up its normal activity. "He was the most eminent and holy prophet, reserved for the backslidden and most corrupt age."

We have no idea to which tribe of Israel he belonged. The fact that he was of the inhabitants of Gilead makes it likely that he was either from Gad or Manasseh. The land of Gilead was split between those two tribes. Gilead lies east of the Jordan, wild and rugged with its hills covered with deep forests. The cold solitudes were only broken by the splish splashes of mountain rivulets and gorges, the tributaries and ravines that were the hangout of various vicious wild animals.

It is "Eliyahu hat tishbi" in Hebrew! Elijah's name means "My God is Yahweh". If he or his parents chose this name, it was a courageous act to choose such an appellation in a kingdom dominated by Baal worshippers who conflicted with all who worshipped Yahweh (1 Kings 18:12-13. 19:10). The scripture at times refers to him simply as, "the Tishbite".

ELIJAH'S PROPHETIC WORD WAS AUTHORISED AND DELEGATED INTO HIS HANDS BY YAHWEH HIMSELF.

Man cannot discover new oceans if he does not lose sight of the shore. Elijah believed this. He didn't just lose sight of the shore; he lost sight of the planet. He left spiritual, doctrinal, cultural, racial, and national shores far behind. This man took prophecy and the delivery of "A Word from God" not only to a new dimension, but into another galaxy, light years away from even the likes of Moses and even Samuel. He himself took upon his own shoulders a taste of imparted divine responsibility and stepped into the divine will and preference in his contemporary "time-space world". The world would never be the same after his interaction with the idolatrous King Ahab and his infamous spouse, Jezebel. To misquote the Rev. Sykes in Harper Lee's novel "To Kill a Mockingbird", whether your name is "Miss Jean Louise" or anything else, "Stand up! Elijah the Tishbite is passing." Through these pages, my prayer is that Elijah is coming your way. Listen for the patter of his feet.

This initial prophetic explosion which is bigger and louder than Krakatoa, takes less than thirty seconds to read. And in those thirty seconds, the Tishbite had appeared to the king, dropped his world-shattering prophetic message, and gone. Leaving all and sundry present in a state of total shock. PTSD. "Post Tishbite Stress Disorder." Or better: "Post Tishbite Blessing Re-order." It was contemporaneously real and wildly surreal. I can imagine Ahab and those of his court that were undoubtedly present, in a state of tremor and astonishment, asking each other, "Did I really see and hear what just happened?" "Was it a man, or a vision?" "He was far too hairy and rough-looking to be an angel!" "Where did he come from?" "What was it he said?" And the most mysterious question of all; "Where did he go?"

Such was the lasting momentary vision of this rustic, austere Tishbite as he appeared and arrived at the rescue of Yahweh's own nation: to defend a purpose that humanly and circumstantially seemed to have vanished into the ether, to position himself solitarily against a mammoth, widespread and heinousness, to confront Ahab and Jezebel in the palatial stronghold of their shameless demonic indulgence, in the very epicentre and ground zero of their idolatrous seeming-supremacy. He had come like the flash of a cutlass, articulated his horrifying divine memorandum, expressed the fury of Almighty Yahweh - and was gone. All in a moment.

Grasping at clues concerning his escape from the royal presence, I shall shock you even further with my best possible solution as to how the Tishbite "escaped" the palace in one piece and still alive. Three and a half years later, a period of time in which nobody in Israel had seen Elijah or known where he was, he stands before a godly little man called Obadiah. (definitely NOT the Old Testament prophet who has a single section of the scrolls amongst the minor prophets) See 1 Kings 18:12. Obadiah is told by Elijah to bring King Ahab to speak to him. Obadiah was Ahab's right-hand man and was undoubtedly present in the real-time of 1 Kings 17:1. He fearfully responds that he is afraid of obeying the man from Tishbe, worried that in the time it takes to find Ahab and bring him back to Elijah's present location, "the Spirit of the Ever-Living will carry you to who knows where". And Obadiah knew that if he brought Ahab to this point and Elijah was absent, Ahab would kill him. Oh dear, Ahab was as desperate as desperation can take a human being in his 42-month search to find the prophet from Gilead.

Why do I interject this account at this point? I bring it forward in order to offer the question: Why would Obadiah suggest to Elijah such a weird and surreal scenario ... unless such a thing had already occurred? It seems to me to be an illogical remark unless Obadiah was present when that very supernatural transportation had already occurred at the closure of the real-time that enveloped 1 Kings 17:1.

Was that how Elijah left Ahab dumbfounded? Had Obadiah witnessed such a phenomenon? Utter and total conjecture on my part, I know. Yet, reading the text over and over, I cannot help but suspect.

Was Queen Jezebel present at "the 1 Kings-17:1 moment"? From what we understand of Jezebel's character and philosophy of life, if she had been present, she may have turned purple or had cardiac arrest on the spot, or, then again, she may have just laughed and ordered Elijah to be killed ... if she had been present, that is. We leave the answer to that query to your imagination. However, I fancy not.

ELIJAH'S PROPHETIC INSIGHT FORESAW NEW TESTAMENT PRACTICE OF FREEDOM.

It seems that everything about Elijah defied the contemporary popular narrative of dress sense of his age, social protocol normalcy, dietary intake, religious understanding, and spiritual perception, especially in the court of Ahab and Jezebel, where self-indulgence, soft silks and fine dresses would have been the predictable norm. Why do I say this? Because of the description of Elijah is given in The Book. In 2 Kings 1, when he contradicted one king's messengers and sent them back with their tail between their legs, the king, Ahaziah by name, angrily asked the messengers what the man looked like who had stopped them on their royal errand. "He was a hairy man, with a leather belt around his waist," said the messengers. "Ah! It is Elijah! The man from Tishbe," said the king with assurance (2 Kings 1:8).

Because of the parallel drawn by Jesus Himself and other scriptures, the Tishbite is always seen as a dress-style prototype of John the Baptist in the gospels. Matthew 3:4 states, "John himself had a camel-hair garment with a leather belt around his waist." This word picture is embellished by Zechariah the prophet who, in a certain context, writes, "And on that day every prophet who prophesies will be ashamed of his vision, *and he will not put on a hairy cloak in order to deceive.*"

On top of these morsels of information, because of poets, professors, scholars, and preachers reading between the lines, it has been generally assumed that Elijah was a huge, muscular, hairy character. The word-pictures describing his activities through his biblical biography suggest he was a man of great energy, a presence that caused people to stand back in awe, especially because of the tangible presence of Yahweh that brooded around and over him. Gilead had already nurtured two judges leading Israel in history long past, Jair and Jephthah. We find in Gilead, from the earliest times through to the Assyrian Captivity of 722 BC, Hebrew communities, centres, and rallying places. The Gileadites were the Highlanders of Israel, and the whole bearing of Elijah speaks of the unconventional manners and the free life of a rustic mountain-dwelling people.

ELIJAH'S PROPHETIC INSIGHT WAS NURTURED BY THE SPIRIT WITHIN HIM.

He must have been a striking and almost shocking sight to those who ever caught a glimpse of him. He was known – initially because of this opening line in 1 Kings 17:1, to be a prophet of Yahweh. However, he did not at all carry the appearance, the life, the dress or even the talk of other religious leaders. There was no frame of reference that could be used to define or describe him. All other leaders were properly, fashionably, well-dressed, well-fed, sophisticated, and worldly. Elijah obviously, by all we read of him, cared for none of those things and even made a point of separating himself from them. His garment of camel's hair and his leather belt about his waist were as plain and drab as Gilead, the place he came from. His clothes were, remarkably practical and long-wearing and far from being comfortable or fashionable.

Elijah's very dress, food, and lifestyle were in themselves a rebuke to the self-satisfied and self-indulgent Baal and Asherah-worshipping religious leaders of Israel and Ahab's court. It was also a rebuke to most of the people, who, though they may not have been able to indulge in the privileges of their leaders, nonetheless admired and longed for the same advantages.

We need to state that Elijah's purpose was not to turn the people into hermits or retire into a life of asceticism, like he appeared to model. He called on no one, not even his servants or later, Elisha, as well as the schools of the prophets, to live or dress as he did. But his manner of living was a dramatic reminder of the many loves and pleasures that keep people from exchanging their own way of life for God's lifestyle. The character and point of Elijah's clothes and diet was to be plain, durable, merely sufficient, and possibly also to rebuke the indulgent garb and diet of his respective nemeses Ahab and Jezebel.

This unique man did not have any equivalent of a Levitical background or any equivalent seminary degree or Hebrew *yeshiva* education. He claimed no following or prophetic school under his belt. He was utterly uncredentialed. He was unorthodox in every human perspective. He was, humanly speaking, an authentic "outsider." A social weirdo. A religious outcast.

Elijah appears from "nowhere," makes a single simple statement assuming authority over the very climate of the entire Levant, and then "disappears" as suddenly as he arrived. No one in the court, assuming the royal court was his theatre, would know much, if anything, about him, for he had just emerged from the obscurity of distant Gilead, to stand before king Ahab with the keys of Heaven and hell in his hand. This man from Tishbe exhibited and validated charge of the very cosmos.

All revelations, when perceived, seem to us to be sudden. The first words in the text of 1 Kings 17:1 are, "And he proceeded to say". The verb is imperfect—we are immediately in his presence, witnessing his speech. His speaking precedes the very brief description of who he is;

in fact, his speaking even precedes where he is speaking. Elijah knew out of his personal experience that God was alive. A true servant first sits before God. And then, being spoken to, stands before God, waiting upon the Lord. If you want God to hear you authoritatively, there is a prerequisite—you must hear God first. And to hear God, one needs to sit with Him and get used to His voice and timbre.

We know nothing of Elijah's background or training, and we guess Ahab was in the same predicament. Because of the Tishbite's lack of credentials, Ahab may not have taken him seriously at first. Human society loves credentials at every level of position and industry. Elijah had no certificates. And yet, the judgment he proclaimed didn't deal in hours, days, weeks, or months. It was a judgment of years.

17

LET'S JUST STOP AND STARE FOR A MOMENT AT THIS WORLD SHAKING THREE SECONDS OF HISTORY. (NO RAIN UNTIL I SAY SO...)

"... No rain until I say so?" What?? You can't be serious! Can you?

What kind of a person could seriously say that? What kind of person would in serious tones say that? Isn't that presumptuous? Not at all. Elijah could say, "There will be no rain nor dew all these years, except by my word." Why? Because he had a word from God in his mouth, and he was one with God. He was in full alignment with Yahweh. There was absolutely no self in that person. He represented the Almighty and his will, fully. All the thoughts we have previously run through, we need to observe that the beast of the prophet gift was raging in his bones. H had read the scrolls of Deuteronomy; he had believed the monster of a thought that to turn the hearts of Israel back to God. Those lines that talked of a hard sky and ground as a divine response to the intensity of the idolatry was overdue. He had taken personal ownership of those biblical words and had spent time – and who knows how much time he had spent there - bringing God's word to Yahweh Himself. This is the stage I believe that would have taken the longest of hours, the self-denying agony of seeking the face of God Himself. He would have fought, laying hold of God with his head between his knees until the dialogue with the Almighty became a two-way interaction. As the confidence and the anointing of power grew, the event was climaxed as the entire message and line of action was engrafted into his being. And the result of the event of that dialogue resulted in 1 Kings 17:1.

This statement, "except by my word," is tremendous. It is groundbreaking, as well as ground shaking. If Elijah were a little bit more conscious of himself, if he were a little bit considerate of himself, he couldn't have brought that message to King Ahab. Why? Because if there should be no rain or dew upon the land, what would happen to him? He, too, would suffer. And he certainly was not a man of means. He never would be, and who would support him? So, when Elijah declared the judgment of God, he had forgotten himself altogether. I do not mean that he was to any degree not himself! No! Not at all. But without a doubt he was more conscious of the present of God that sat on his life is what he was concentrating on.

Statement made. The word heard. That's it! Job done! War declared! Ground taken. One small step for a man. One giant step for prophetic mankind. Authority of an absolute nature is enforced, and unleashed by a human being that the inspired writers of the New Testament trouble themselves to declare that he was a man of like passions such as we. So let's follow the inner temptation to back off and say things like, "This is a biblical prophet that lived in realms we can only dream of." A pox on that logic. The voice of heaven has tangibly invaded earth. No, "softly softly," here! God has commissioned this man, and by the language he utilised, Yahweh has left it to this man's own volition. He was a conscious agency that was saturated, soaked and marinaded in the Spirit of the ever-living God to take charge of the war that Yahweh and all of heaven had sanctioned and was actively endorsing. On earth, he was clearly God's Commander-in-Chief. Like Potiphar, and later like Pharaoh leaving the rule of all he had to Joseph, Yahweh, so it seems, left this issue to the man from Tishbe. Yahweh had revealed His will, His plan and purpose from the books of Moses, and, by those means, placed the entire resolution of Baalistic idolatry in Israel into his hands. In the realm of prophecy, there is deep, deeper, and deepest. Elijah had gone deeper than anybody previous to himself.

ELIJAH'S PROPHETIC WORD IMPACTED AN ENTIRE NATION.

We need to reutter in this watershed moment of Israel's history. After pawing over dictionaries, lexicons, varied translations, scholars, and Hebrew professors, "little old moi" has come up with my own expanded and qualified paraphrase - that reads:

"And Elijah the Tishbite, (foreigner? Stranger?), from amongst the Tishbe settlers in Gilead, said to Ahab, "As surely as Yahweh, the God of Israel lives, in whose presence and before whom I stand, that is, the God whom I serve, there will surely be neither dew nor rain in the next few years (which turned out to be three and a half) except at my word – meaning, until I personally give permission and the word of command for it to do so."

It's impossible for the amazement of Elijah's first recorded words to remain calm in one's mind. What the...? Who the ...? How the ...? Let's stop and take a calm deep breath. Clearly, servants of this breed serve Him (God) continually while seeking and seeing His face and/or hearing His voice. The Tishbite's inner life, his spirit, was echoing with the voice he had heard instructing him from the throne of heaven.

See it. Feel it. Enter into it. People would just not have known what to conclusively think! Was this hairy, ill-clad man mad? Nobody would talk to the king like that – would they? If he wasn't mad, he was clearly wildly eccentric. Or was he genuinely delivering a word from God? Was he, is he, an authorised mouthpiece of Yahweh? After all, that is what prophecy is, i.e., an utterance made by an authorised mouthpiece of the Almighty. Astonishingly, he carried more authority than the king. Like Moses, like Samuel, he was not a king – yet he walked, acted, and spoke more like a king than any king that had ever lived before him. Up to this moment of time he had done nothing but speak one full sentence. That was all the king and population of Israel knew of him. The fact that the scripture starts in 1 Kings 17:1 by telling us his name, we are left with the question that students over two millennia and more have been asking. That question is: Did Ahab and his court know who this man was when he made this opening gambit of input into Israel's history? Or did the editor or scribe who wrote the inspired text (possibly years later) know who it was, purely by commonly known retrospection at the time of writing?

If nobody had ever seen or heard of this man before the "Real Time" moment of 1 Kings 17:1, the gossip and conversation of the population for the next three and a half years – whatever the equivalent was of social media in those days – must have simply chronicled this man's record of a single statement spoken in the awe-struck face of the king, and laughed.

From the moment Elijah spoke those words, it did not rain in Israel (or the whole Levant?) for three and a half years. We only know the time span of 1,277 days (or thereabouts) because Jesus Christ Himself informs us so. (Luke 4:25, James 5:17) Then … as time passed by, and the early and late rains didn't come over a few months, people would have recalled. "That silly, strange, bohemian, ill-dressed man was, perhaps, not silly at all." And as time passed, the masses of the land stopped referring to the Tishbite as "the strange man" and slowly became the national legend known as "The Prophet Elijah."

Later, after a full year of dryness and drought creeping over all water sources, this man with a Gileadean accent would have begun to fill the man on the street with deep respect and mystery. Up through all the different classes of society and into the very court of the king and his Baal-worshipping, Asherah loving apology for a queen, the gossiping, chit chatting, and news-carrying populace would have spread the news far and wide. "It seems that Yahweh is not as dead as her majesty Queen Jezebel would have us believe, folks. This prophet has king Ahab in the palm of his hand, and he has told Ahab that he and Yahweh were on our case. It seems as if this man was the ruler, and Ahab (and Jezebel) are subject to him. But "Shush!" Whatever happens, do not let the Queen hear you talking like this." 1 Kings 17:1 was legendary in pubs, clubs, and meeting places – whatever was Israel's equivalent at the time before the words were ever written down.

ELIJAH'S PROPHETIC WORD IMPACTED BEYOND ISRAEL.

The national gossip stream would have travelled across the Jordan and carried itself into the rough highlands and rustic fields of Gilead. The talk would have been filled about his, "East of Jordan accent." Gilead, properly, "The Rocky Region," lay east of the Jordan river, between the Yarmouk River and the valley of Heshbon. It is part of Jordan today. Gilead was open to the desert on its east and is substantially a wilderness. With but few cities scattered within its borders, it suited well to developing the reclusive Tishbite as a "dweller in the wilderness". If the people in Israel did not know it at first, surely the returned echoes of the news from some of the travelling rustics of Gilead, those that knew the Tishbite who wore camel hair and a leather belt, would have messaged back an animated response through the Hebrew grapevine of the day: "Oh yes! That sounds like Elijah the Tishbite. He is the only one that dresses like that – and speaks as directly as we are told. Be careful! Don't mess with him! He walks hand in hand with Almighty Yahweh!"

At first, there was no alarm. Only headline news bytes fed conversation and social interaction. The farmers continued to sow their seed in hope. The trading caravans trailed through and then toward the horizon. Then the rains were late. Anxious eyes scanned the middle eastern sky. Then, gradually, the streams became gravel beds. The wells became dry, and the vineyards began to wither in the burning sun. The temples and shrines began to resound with prayers to Baal, and great pillars of smoke rose to heaven from the altars of Ashtaroth. At last, from out of the fiery furnace, Israel and even the monarchy raised cries of despair. From the king in the palace to the beggar by the wayside came one common, desperate scream: "Where is Elijah the Tishbite?"

After eighteen months, then two years, and then three years of no rain, drought had pressed Israel, Judah, Tyre, Sidon, and Zarapheth in Lebanon into desperate days. The man from Tishbe, known and seen by so few, was a living legend throughout the middle east. All on the grounds of a single sentence that proved to have the authority of God Himself.

ELIJAH'S PROPHETIC MYSTIQUE AND MYSTERY WAS THE ESSENCE OF HIS CHARACTER.

So, here we are ... and there we were – the Bible reading public – happily browsing through the book of First Kings, happily educating ourselves in God – or, perhaps, disgustingly - reading through the division and split of the kingdom of Israel, watching the Israeli nations as they were sliding into the dark abyss of idolatry, polytheism, and a national cultural lifestyle that turned against God. Suddenly, out of the blue, without so much as a hint of this man's development or prophetic calling, without the tiniest clue of his presence, his upbringing, or his native town, God Himself throws the population a curved ball, and this fellow appears in 1 Kings 17:1. Yes! - "appears" is the most accurate word to use – and astonishingly, with just a few words, he challenges the direction of an entire nation and its culture, introducing a new age of prophecy and prophets. Literally – he re-directs the very course of the history of the Hebrew people. And having redirected history by one uttered sentence, he disappears from the scene in Israel and is not discovered for 42 months, when he returns to give the command for the rain to fall - with caveats. This man is a mountain. He is bigger than the Pacific Ocean. Whatever analogy or euphemism one chooses, the world has somewhat changed, and only a handful of people have ever met him, as far as we know.

ELIJAH'S WORD HAD A SUBSTANTIVE SELF-EXISTENCE OF ITS OWN.

Elijah says, "except/mouth of/my word". He characterises his word as having a substantive existence with a mouth of its own. He may have done this to add to the force of his statement. Intriguingly, this is also how Yahweh's word is characterised in the next verse, and later, when Elijah visits Hebron, "Look! there was Yahweh's word coming to him". 1 Kings 17:3. 1 Kings 19:9. "The word of the Lord approached him."

THE IMPARTATION OF THE DIVINE WORD AND BURDEN.

"We can imagine Elijah seeing the idolatry of the nation all around him and feeling the same as Yahweh Himself. And, as Elijah read the words of what we refer to as the book of Deuteronomy, he developed deep moral indignation. He prayed with depth, passion and faith. As a result, his prayer was in perfect harmony with Yahweh's feelings and will. His anger at the nation's idolatry matched Yahweh's anger, and so his prayer was favourably received, heard, and answered. "And this is the boldness which we have toward him, that if we ask anything according to His will, He hears us." (1 John 5:14) even though he was an imperfect man, "with like passions as us". If we share Yahweh's attitude, we may well go on to share His feelings and His inner responses. Yahweh loves to include others in his work. Christ's followers "are God's fellow-workers"(1 Corinthians 3:9). Elijah's prayer that Yahweh would "shut up the heavens so that no rain would occur", was Elijah's moment that was equivalent moment to Isaiah 6, when Isaiah said, "Here am I! Send me" (Isaiah 6:8).

Ahab forged a marriage alliance with the Sidonian kingdom on his northern border and solidified a religious alliance with their god, Baal. Baal worship legitimised and encouraged sexual immorality. It was believed that widespread immorality would encourage Baal to ensure that the rains would fall and that the land was fecund. Elijah's pronouncement was a direct attack on the central promise of all Baal worship. Elijah's opening word was an important assertion. To carry out their carnal desires under the auspices of Baal worship, the Israelites had to believe that,"Yahweh had left the land," (Ezekiel 8:12), and that He was "dead," to what they were doing.

Elijah follows the declaration that Yahweh is alive, with the word, "the God of Israel". Singular "God", the *only* God, the God of

Abraham, Isaac and Jacob. No room for syncretism. Yahweh had told Israel: "I am Yahweh your God, who have brought you out of the land of Egypt, out of the house of slavery. You must not have any other gods against my face" (Exodus 20:2,3). Yahweh deserved their allegiance for bringing them out of Egypt long ago, but especially just because of who He is. Elijah was "the messenger of the enthroned Jehovah" (Campbell Morgan). What a privilege!

All men are at the mercy of God, but up to this moment, Ahab refused to believe it. Now, he was being forced to experience it. The nation was also to know that it was at the mercy of God and his prophet.

Elijah's announcement about the cessation of dew and rain would only be noticed if he made this announcement when the rain was expected. From April and into September, there was a period of continuous rainlessness. The land would go completely dry, and the vegetation would become utterly parched were it not for the heavy dews that fell at night in the cool of the day. The dew formed and soaked the vegetation during the months of April, May and, August and September. None is mentioned as occurring during June and July". We are safe to assume that Elijah made his announcement mid-October.

"Both Jesus and James say that it did not rain in the land for "three years and six months." Yet, Elijah is said to appear before Ahab to end the drought "in the third year"—no doubt counting from the day he announced the drought. Thus, it must have been after a long, rainless dry season when he first stood before Ahab. (Luke 4:25; James 5:17; 1 Kings 18:1".

"In the Ras Shamra texts, Baal...is referred to as... "the Rider of the Clouds." Elijah was putting himself in an open confrontation with Baal. "Year after year, the rains came. Year after year, Baal got the credit". Jehovah could not stay silent. He had promised at Sinai, six hundred years before, "I shall have to break the pride of your strength and make your heavens like iron and your earth like copper" (Leviticus 26:19).

Elijah's confidence reverberates down through history. Indeed, the angel told Zechariah that his son, John, would go with "Elijah's spirit and power, to turn back the hearts of fathers to children and the disobedient ones to the practical wisdom of righteous ones, to get ready for Yahweh a prepared people" (Luke 1:17). "Elijah's spirit," would refer to his conviction, his determination, his dynamic, enthusiastic love of Jehovah and his courageous stance against opposers. At Horeb, Elijah later said: "I have been absolutely jealous for Yahweh the God of His own armies" (1 Kings 19:10). Elijah was passionate in his call for people to come back to the covenant, forthright in his condemnation of unrighteousness.

"How did the king respond? The king's wrath might provoke an outburst of sullenness, but he contented himself with menacing and reproachful words. It was otherwise with Jezebel. A genuine idolatress, she hated the servants of Jehovah with implacable hatred and did her utmost to suppress them by violence" (Dean F. W. Farrar). In time, Obadiah would later say to Elijah, "As Yahweh your God is living, there is not a nation or kingdom where [Ahab] has not sent to look for you" (1 Kings 18:10).

Oh, to have been the man who poured water on Elijah's hands, to have heard the entire prayer that closed heaven and imparted the prophetic reality of authority on Elijah. Like Joshua hanging behind in the Tent of meeting overhearing what the manifest person of Yahweh was discussing face to face with Moses. Like Gehazi standing by the door of Elisha's room waiting for every sound of his master's groans and cries whether it be aimed at Yahweh or he himself to valet his master. Perhaps even a person like me could have turned out as mighty as Elisha if I was following Elijah around as attentively as farmer Elisha did in years future to the time we are considering. Elijah just prayed what the Bible promised - and the normal routine of nature and sky was halted.

How simple and pliant was Elijah's spirit to the statements of the holy scrolls? How tender was Elijah's heart to what Moses had written centuries before? How violent was he to bring such cataclysmic results to his prayer? One man praying for the fulfilment of scripture brought an answer that impacted whole nations and possibly millions of people. It is almost surreal when templated over the comparatively insipid prayers and lifeless cries of my own soul. This man was aligning with the scriptures, and even though he may never have seen a miracle in his own district of Gilead, he had strong convictions concerning the absolute veracity and integrity of the scriptures that the people of Israel treasured.

The prophet was supremely confident in claiming that his own volitionally spoken words would just as easily bring the rain and dew as they would first stop it from falling. In that one line, Elijah revealed and manifested the fullness of the divine, enabling imparted to him to stand against the evil spirit of the age. His words imply that his authority was backed by the presence of Yahweh that was surrounding him. The announcement was supremely heavenly.

Finally, we cannot miss the point that Elijah's statement suggested that he would be carrying the promise of the word with him for years to come. He does not give a date. He does state that there would be no rain or dew for the next few "years." He was choosing to withhold his word. The impact of drought for one year would be cataclysmic. Elijah's word was plural: "years". Elijah was choosing to endanger his own life in the drought as he lived with the weight of his own prophetic word resting on him and all he did and everywhere he went.

What awesome responsibility on a man's shoulders! What an awesome character to carry such a weight! What an incredible anointing to consciously be aware of such authority. The future of the Hebrew people was in the hands of Elijah the Tishbite, the man that was continually standing in the presence of Yahweh the Almighty.

There are a few scholars who vaguely suggest that the drought had perhaps begun sometime before his appearance at the Court of Ahab. For when he does appear, it is not necessarily to proclaim the beginning of the drought but to declare that it was the work of Yahweh, and that it would not end except according to the word spoken by the servant of Yahweh. The veracity of Elijah's authority dispels this theory. The word of the prophet that started the drought, is the same word that broke the drought.

P.S.

A quote I have in one of my notebooks, without the source being written, says:

"Such was this rude, stern, volcanic Tishbite as he comes to the rescue of his country; to champion a cause that seemed lost; to stand alone against a huge and dominant iniquity; to challenge Ahab and Jezebel in the palace of their licentious pleasure, in the citadel of their idolatrous power. He came like the flash of a scimitar, uttered his appalling message, voiced the wrath of the Almighty, and was gone."

.

18

SELF ISOLATION AND WITH NOTHING ELSE TO DO? (1 Kings 17:2-4)

"The word of the Lord now came to Elijah, saying, "go away from here, turn eastward and hide yourself in the Kerith torrent ravine that is east of the Jordan. And it must occur that from the torrent valley you should drink, and the ravens I shall certainly command to supply you with food there."

Absenting himself from the public view and whatever was the equivalent of social media in Elijah's day, and secreting himself by a brook outside of Ahab's reignal jurisdiction that nobody knew of, is the last course Samuel would have selected. If Elijah was told to wait for the further manifestation of God's will, he waited patiently. As blind John Milton discovered and sang: "They also serve who only stand and wait."

The reason for Yahweh's instruction to go to the brook called Cherith was to withdraw the most precious thing, i.e., the prophetic word of God, from the land, as well as, undoubtedly, to keep Elijah alive and safe. The drought and famine blanketing Ahab's kingdom (and beyond) were Divine scourges in keeping with Yahweh's terrible action toward Ahab. It should be pointed out that the Hebrew word for "hide," (1 Kings 17:3), is an entirely different one from that which is found in Joshua 6:17,25 (Rahab's "hiding" of the spies) and in 1 Kings 18:4,13. The word used in connection with Elijah might better be rendered "turn eastward and *absent yourself*". So, the thought of Elijah "hiding" does not seem to be properly appropriate.

Elijah's journey emphasizes the value of obedience, especially in solitude. God commands him to leave his homeland and go to the brook Cherith, where he would find sustenance.

This highlights a profound lesson: sometimes, divine direction cannot do anything but lead us into isolation. In our contemporary cultural context, isolation can be perceived negatively; however, it can also be a divinely ordained personal space for spiritual growth. It allows for introspection and a deeper understanding of one's own purpose. Elijah's obedience in a seemingly barren place, or if not barren, a place void of humanity, illustrates how isolation can be a sanctuary for divine communication, and clarity of thought and motivation.

The presence of the man from Tishbe, and the possibility of him being pursued by the masses, be it for good or evil, was to be prevented. The only thing that the King, queen and population of Israel had to chew on was not the strange human being that precipitated the 3-and-a-half-year drought, but the naked spoken word of God that suspended the natural and divinely ordained mechanisms of nature and the whole of creation that drove the climate over the Promised Land and the entire Levant. Even in the darkness of the idolatrous world of Israel, no priest or prophet of Baal could emulate such a predictive statement with such a sustained accuracy and longevity of intention. It was a 42-month sustained restraint of rain. Any open mind would relate the burdensome climate to the statement of the prophet. Whether it was perceived in a positive or negative perspective.

All dew and rain was to be withheld from Ahab's temporal domain, not only literally but spiritually too. The man who delivered Yahweh's most relevant Word for generations was removed from the scene of public action. The prophet was directed to a place outside the popular camps of Israel, away from the entire religious system. Joseph was brought to blossom in prison. Moses grew to full stature in the back side of the desert. David learned Kingliness was being pursued by a most unkinglike monarch. Elijah's anointing was to be honed to perfection at a completely depopulated wild place called Cherith.

The commission which now challenged the Tishbite, was no ordinary employment. It called for something a million miles north of extraordinary valour. For an uncredentialed, untutored agrestic of the hills to appear unsolicited before a monarch who defied Yahweh and his heaven was sufficient to quash the bravest. The mission was made even more of a brick wall when his heathen consort from Sidon leapt at the opportunity to slay any who opposed her will. At this point of the story, in real-time, she had already put many of Yahweh's prophets to death. What likelihood was there of hope for this lonely Gileadite escaping with his life? We have the scripture and know the outcome. Elijah had no such privilege.

There was no mention of Jezebel in verse 1. If she was not present for Elijah's previous sudden edict, she undoubtedly would have been informed soon afterwards. Had Elijah not hastened to go, she would have wanted to seize the prophet.

Testifying to the truth can be terminally dangerous, as many twenty-first century Christians know too well, declaring various particular biblical truths only within the open yet secluded doors of Christian fraternities and expounding certain biblical concepts concerning sexuality and/or morality and free speech together with preaching the gospel on the streets. All those facets of biblical truth can in some cases reap a whirlwind of legal indictments. Like the 7,000 prophets that hid in caves, away from the presence of Ahab and Jezebel, the modern equivalent that is much bigger than 7,000, hide in plain view of church buildings and stay quiet. God knows this (Acts 22:18; Revelation 12:17). In a land steeped in false worship, it was not just the king and queen who were now Elijah's enemy. The Tishbite was, by Divine choice, to be cut off from any social interaction with people who might betray his place of abode. The divinely ordained concealments of the man from Tishbe would last until the punishment of the drought was over.

There would, undoubtedly, have been masses of people wanting to question Elijah about what he had prophesied. "What about my farm?" "What about my family who will starve if there is no rain for more than a year?" "What about my livestock?" "Are you being serious?" "Did Yahweh actually approve of what you have just spoken?" "Are you suggesting Yahweh is more powerful than Baal?" "Are you really contradicting the king and queen?" "Why did you seem to have so little respect for the king's wishes?" "Which tribe and clan do you come from?" "Are you a true Hebrew to speak such damaging nonsense?" "Why do you dress so weirdly?" The King, his courtiers, and, as the word spread around the country, the population of Israel would have had so many questions. Couldn't Elijah pause and stop and answer the cries of many. Just a brief social-media interview.

Having delivered one message that would, by its own content, be left hanging for at least a couple of years, Elijah hears another message from the same source as the decree of the drought. "Leave here!" "Absent yourself!" "Go to the stream Cherith." As was Elijah's word to Ahab, so was God's word to Elijah thereafter. No explanation! No qualification of the divine statement. No questions were posed by the Tishbite concerning the minutiae of the statement he had made to the king of Israel. There was no small print to the divine decree …or was it Elijah's decree?

Fascinatingly, the scripture states that Yahweh sent His Word to speak to Elijah directly, or rather, "the Word of Yahweh" spoke to him. The apostle John reveals the profound truth that the Word was with God and was indeed God Himself. It was Christ Himself talking to Elijah. We see the different persons that constitute the One true God. Jewish scholars would refer to it as the unspecified "second power" in heaven. It is clear in the Hebrew that the Word of God came to him, and having arrived, the Word of God spoke to him.

When the Almighty says, "Leave here", I am left wondering, "Where was 'here'"? Did Elijah hear that instruction while he was still in Ahab's presence? Was he out in the street or on the steps of the royal palace? However, if God considers telling us where he was as classified data, we are at least, thankfully, allowed in on the plan as a whole, as God looks after His prophet. God is aware, as was Elijah of course, that his life would plainly be in danger if people had a clue where he was at any time. With Jezebel on the throne and dominating her husband, this kind of situation could clearly degenerate into a violent matter of death for Elijah.

A LEARNED HABIT OF IMMEDIATE OBEDIENT RESPONSE.

"Immediately he went and did according to the word of Yahweh, and so went and took up dwelling by the torrent valley of Cherith that is east of the Jordan."

Biblical Hebrew does not have a word for "immediately." Nonetheless, Elijah would have departed the court of Ahab, "immediately" after his obloquy in order to avoid capture; so, one could defend the use of the word here as deistic. The verse, word for word, literally reads as "And he was going/and he was doing/according to the word of/Yahweh/and he was going/and he began to dwell/in the wadi of/Cherith/upon the face of/the Jordan". All the verbs in this verse are, I am told, imperfect in tense. This means that we have here a described ongoing, ever active process. The repetition of these imperfect verbs also creates an inclusive tense around the whole sentence. "And he was doing/according to the word of/Yahweh". This emphasises Elijah's ready obedience to Yahweh's command. As Moses would have said, "he did just so." (Genesis 6:22; Exodus 7:6; 12:28, 50; 40:16; Numbers 1:54; 17:11).

"Go away from here, and you must turn your way eastward and hide yourself in the Cherith torrent valley[i] of that which is east of the Jordan."

East of Samaria, the land drops away into gullies that feed the Jordan. Samaria is at a height of around 1,500 feet above sea level; the Jordan to the east of Samaria, some 25 miles away, is at 260 feet below sea level. For self-preservation's sake, Elijah descended towards the Jordan. We may not know where Cherith was, but there is no doubt that Elijah knew. We are told that it "faced the Jordan," in other words, flowed into it. It was on the east of the river, further away from Samaria and in an area of Gilead where Elijah had been previously dwelling (1 Kings 17:1. Tishbe is believed by the majority of scholars and historians to have been on the Eastern side of the sea of Galilee in the rustic land of Gilead Gilead.).

"Leave here, turn eastward and hide in the Cherith Ravine, east of the Jordan." This was, to Elijah, the tangible evidence that he was not alone. "As Yahweh lives, before whom I stand." He was still standing before the Almighty when there was no other human being present or visible.

We get the picture as we survey the whole text. People of Israel, especially the king and Queen, were, scouring the country and every conceivable corner or possible hiding place, looking for the hairy man with the camel skin top and the leather belt. It would seem, however, that east of the Jordan was not on Ahab's search map. East of Jordan, strictly speaking, was still part of Israel. However, East of Jordan was not considered in their scouring. After all, no sane, sensible person would go into that rough terrain, would they? God knew Ahab's mind and He arranged that Elijah would be safe from the vitriol that was ever developing between Ahab, Jezebel, and the Tishbite.

A PERIOD OF TOTALLY DIVINE CONTAINMENT.

"And it must occur that from the torrent valley you should drink, and the ravens I shall certainly command to supply you with food there." The raven was an unclean animal according to the Mosaic Law (Leviticus11:13,15; Deuteronomy 14:12,14). God caused birds of prey, which lived on carrion, to feed the prophet. However, Elijah was not going to be eating the ravens. He was only, miraculously, going to be fed by them. If Elijah had any religiosity that would have precipitated rejecting the Ravens, it would have been concerning the food that the ravens would bring him. Even if Elijah had wondered

about the type of food he was to receive, I do not think he would have spent much energy on the issue. The choice of the raven was also appropriate since it is usually a bird of the wilderness, often inhabiting mountainous regions and even deserts. It was among the creatures envisioned by Isaiah as inhabiting the emptiness and wasteness of ruined Edom. (Isa 34:11)

In verses 4 to 6, we see that God commands ravens to bring Elijah bread and meat. This act of using unlikely agents for provision serves as a powerful reminder that resources can come from unexpected places. In our lives, we may often overlook potential sources of support and nourishment. This lesson encourages us to remain open-minded and vigilant, recognizing that help may arrive through unconventional means or through individuals we least expect.

Yahweh was going to cause Elijah to be self-contained in his isolation in the ravine of Cherith. He would have no need to depart from it for any supplies, thus avoiding any of Ahab's scouting troops. God's servants should feel confident of His ability to provide for them. Elijah was fully "contained" in Yahweh's love and care. A hiding place is the God of ancient times, and underneath are the everlasting arms (Yahweh would ensure that Elijah would be the "blessed man" described metaphorically in Psalm 1:3: "He will certainly become like a tree planted by streams of water, that gives its own fruit in its season."

The cyclical nature of receiving provision is another notable lesson. Elijah is instructed to drink from the brook, while the ravens continuously bring him food. This rhythm of receiving - trusting in God's provision while actively engaging with it - can be applied to our own lives. We often seek immediate and abundant solutions, but Elijah's experience illustrates that trust is often built in a process of repeated acts of faith. Each meal brought by the ravens reaffirmed his trust in God's faithfulness.

Note also the significance of the place. The brook Cherith is more than just a geographical location. It symbolizes a divine appointment. God leads Elijah to a specific place for a purpose. This teaches us that our locations - both physical and metaphorical - are significant in our spiritual journeys. Whether it's a job, a community, or a season of life, understanding that we are exactly where we need to be for growth and preparation can shift our perspective on the challenges we face.

A PERIOD OF NON-PRODUCTIVITY IN THE PHYSICAL REALM.

"And the ravens themselves were bringing him bread and meat in the morning and bread and meat in the evening, and from the torrent valley he kept drinking."

Take note that very little about Elijah was kosher. It is true. According to the established religion of Israel in the Mosaic scrolls there were certain protocols that we have no clue of Elijah following. Chew on this. Unclean ravens fed him. Later a Gentile widow sustained him. According to Moses law, nothing about Elijah was ceremoniously clean. But noticeably, what made all of this clean and acceptable to God (ravens, Gentile widow, camel's-hair cloak, unclean food, etc.) was the pure, clean, and faithful heart inhabited by the life and presence of God who was active within Elijah.

"Contained" in the wadi's ravine, Elijah was more than well catered for. He may also have been able to eat some of the vegetation growing next to the stream. Yahweh provided a good diet as Elijah sat by the Cherith. Spurgeon sums up that Elijah may not have dined on the dainties that the palace would have supplied for the prophets of Baal and royalty, but God ensured that he would eat better than the prophets hiding in the caves that were given only bread and water by a man named Obadiah. They *only* had bread and water. Elijah had bread and meat. And that bread and meat was delivered as a daily supply, with no bulk carrying. The Ravens did not allow Elijah to hoard up a surplus. Ravens hold a passion for picking out the eyes of men and animals. They love to maul the sick and the dying. They swallow, with vulturous gaggling, everything they can put their beak on. However, miraculously, all the food Elijah gets while at Cherith is from ravens.

Meat is good source of vital elements for the body. Rich in niacin, vitamin b12, vitamin b6 and the mineral nutrients; iron, zinc, phosphorus, potassium and magnesium, all vital for health. It is also worth remembering fish as part of a raven's diet. Since Yahweh had commanded this provision, Elijah did not need to be concerned that the meat was from an unclean animal or whether it had been bled properly when it had been slaughtered. Although ravens are carrion eaters, this meat must have had a different source because Yahweh had been strict on this matter, saying to his people: "You should prove yourselves holy men to me, and you must not eat flesh in the field that is something torn by a wild beast. You should throw it to the dogs" (Exodus 22:31). Is it possible that the Ravens stole food from the kitchens of Ahab and Jezebel?

The repetition of the phrase shows how very reliable the delivery service was - every morning and every evening, there was bread and meat.

A PERIOD OF DEEP RICH PRODUCTIVITY IN THE INVISIBLE REALM.

As far as we understand from the narrative, Elijah had absolutely "nothing" to do but eat the food delivery and sleep whenever required. Other than that, no matter how long Elijah was actually living at Cherith, there was nothing for him to do that we are told of, apart from waiting on God. I think that waiting for instructions while worshipping Yahweh was more than a full-time job for Elijah, with long days and lots of expectance over time. It is a biblical concept that has been emphasized and modelled by several biblical characters, that waiting on God alone and in silence is a door opener to the presence of God, as well as an ear-opener to what he was saying at that moment.

I have always understood that the term "waiting on God" has two distinct significations as it is in English. One can wait for a bus. In such a situation, one is quite literally doing nothing but eagerly, yet idly, waiting for somebody or something to arrive and deal with. Indeed, this kind of waiting is necessary for us all. Yet the same English terminology is used when dining out. The waiter in the restaurant is physically extremely busy. In this circumstance, the person who is waiting is extremely busy serving. So, Elijah was surely performing both aspects of waiting on God. Waiting passively for further directives and waiting actively in prayer and worship, aligning himself with the plan, the cause and the Spirit of God and His purpose.

A PERIOD OF TOTAL SELF ISOLATION FOR AN UNDEFINED PERIOD.

The prophet Elijah hid on the banks of the Cherith stream and was fed by ravens during the early part of the three-and-a-half-year drought, which he announced to King Ahab. Most commentators play it safe by suggesting things like Elijah needed to take one step at a time, i.e., Cherith for a while, Zarephath later while leading slowly to the ultimate battle at Carmel. A man of God must be taught how to trust God for the most essential yet mundane things, like food. God's people need to learn the secret of "the hidden life," making the point that one must have treasured times alone with the dialogue of Yahweh before he utters a word in public. They exposit that while waiting on God, the Christian may be called to sit by drying brooks.

Note how God enlists all levels of creation to obey His will. I believe it was Spurgeon who highlighted the unclean ravens were like good and kind people who did not know Christ yet were doing God's will in some dimension. An unclean creature serving God in some way and yet remaining unclean still. So, we may be serviceable in the Lord's cause to some extent and yet, after all, be utter strangers to the things of Christ.

A PERIOD OF TIME EXPERIENCING THE JUDGEMENT OF HIS OWN PROPHETIC WORD.

Elijah was not only the messenger of the drought but, in some sense, the cause of it. That was where his anointing and power was manifested. The brook was drying up little by little.

The Divine direction to retreat from public view at Cherith reveals the Divine sense of protection. It seems nothing but the Ravens and nobody but the Word of God knew where Elijah was.

Cherith, for Elijah, was also a place of training on the experience of divine communion. Yahweh's goal was that this man was to enter glory, omitting death and burial from his agenda. Such a programme of intention in the heart of Yahweh surely demanded a level of relationship and interaction with such a man who carried and bore such a high calling and purpose. Preparation was also required for the battle with hell (quite literally) on Carmel that was to be fought sometime later. Life in the Spirit, with the manifestation of the Spirit was to be intense both at Carmel, in Zarapheth, as well as later, on the eastern bank of the Jordan in the whirlwind where God was to elevate the man from Tishbe to a whole new dimension of relating to God and the universe. Training for ongoing mindsets in faith and preparation to subjectively miss the death process that none but a man called Enoch ever previously engaged with may have been unknown to Elijah but was clearly part and parcel of God's dealings with him all through his life.

So, we conclude that Divinely sent food and daily interaction and intercourse with heaven, developing a different dimension of faith and dependence on Yahweh, was also engrafted into the man from Tishbe at Cherith. It becomes ultimately elementary in the prophet's ever-growing knowledge of Yahweh that God's sending of Elijah to Cherith was part of His divine plan to prepare Elijah for his unique future.

Unique futures planned by heaven require unique preparation of each character on the planet. Whether you are goaled by God to be a world-wide evangelist, or a local postman to your area, God has a training course experience for all who strive to serve Him.

How outwardly tranquil was life while watching the torrents become a trickle. How violently war-like was the mental and spiritual preparation of the inner life, coming to terms with the word that he had carpeted the whole Levant with. The "1 Kings 17:1 pronouncement" was busily constantly active. The weight of the responsibility must have been intense.

God's servants must be taught the value of the hidden life. The man who is to take a high place before his fellows must take a low place before his God. Every saintly soul that would wield great power with men must win it in some hidden Cherith. We cannot give out unless we have previously taken in.

There is a strong emphasis on the word "there." "I have commanded the ravens to feed you "there."

Elijah's experience also illuminates the interplay between divine sovereignty and human agency. While God orchestrates the provision, Elijah must actively engage with his environment. He must drink from the brook and accept the food offered by the ravens. This duality teaches us that faith is not passive; it requires action and engagement. We are called to participate in the unfolding of God's plans while trusting in His overarching control.

The drought that was impacting millions of others was impacting the Cherith torrents. The land was drying up. So was Cherith. The Cherith stream had lost its torrents because of the prophetic word uttered by Elijah himself. If he hadn't said that word, it would not have failed. Prophecy makes things happen. He was suffering the profound validation of his own prophetic utterance. His own water supply was subject to the power of the prophetic. It was the water that failed, not the ravens. It was the natural, not the supernatural, provision that had come to an end. Drought had finally reached and impacted Cherith.

The torrents had reduced to a trickle, and the trickle had reduced to a trail of dry sand. The ravens were still flying in with the food supply.

This passage serves as a precursor to the greater challenges Elijah would face, particularly as he confronts the prophets of Baal. The time spent at Cherith is not just a survival mechanism; it is a preparation phase. God often uses periods of relative quiet to equip us for future challenges. The lesson here is that times of waiting and provision are not wasted; they are crucial for our development and preparedness for the tasks ahead.

19

ELIJAH, THE HEALER OF A NATIONAL TRAUMA.

"All ideologies are both intellectual and Philosophical spongers nourished by perverting pure biblical Judaistic-Christian thought," says Dr Jordan Peterson. That seems to me to be a fact. As usual, once the divinely stated Word as a model, with its teaching and guidance, is humanly "edited", no matter what the context, be it philosophic, religious, political or even scientific, the original dream received from heaven crumbles when added to or subtracted from by fallen man. Moving the doctrinal rails and replacing the rock with soft, gooey sand produces hideous, ghastly portrayals of a vicious, submission-demanding, "local" deity or paradigm that will be remarkably perverse and destructive. Under the fascist and ultra-religious immoral regime of Baalism, the fact that the idolatrous paradigmatic system was a parasitic worldview without arms and legs – and as it is revealed, also without a mouth - the submissive practices of the people of the Northern state of Israel showed that the population, generally, was acting-out things they did not deep down believe. If you have read and understood the somewhat diluted explanation of the definition of Baal and Asherah worship, you will easily grasp the truth of it when I say that with the onslaught of Baal institutions across Israel, the families and general population were traumatised and thrust into broken homes, broken families and broken society. Truly, this writer perceives Jezebel as larger than Hitler, Saddam Hussein and any other Totalitarian dictator one can think of.

In fact, it was fear of the dominating woman, Jezebel, that led to a national wimpish response to the queen's demands. There were even 100 prophets of Yahweh who simply zipped up their mouths and hid for their lives. I have never really understood how the 100 were still comfortably referred to as prophets. A gift is still a gift, of course, no matter how 100 of them were restricted by the vicious governmental authority. i.e. the Queen. A prophet is still a prophet, of course, despite the threat of death for speaking hope to the ten-tribed hegemony of Israel. But not only would the 100 prophets have been somewhat traumatised, but the population being starved of the Yahwehistic daily, regular ministry would have left the population floundering for comfort, inspiration and faith. The queen carried demonic authority at that time that was more substantial than any known follower of Yahweh, it seemed. That was until the man from Tishbe came to town. (However, we need to postscript this paragraph with the reminder that later on in these pages, we shall be negotiating the whys and wherefores of Elijah - the man who called down fire and defied the demonic powers of Baal - fleeing the country simply because Jezebel was heard to say, "God do so to me if I haven't killed Elijah by this time tomorrow. No difference between the 100 prophets hiding in a large cave, while Elijah did exactly the same in a much smaller cave).

The entire nation was submitted to Jezebel's orders. She was the State's dominant power at that Moment in Israel. Mindlessly, without conviction or spiritual insight, people acted in a manner shaped by the world that they lived in. They sadly submitted and were like sheep being dragged astray, not knowing how to handle fascist politics and religious manipulation.

Elijah was to arise as a divinely sent body that firmly and solidly dreamed beyond the articulated knowledge of anybody that lived at that moment. Or was it that the commonly accepted articulated belief system had not read the Mosaic sacred scrolls properly? Fear of death being managed while suffering beneath a cultic slave mistress would have unbalanced and traumatised the majority of Israel. Elijah had clearly read the Mosaic scrolls and dreamed of freedom. The visualised dream is the birthplace of revolutionary thought and world-changing motivation. It is my personal conviction that the Bible teaches that there is nothing random about dreams. Whether the dream simply brings fresh knowledge and vision from heaven to its recipients or whether it simply surfaces from the unconscious things that are held in unsuspecting memory recesses, I have no idea. But I do know Elijah must have imaged, seen, and inwardly experienced freedom for his people before he took hold of the responsibility that was initially God's alone.

Elijah must have immersed himself in the dream/vision of breaking and burying the spiritual binding of Baal and Jezebel. Like any dream and aspiration, his visualisation was conceived initially as fiction. However, prophets, listening to God speak, are wombs for such dreams and visions, immersing themselves in the obsessed fiction of the pictures and spectacles of the unconscious night. The spiritual man of faith sees many a phantasmagory with lucid dreams and cannot but hold them as factual evidence of what is to come. Faith is the substance of things hoped for and the evidence of things unseen. And isn't that also the definition of dreams?

Elijah was not in the order of misogynistic at all, but his hatred of what dominated Jezebel was a consuming drive that is made clear in the later episode and reason for Elijah fleeing to Sinai.

The nationally experienced trauma was not an immediate, physical, life-and-death issue. Few periods in ancient history are better documented than this kind of scenario that was swamping Israel, especially after the middle of the 8th century. If the scholars are correct and Edwin Thieles', *"The Mysterious Numbers of the Hebrew Kings"* which has seemingly been tweaked by so many other authors, is finally accurate, Ahab and Jezebel reigned together from 874 B.C. to 853 B.C (22 years), while Jehoshaphat reigned down south in Judah. We are talking of a national, cultural, spiritual and emotional disaster carrying a tankerful of overwhelming suffering that brought a tsunami of incipient death to all people in the area of the ten northern tribes. But what started as a shock of a gestating spectre when Omri, Ahab's father, was over-friendly to the kingdom of Sidon and its horrifically sensuous cult of Baal and the Asherah. Immigrants from Sidon brought in the false worship and sexual debauchery of the Asherah was developing into a horrific creeping death of a culture, of faith and of self-dignity throughout the northern kingdom of Israel.

The declared war for spiritual purity and Yahweh was to be frightful for some, and I don't mean with horsebound troops on a battlefield.

The context was several invasions by marriages and social link-ups rather than military forces crashing through the land. Solomon, of all characters, started the downhill slide. He married many princesses and queens who worshipped nonsensical mythical gods and then built high-profile altars and temples to facilitate their religious darkness. The seven kings of Israel that sat as leader and King in the Northern Kingdom from 930 to 874 (a mere 57 years since Solomon's death) and the way in which most of them vacated the post, Ahab arrived as king number 8. Things were dark and recreant already. But the evil cherry on the demonic cake was Ahab took a wife. He married Baal's apostle, Jezebel, who went even further than Solomon's many wives ever did.. References to such conduct predicted national disaster in the Pentateuch. Israel had already had deeply cutting traumatic spiritual catastrophes that readily made its strike on the national Israeli psyche. For that we give thanks to Solomon in his latter years. The pain and terror introduced in those days manifested expression to the horrors that were brought to Israel by the same biblical scrolls that carry this narrative. The Jewish moral and spiritual descent had by multifarious tidal waves, of heathen marriage after heathen marriage seeped its way into Israeli and Judaistic normalcy. Whirling dislocation of the populations spirituality ever deepening from the Solomonic days brought repeated ever damning trauma ever worsening, and the reigns of totalitarian king after king.

Traumatised people cannot often recall the chronology of their distress and upheaval – and when at its worst they have no language to express the agony and sometimes even turn mute as they contemplate the historical, unmentionable abuse. At least we cover it with a title these days. PTSD states nothing but, but in substance, it explains everything. The evil queen and insipid king had killed and tortured, demanded and commanded, stole and grabbed. The people were broken. Like limbless soldiers home from a war, what is unspeakable, literally, can strike grown strong men dumb, drive the intelligent and eloquent to imbecilic silence. War and violence in biblical days was no different to the Twenty-first century, perhaps more damnable. Israel's status was widespread emotional trauma, and Ahab and his wife were two of the major perpetrators. The emotions of the populace, it seems, had closed down and they were utterly unable to discuss and interact about the issue. The spiritual leaders – the prophets, aided by Obadiah, Ahab's secretary, seem to have all gone into hiding apart from Elijah. The true priesthood (the Levites) were all in the South, where the Temple was. Such disasters remove societal anchors and stays. Jezebel and fellow conspirator Ahab had destroyed the entire spiritual fabric of the people of Israel. The end of the world could be clearly outlined in the future of Baalistic Israel.

1 Kings 16 is a pathetic soul-destroying history. Reading Kathleen O Connor's heart stirring book diagnosing and itemising Jeremiah's PTSD, she graphically illustrates people and populations that go through what the northern tribes of Israel were going through, when the Tishbite appeared to bring healing – seemingly from nowhere.

Ms O Connor lists three-dimensional inserts that are required to recover and sustain a society that has lost its dignity, culture and traditions and is crying out for a divine lifeguard to step up front. A David to behead a gigantic monstrous Goliath that has everybody terrified and frozen.

First: Language. The need to recount the trauma without being re-traumatised in the examination of the injury. Language is needed to speak about the personal and/or national catastrophe. The sadness and misery of the history makes people cry for themselves, not for others. It is more than Cathartic. War is rape on a national scale. The visual horrific news reports of the rape of Gaza and the Ukraine have no difference to the spiritual and political wipe-outs of Israel and Judah. Ahab, Jezebel and her "prophets of Baal" had raped Israel, a nation that had already experienced 70 years or so of spiritual rape prior to Jezebel's rise. A nation's new language and expression was required that would run the reel without re-experiencing the trauma.

Second; there is a need to explain the cause, the rationale, of the catastrophe. Why did it happen? Blame is needed. Cause and effect needs to be perceived. In those days, Israel was a people neglected and without any legitimate leadership. Coups after coups. Assassination after assassination. Israel had no true head. Yahweh had been deserted. Demonic religions were welcomed by murdering dictator king after murdering dictator king. And now they had a murdering queen with a heartless murdering profile more horrific than any of those that had gone before on Israel's so-called throne. The people were left to follow thoughtlessness and purposelessness. To weak and occultic thoughts, the car crash of life that was Israel at this moment suggested, to religious views of the time, a weak god. At least, that was the pathetic theology of the time. Elijah insists and proves that Yahweh will never lose the war. God was confronting evil to arrive at good. The man from Tishbe affirmed that God was greatly and positively in control of all things.

A bad explanation, or a false one, can be initially discussed, but in reality, there are many reasons that explain national collapses. In blaming the people, the prophet can help them. When people take responsibility it is helpful. If it is, "My fault!" That is good in as much as it suggests, "I can change things." Used as an ad hoc first discussed theology, it is a good temporary bus stop, holding back confusion. It helps bind people to God and mourn the loss. There are some things, people, and even a sense of being, that will not easily maintain themselves. Grief and mourning require touching, surfacing and expression. The three-and-a-half years of drought and the legendary mystique that the nation held concerning the man from Tishbe, instilled a turnaround within the nation.

Third; Grief must be accessed. Tears from all and everything pervade the days of Elijah. The speaker that is assisting also needs help to weep as did Jeremiah in a generations later catastrophe that was actually the summit of the social tragedy in Jezebel's era. The grief-stricken speaker, i.e. the man from Tishbe, undoubtedly, to my mind, would have wanted to weep but could not. In Old Testament days it was the women's job to provoke grief. Tears for the nation was an enormous job to negotiate and enact.

It was the anointing of power and strength that sat on the life of Elijah that would build faith in God and defied the negative purpose of the trauma that had crushed the nation. In time of disaster the ancient traditions by themselves did not protect the people.

Jeremiah and Elijah provide an explanation of all 3 points above. They honour sorrow by presenting all 4 aspects. They mirror grief back to the public. It replaces speech from facticity. Speech staggering towards the unsayable removes the self-sustaining pain.

20

SEEING, HEARING AND EXPERIENCING OTHER DIMENSIONS. (1 Kings 17: 8-9)

It is my conviction that whenever a prophetic word is received and delivered, its source, as Walter Brueggemann refers to it, is "elsewhere." "Elsewhere" in this context is a simple euphemistic expression of the English language, meaning, in the framework to which we are thinking, "from some other unknown and unseen world", that is, *not* from a visible and physically logical source.

Angels come from "elsewhere." This is a word used for somewhere that we cannot explain to any degree of detail. We know the angels are active in heaven. But we cannot supply details as to where heaven is or their addresses in heaven - if they have addresses. Where do angels live? The realm of the spirit is "elsewhere". Where do spirits dwell? Whatever and however one reads the Hebrew Bible along with the New Testament, one cannot escape from the concept of other worlds and dimensions, which are briefly revealed in chapters scattered throughout the scrolls as being full of activity, and, sometimes, they are going through even hard-fought wars. "Yahweh is the Lord of hosts". To be consistent with scripture, "the hosts", of which Yahweh is Lord, are fighting armies. Where do those armies of Yahweh camp? Where do their battles take place? If you know, please email me with that intelligence. I tell you, there are other worlds.

Paul talks of the third heaven. I have read dozens of different authors defining what the first, second and third heavens are. All say something different. In other words, we are not sure. But what is accepted by all Bible believers is: There are at least three heavens. That means other worlds.

The apostle Paul teaches that an active faith in Christ translates the Christian believer to a seat with Christ "in Heavenly places." Why is it plural and not a singular "place". There are clearly other worlds, other dimensions. In Isaiah 6, the prophet Isaiah states that he saw the Lord "high and lifted up" with his train filling "the temple". This could not have been the stone Temple of Solomon on planet earth in Jerusalem. Isaiah was not a Levite, and only Levites could legitimately be in the Jerusalem Temple. So what Temple, and what world was Isaiah in when he visited "the Temple" seeing the Lord high and lifted up, with cherubim and seraphim surrounding Christ and his throne. I say yet again; There are clearly other worlds.

The prophet Daniel talks of an Archangel battling over 21 days to get Daniel's prayer answers to his eyes and ears. He was fighting and struggling with the powers of darkness "elsewhere". How do our minds handle these biblically revealed existences.

In 2 Kings 6 we have a certain narrative that opens up a closer cosmos of insight and understanding of how, why, and where the prophetic "elsewhere" actually is. And it reveals the interaction of this "elsewhere" with our time-space physical world. In Elisha's day, years after Elijah had left the planet to God's "elsewhere", the King of Syria fully intended to attack Israel and injure their international status and armed capability. Several strategic attempts were made after having found out where Israeli troops were situated. However, on each of these occasions, when Syrian forces shouted, "Attack!" they found that the Israeli troops had left their reported camps and fled. The blazingly angry King of Syria held an enquiry as to who the traitor was that was betraying him, assuming one of his own was letting the King of Israel know of the Syrian strategy. One man advised the king that nobody was betraying him but that, "Elisha the prophet tells the king of Israel what your majesty says in your bedchamber." We shall ignore the humongous issue of how Elisha heard what the Syrian king was discussing in his bedchamber. The king had to act. So, Syria sent spy's out to find out where Elisha lived, and when they completed that task, Syria's king sent a great host of armed soldiers to kidnap Elisha and bring him back to a Syrian prison. The Syrian army was lined up to take Elisha captive from the city of

Dothan to Syria. Elisha's servant is panic-stricken in fear for his life. Elisha calmly states to him that there was more forces *for* him than there was *against* him. On asking Yahweh to allow his servant sight to see what he himself saw; it is stated that the surrounding hills were utterly thronged with horses and chariots of fire. And there was more in the fiery flames and chariots than there was of the Syrian soldiers. So, there is clearly another world that is curtained from our normal earthly view, yet nevertheless within time and space of our physical world. If we could open the invisible curtain, perhaps we could see the Chariots of fire too. Oh! If only we could see as Elisha saw!.

When God made man in the opening chapters of Genesis, there was a confluence of worlds for Adam, Eve, angels, Satan, and God Himself to enjoy and to live in, and to visibly see each other. Seemingly each world and realm was congruent with and visible to all, and they were interacting together. It was only after the disobedience of the human couple that a disjunction took place, causing division amongst each divinely created section of the cosmos.

Throughout the entire 66 books of the Bible there are accounts that refer to worlds that are sometimes called dimensions, realms, dominions or principalities. I am unaware of any specific title for all but a few. I am talking about dimensions that could be said to be accessible from our time-space world on planet Earth. These references to various "unearthly" worlds, realms, and dimensions are sometimes described explicitly and sometimes just lightly alluded to, as if the human being that was writing the text takes it for granted that readers of his text will surely know what he is talking about, leaving us to meditate and to draw conclusions about what, where and how we should conceptualise these "places".

Some of these references have been interpreted in different ways by scholars, theologians, and believers through the ages. While the concept of multiple worlds or dimensions in the Bible may not be as systematically developed as in some other religious or mythological traditions, there are several key references worth exploring merely to aid our grasp of the universal cosmos. I believe this brief and cursory exploration may aid us, especially into understanding some of the contexts of both Elijah and Elisha and their words and responses. It may also aid us to a comprehensive understanding of "elsewhere" and its relevance to twenty-first-century Christians.

To start at the basic reality that nobody can argue with, the initial realm where Elijah and Elisha lived is the same place where you and I live, i.e., the physical world - the planet Earth.

In Eden, Satan, the devil, was at home also, although in a perfect, unfallen world, the visibility of the devil and the angels, as well as god Himself, suggests that there were multifarious worlds, thrones, principalities and dominions. To Satan's consciousness, he was in touch with, or perhaps, as is commonly believed and accepted, he was visiting then alien realm to soil the newly created human race and the part of God's creation that he was given. He appears as a serpent living among the greenery, tree-gazing along with Eve. God Himself (undoubtedly Christ) was at home in Eden as He walked in the cool of the evening to socialise with Adam and Eve prior to their fall. And a sword-carrying angel was visibly present - on guard, we know, as the humans were later cast out of the garden. There was so many "elsewheres".

The real-time of Genesis 3 took place. Thereafter the physical visibility of the different realms between each dimension began to fade and fail. Occasionally, bands of angels were seen and engaged with. Sons of God (i.e. Angels) were visibly seen and related to, and some sinfully co-habited with women. In Genesis 18, Yahweh Himself dines with Abraham, being accompanied by two angels. In Genesis 19 the same two angels are seen and sexually threatened in Sodom.

In Genesis 32:2 Jacob encounters "the angels of God" at Mahanaim. Was Mahanaim an angelic "portal"? Some think it was indeed a "thin" place. (A "thin place" is the epithet to describe physical locations where angels are reported to be seen, or manifestations of healing, or Christophanies are reputed to occur.).

There are three appearances of the Angel of the Lord throughout the book of Judges. Each appearance is in our natural time-space world. Apart from these singular appearances of angelic beings visibly active amongst men, we leap forward to Elijah and what we shall be discussing in later pages of this volume. In 1 Kings 19:5-8 Elijah is depressed and asking God to take his life. An angel fed him and encouraged him. That is, the invisible becoming visible.

These extremely cursory observations clearly reveal and open to us that the Bible contains a rich tapestry of references to various worlds, realms, and dimensions that collectively contribute to its theological and cosmological outlook. These references invite believers to contemplate the mysteries of the divine, the complexities of human existence, and the ultimate purposes of God's plan for creation as a whole.

These spiritual realms are depicted as invisible to human eyes but exerting influence over earthly affairs. For example, in the book of Daniel, angelic beings are depicted as operating in the heavenly realm. The text in the book of Daniel strongly suggests that there were times Daniel had been translated to angelic "territory". Not only does he visit angelic dominions but is given the grace to hold dialogue with them concerning what their activities were about.

This is to highlight the fact that, whenever the word of Yahweh comes to anybody, that word comes from another world – from an "elsewhere". And the word came :

Then the word of the LORD came to him: "Go at once to Zarephath in the region of Sidon and stay there. I have directed a widow there to supply you with food." 1 Kings 17:8-9

Elijah's route from Kerith to Zarephath, as described in the Bible, specifically noted in 1 Kings 17, is not detailed in terms of specific landmarks or routes. However, it is generally believed that Kerith (also known as the Brook Cherith) is located east of the Jordan River, while Zarephath is situated near the Mediterranean coast, north of Sidon. The approximate distance between these two locations is around 80 to 100 miles (about 130 to 160 kilometres), depending on the exact route taken. The journey would likely have involved travelling through hilly and mountainous terrain, which could have affected the actual distance and time needed for travel. Perhaps, if Elijah travelled Northward following the banks of the Jordan it would have been easier to hide from any passers-by.

1 Kings 17:8-9 marks a pivotal moment in the narrative of the man from Tishbe. To fully appreciate the weight of these brief verses, it is necessary to consider the broader context. As we have been explaining, this passage occurs during a time of severe drought in Israel, a consequence of Elijah's own prophetic warning to King Ahab regarding the nation's idolatry and moral decay. The drought not only signifies a physical scarcity but also symbolizes a spiritual barrenness in Israel. In this setting, God's command to Elijah to go to Zarephath—a town outside of Israel—introduces an intriguing juxtaposition of faith against a backdrop of desperation. We witness a pivotal moment in the life of Elijah as he is directed by God to the town or village, or was it merely a hamlet, known as Zarephath of Sidon.

This choice is significant as it challenges the accepted boundaries of God's care and provision. It is outside of the Promised Land. God's work is never confined to a particular culture or nation, not even in the Old Testament. Elijah, a prophet of Israel, is sent to a Gentile territory, which foreshadows a broader divine plan that transcends ethnic and national restrictions. This concept resonates with the New Testament themes of inclusivity and the universal scope of God's love and mission.

By this instruction from Yahweh, Elijah found divine providence in the most unlikely place. The choice of a widow in Zarephath, a district of Sidon, highlights God's ability to provide in unexpected circumstances. It was in a gentile nation, a people that worshipped the very god that Elijah was raised up to remove from the Israeli culture. Christ Himself, recalled this event to the disciples and others how there were many widows in Israel, but the widow in Zarapheth was the woman divinely chosen to sustain the prophet until the drought was about to end. Widows in the ancient Near East often faced extreme vulnerability and poverty. By choosing a widow, the text underscores that divine provision can emerge from the most unlikely sources, challenging prevailing notions of strength and security. God had chosen for this gentile woman to be an actual living witness that Yahweh was the God of resurrection. He is indeed the Lord of life and death. Life and death was in His hands, and therefore in the hands of His prophet. (Luke 4:24-27) Through the widow of Zarephath, God would declare himself not only to be the giver of life (in terms of making provision for the needs of his children), but as the Giver of Life who could do what no person could ever do - defeat death. It also suggests that there was an effective faith in the heart of the widow in Zarapheth than there was in the widows of Israel.

Elijah's obedience to God's command emphasizes again the theme of faith-in-action. He does not hesitate. He rises and goes. This immediate response illustrates a profound trust in God's word, embodying a faith that is not passive but dynamic and continuously seeking for expression. It invites readers to reflect on their own responsiveness to divine calls in their lives, especially when circumstances seem dire, as they did at this moment in Elijah's life.

Note the symbolism of Zarephath. Zarephath, meaning "refiner's furnace," carries rich symbolic meaning. The act of refining is a process of purification and transformation. By sending Elijah to this location, God not only provides for his prophet's physical needs but also sets the stage for a transformative encounter. This underscores a critical insight. Moments of need can lead to profound spiritual refining. The journey to Zarephath becomes a metaphor for the trials and tribulations that often precede divine revelation and personal growth.

The inclusivity of God's Grace is an aspect to behold in this narrative. The choice of a Sidonian widow as a key figure in this account highlights the expansive nature of God's grace. It suggests that divine favour is not confined to the Israelites but extends to all humanity, regardless of nationality or status.

In times of personal or communal crises, individuals are encouraged to open their eyes to the unlikely sources of help and support that may arise. This passage reveals that divine provisions often come disguised in humble circumstances, urging from the believer a posture of humility and receptiveness.

Zarephath was something like 130 miles away from where Cherith is generally considered to have been. It stands on a long ridge, backed by the snowclad steeps of Hermon and overlooking the blue waters of the Mediterranean. Googling Elijah's trip from Cherith to Zarephath is, in contemporary language, a journey from Wadi-al-Yabis (Cherith) in Jordan to Sarafand (Zarephath) in Lebanon. We are talking of approximately a 132-mile trek. That is, according to Google, a 45-hour walk. Playing with the idea that Elijah walked 7-8 hours a day, I am suggesting that the prophet's trek lasted something like a week. He was to go and remain in this place till further notice from heaven. No time parameters were given concerning the longevity of his stay in Sidon's suburbs. Elijah was to be in the district of Baal's headquarters, Sidonian Baal temple territory. As Matthew Henry says, "To show Jezebel the impotency of her malice, God will find a hiding place for His servant even in her country."

"... I have commanded a widow woman there to sustain you." (1 Kings 17:9b)

It would seem by the text that Yahweh had spoken to the widow prior to Him talking to Elijah, i.e., "I have commanded a widow..." No name. The command given to the widow was that she was to provide for the prophet. How would she know the person when he turned up? How would Elijah know who she was? Perhaps she did not quite believe the Divine instruction. Her first words to the Tishbite were that she was "collecting firewood, to light the fire for her very last meal prior to she and her son taking space to lie down and die." Christ Himself had memories of this real-time moment in Elijah's biographical timeline, when He said, "Of a truth I say unto you, there were many widows in Israel in the days of Elijah, and to none of them was Elijah sent, but only to Zarephath, in the land of Sidon, to a woman that was a widow." There is a constant hint of New Testament gentile inclusion (Luke 4:25-26) and resurrection activity (Luke 7:11-17) in Elijah's worldview and adopted paradigm. Elijah was to learn lessons there that would fit him for the great place he was yet to occupy in defending the ancient system against the assumptions of the Crown. Surrounded by Baal worship, he would know more clearly the nature of the religion against which he had to contend. Elijah was transferring from being fed by unclean birds to being sustained by an "unclean" gentile. A huge learning curve was being tracked by the prophet.

God's command to Elijah to seek sustenance from a widow reveals an unusual aspect of divine provision—the idea of the "divine economy." In human terms, it seems counterintuitive to seek help from someone who is also in need. However, this illustrates that God's provision often operates outside human logic. It reminds us that in God's economy, sharing and giving can lead to abundance, even when resources appear scarce. This principle invites a re-evaluation of how we perceive and manage our resources, emphasizing trust in God's ability to multiply what we offer, no matter how meagre it may seem.

Elijah's journey to Zarephath underscores the prophetic call to action. It serves as a reminder that faith is not merely an internal belief but is meant to manifest in tangible actions. Elijah's obedience in following God's directive—even when it led him to an unfamiliar and potentially hostile environment—illustrates the nature of prophetic ministry: to act on God's behalf, often in challenging circumstances.

This aspect encourages us to consider how we, too, are called to act in faith, to respond to God's leading, and to engage with the world around us, even when it feels uncomfortable.

From the call to a foreign land to the intersection of desperation and divine instruction, the role of cultural context, the symbolism of the widow, the divine economy of provision, and the prophetic call to action, each point invites deeper contemplation. By engaging with these themes, we can gain a more nuanced understanding of God's work in our lives and the world, challenging us to embrace obedience, compassion, and faith in the face of uncertainty.

O God! Give me just a little bit more of whatever Elijah had.

21

PROPHETIC AUTHORITY OVER LIFE AND DEATH. (1 KINGS 17:10 -24).

"So, he arose and went to Zarephath; and when he came to the gate of the city, behold, a widow was there gathering sticks ..." 1 Kings 17:10a

Yahweh had the logistics of Elijah's transfer of "digs" calculated to the very minute, for as he sat at the Zarephath gate, inside which most towns and cities had their wells situated, he encountered this hitherto unknown woman, who was about to cook her final meal in the horror of the famine precipitated by the drought, that was in turn, precipitated by Elijah's word to Ahab. God has all things in His perfect timing. As the Cherith torrents had run low, so had the widow's oil and flour. It seems the widow would have died of starvation within a day or two had Elijah not turned up at that very moment. The timing of God's instruction for Elijah to travel to Sidon was perfectly timed for the expected "last supper". If Elijah had missed this outing of the widow, she would not have stepped out of her home again to be seen publicly, as she was at that very moment preparing for her last meal before retiring - to die.

Zarephath was a small Phoenician community, we believe, a little way from Sidon on the road to Tyre. It was 22 miles from the walled border of Tyre to the heavy gates of Sidon. Zarephath was a Sidon suburb. Neither here in First Kings nor in Christ's reference to the woman (Luke 4:26) is it said that she was a worshipper of Baal. Nor is the text explicit of any attachment she may or may not have had towards Yahweh. It has been suggested by some, therefore, that she was an Israelite woman who had been married to a Phoenician. There is nothing in the text to support that statement. It is true that the oath she made later was in the name of Yahweh. However, there is nothing unlikely in a Phoenician woman having some knowledge of the God of Israel, especially at this period in the history of both nations, while Jezebel's mission for Baal was in full intensity, impacting Israel and the now infamous story of the prophecy of the strange Tishbite was undoubtedly the conversation piece of the entire Levant. Sidon and Israel were also geographically next-door neighbours and socially mingling in trade and politics. The way in which Jesus makes use of this incident appears to favour the view that she was not a worshipper of Yahweh. However, what she may have become before Elijah left Zarephath is another matter. As a "by the way", there is a Jewish Midrash that insists that the widow's son grew up to become the prophet Jonah, son of Ammitai. Do with that morsel as you will, but it does mean that Jonah must have been 80-plus years old when the narrative that led Jonah into the belly of the big fish took place.

Even though it is not known how long Elijah remained with the widow, it is probable that he spent nearly two years in Zarephath. However, as it was with Elijah's time in Cherith, we have no indication of how the prophet's daily routine was occupied. The linear biblical chronology of the prophet's life is never very exact in its measurements. Our narrative only tells us that he left after being there "many days" and in "the third year',' from his first appearance to Ahab. In the references made by the Master (Luke 4:25) and His brother (James 5:17), the drought is said to have lasted three years and six months.

So, here we are, Elijah had come, we assume by foot, to Zarephath to meet an unnamed woman in a previously unvisited (as far as we know) village in a day when King Ahab was messaging kings of all the local nation-states, asking them to hunt down this strangely dressed character, who clearly would have stood out in any public crowd. God help any other human being that chose to dress as Elijah dressed.

"Fetch me please a little water in a vessel, that I may drink" I *Kings 17:10*b

Whether it is because the biblical text has missed out some dialogue between the prophet and the widow, or whether it was some discernment on the woman's part, she related "Yahweh" to the strange foreign hairy figure in the town gate who addressed her so boldly. She responded hospitably and saw, in the face of death and bereavement, something of Yahweh in Elijah. She was shortly afterwards to remark to the man about Yahweh being, "Yahweh your God". She saw it. She sensed it. As a BTW, I think it is helpful to image the scene by remarking that the woman and Elijah must have been the only human beings on the street at that moment. The seriousness of their dialogue was far too weighty to have been exchanged in company anyhow.

Yet, as far as we know, whether she nodded or waved in acknowledgement, the woman turned to fetch Elijah the drink he had asked for. This was kindly, accessible hospitality under the weight of expectant death and sorrow, and in the district that was central to Baal worship and its temple. This broken woman went for the water, knowing her life was about to end. Her problems in life concerning food, drink and a starving son were about to peak, and her plan in the short time that was left was to provide all she could until she could do no more but die. The firewood she had collected and was carrying was undoubtedly soaked with her tears. She was about to pass away with dignity and grace – yet she will still do what good she can until breath leaves her. The dear soul had not the slightest idea that this "end" to her story was in reality, the middle of the narrative that God Himself was the author of. It was, for her, not the end but very much a new beginning. Perhaps she was carrying shame. Perhaps, if she was consciously aware that Yahweh had commanded her to sustain Elijah, she felt humiliated that he had turned up and that she had nothing to give him. God knows all and is steps ahead of humanity constantly.

Elijah could have walked through the village gates with a skin of water and a bag of food. But he was not given those resources. Although the widow has to entertain and be welcoming to a strange and foreign man in the village, later in her home, there is no question, suspicion or suggestion of any impropriety as there probably would be in modern times.

Elijah had faith to take God at His word. "I have commanded a widow" to take care of you." The context of the setting enables us to see that Elijah was aware she was the widow that Yahweh had spoken of to him. All these aspects of his knowledge, foresight and intuition were fed from "elsewhere". The text also suggests that she had a few twigs of firewood in her hands. Without any clarification as to her dialogue in response, we are made aware that she was going to get the water that the stranger had asked for.

Having shown the stranger, by her direction of movement, her willingness to offer hospitality for his requested refreshment – a natural observation that is not mentioned, yet something is that we have to note, that, because of the drought, water was a rarity at that moment of time. So, it was clearly challenging the woman to the greatest stretch of any nobility of character she carried. Last meal. Son dying. Poverty of the "absolute" kind. Waiting for death. All that is ignored for a glass of water for this stranger. Foolishness or faith?

"As she was going to get the water and bring it to Elijah, he called to her and cried, "And bring me also, please, a morsel of bread in your hand while you are at it.""

In the natural perspective of things, Elijah would have wished he had never asked for the refreshments. He was about to have his "ear bent" with a terrible story of lack, anxiety, and pain. However, he now desires food as well as drink. Next … who knows … he may be asking for a bed.

However, she answered with, "I swear, as surely as Yahweh your God lives, I don't have anything baked, not a single piece of bread in the house. I only have a full handful of flour in the jar and a little olive oil in the bottom of the horn. See! Right now, I was and am gathering just two sticks to take home to dress and cook what little I have, in order to make a meal for myself and my son, that we may eat it, our last meal and then my son and I will die of starvation."

In the midst of drought and famine, in days that were generations before government handouts, this widow without income, who is rearing a son, is told that she would be providing for an unknown and unnamed man. That is scary. The widow's claustrophobic little world was about to become cosmically huge. Both prophet and widow were enjoying divinely ordained strategic timing and positioning. How supernaturally comforting is that!

Clearly, Ahab believed he had encountered a prophet who had spoken the drought into being, and now the king wanted him to undo it. As far as Ahab was concerned, during the three and a half years through which the drought lasted, Elijah was "in hiding". Bible readers are, of course, famously aware of Cherith and Zarephath and their role in the biblical narrative. In the real-time of the scriptural narrative, however, no other human soul had a clue where the prophet was during his "Cherith period". There were only three human beings who knew where Elijah was after leaving Cherith. His week-long trapse to Zarapheth was obviously discreetly made, easterly to the eastern bank of the Jordan, then northwards against the flow of the river, and then across to the west coast from the top of the sea of Galilee. God had said "go" to Abraham, Jesus said, "go" to the apostles. It is clearly one of God's favourite words. It is exciting to be a man of God, especially when God instructs somebody to "go".

There is nothing that Elijah could have been doing as far as ministry to people was concerned. He was in hiding for years. He was the most wanted man in that part of the world. If he was seen by anybody other than the widow, betrayal to Ahab was the likely outcome. Secrecy was the name of the game currently.

The apostle Peter, eight hundred years future to Elijah's day, was taught to call nothing common or unclean by a vision from heaven (Acts 10:15). Elijah was to learn it by contact with those outside the covenant of promise. He was to have a deep exploration into his relationship with Yahweh while living in the suburbs of Baal's leading community - a stone's throw away from "his" main temple and priests.

The opening dialogue betwixt the Zarepathian and the Tishbite has words, sentiments, and a plunging into a whole new galaxy of human understanding of faith. It is, without doubt, one of the most groundbreaking prophetic dialogues in the entire Hebrew Bible, transformed into a form of New Testament normalcy by Christ Himself and the apostolic letters. The fact that it uses six and a half verses in a narrative that is generally extremely scanty on detail, suggests to even a cursory leader that the volume of words allowed for this dialogue is weighty. They are voluminous utterings of New Testament revelation, with Elijah bringing the Kingdom into being in this time-space world eight centuries or so before the Word was to become flesh.

So, choreographing the dramatic landscape, we start with Elijah having entered the gates of Zarephath. Some academics suggest that Zarephath was a mere hamlet of a village. I ask if it was common for a small village to have gates at all. I think not. Elijah is, I propose, sitting in the marketplace or by the village well (probably dried up), seeing an elderly woman passing by. She had some firewood already in her hand. There was nobody else to be seen about that could witness the dialogue that was about to take place.

Some translations have the text as: "Indeed! *A* widow woman ...", suggesting that by her dress and cultural clothing it was clear that she was a widow by visual observation. Other translations have, "Behold!" or "Indeed! *The* widow woman..." suggesting Elijah knew it was *the* widow that Yahweh had referred to, be it by discernment or by the word of Yahweh Himself.

We are told by an infallible source that there were many widows in Israel at that time, but by the divine choice of Yahweh, Elijah is sent to this gentile land and this particular gentile woman who was acutely poor, acutely in crisis, and acutely in total social lack. Why would Yahweh send Elijah to a woman who had less resources to the sustenance of life than the Ravens did?

The text has the air of immediacy about it when we read that *"Elijah called out to her and said, "Fetch me, please, a little water in a jar so I may have a drink?"* And yes! the tiny Hebrew word that is pronounced, "na" is definitely similar to, "please". (Or, "I pray", "I implore" or something politely similar.) We are reminded of another Jew who sat at a well and, against all contemporary culture, asked a woman of another race for a drink of water.

In reaching out to the woman, Elijah crossed contemporary social norms, speaking as a stranger in a foreign culture, publicly, openly, forwardly to a gentile woman, and blatantly imposing on her concept of hospitality – if indeed she had any sense of such a thing. He was in Sidon. It was enemy territory not only politically but spiritually and historically. The man Sidon was the firstborn of the cursed Canaan (Genesis 10:15). Noah had predicted that the sin of his son Ham would continue and develop through Ham's son Canaan. The seed of the Nephilim it seems, was continued in the ark via Ham's wife to the far side of the flood.

We must keep in mind that although the predicted famine and drought were spoken only to the king of the small land named Israel, as far as we know, the entire Levant was impacted by the Tishbite's prophecy. The dearth and scarcity were bigger than Israel. If only Ahab could understand. When he later accused Elijah of being the one "who troubled Israel," the world would have been a different place if he had seen that it was he, King Ahab. that troubled the nation – and not only Israel but all the neighbouring nation-states, Edomites, Ishmaelites, Moabites, Hagrites, Gebalites, Ammonites, Amalekites and people of Tyre, Philistia, and Assyria. It would seem that only Elijah knew via heavenly intelligence who the world "troubler" was.

Elijah had arrived at the very moment of the finality of the widow's hopelessness. She had come to the end of her resources -

human and natural. It is obvious that she had no social assistance from the people of Zarephath. Her son was starving. The grass had lost its greenery. The rivers and streams had become dry wadies. She was in a dark cocoon of grief, sorrow, and motherly worry. This woman was no stranger to death and the sorrows and hardship that trailed widowhood in those days. Elijah carried prophetic matters of life and death with him, no matter where he went. Poverty was rife in women of such desperate bereavement. Whether she was a believer or not, Yahweh had allowed her particular and personal distress during the prevalent and widespread anguish. As Arthur Pink states, "Observe that once more God sent Elijah not to a river, but a "brook" - not to some wealthy person with great resources, but to a poor widow with scanty means. It takes serious pressure of circumstances to make us bow to what is repugnant to our natural inclinations."

She had truly, in a way that most of mankind know not, lost hope. Last kitchen resources. Last chance to eat. Last act of pathetic sustenance with what little she had. She was to cook the morsels she had, after which she was resigned to dying, lying next to her son. Do not allow the lucidity of her words to Elijah to fool the reader as to her state of mind. This woman was lost, confused, and at death's door. As a widow and a devoted mother, her grief was more for her son than herself.

How incredible that Elijah had been instructed to come here. See it clearly. Yahweh had arranged for a poverty-stricken widow without income and with only a fading son to meet Elijah's needs for the next months – or was it years? There is nothing "natural" about the narrative. The widow and her son were being plunged into the supernatural provision of Almighty Yahweh.

God had instructed Elijah where to go and had assured him that a relict would maintain him. However, what her name was, where her house was situated, and how to distinguish her from others he was not informed. He relied on Yahweh to give him additional light when he arrived there, nor was he disillusioned. He was immediately reassured from any uncertainty as to the identity of the person who was to befriend him. Seemingly this meeting was quite spontaneous, for there was no appointment made between them. The text in the scroll states, "Behold the widow woman was there." Yahweh, in His providential forethought, overrides all events, so that this specific female was at the gate at the very moment the prophet arrived! She comes forth to where Elijah is situated as if on purpose to meet him. Yet he did not know her, nor she him. It has all the appearance of being pure fortuitousness, and yet it was decreed and arranged by God so as to make good His word to the prophet. But how was Elijah to know she was the one whom God had ordained to befriend him?

Whatever God had commanded her to do, whether she was conscious of what had been "commanded" or not, I really must note the obvious with the graphic verbally painted scene that screams at us, saying - she quite obviously and clearly was not expecting guests.

Elijah's call, request – or was it a command (?) (I think it depends in what tone one reads Elijah's words) brought her to a moment of decision. She was caught red-handed in her concentrated effort to die gracefully, with the Eastern social demands of hospitality. Elijah's words were dethroning Baal on his own turf.

We have no indication as to how Elijah spent these days. Strangely, John Milton said in his blindness, in blustering total conjecture, "It is not unlikely to assume that Elijah made his way more than once back across the Israeli border to learn for himself the progress of the famine and the effect upon the people." Really? I think not.

Every day, the widow and her son, having settled down with the bohemian strange prophetic lodger in the home of erstwhile poverty, could peek into her decanter of oil and her tub of flour and jubilate in the miracle power of Yahweh. There was still a tiny sample of both, that would hardly fill a spoon. Yet still, the lodger (Israeli ex-pat,

Elijah the Tishbite) and her son were gathering together with her at the dinner table and having at least two nourishing meals each passing day. (I am not sure the middle eastern culture holds lunch.) It was a period of wisdom gleaning. How much mother and son interacted with the prophet, we will never know. However, I am confident to suggest that the presence of the prophet was beneficial to everyone and everything in the home. Oh, to get our hands on a transcript of any dialogue that transpired between them. It was a season of light, inasmuch as the mother and child were learning that Yahweh brought nothing but peace and tranquillity while death and starvation were rampant in the rest of the nation-state that was supposedly sustained (as the population conceived) by helpless Baal.

It is one thing to communicate with Yahweh in private, alone in the secrecy of the wilderness of Gilead and what used to be the stream called Cherith, and even to accomplish Godly acts of dedication and fervour in the presence of many spectators as with leading prayer; however, it is something else to align with Yahweh and manifest His grace and character every day in the midst of home and family life, with its many demands for the "continual self-sacrificing of daily routine chores."

Then suddenly, it would seem. A hastily developing diminishing of health shrouded the widow's life. The source of life and hopeful expectation dissipated hastily leaving the darkness of death and despair gathering over the woman. The man filled with the Spirit and words of Yahweh, who had brought the miraculous into her home was still present. The glow of Yahweh's anointing was still sitting on the Tishbites life. But the much treasured and deeply loved son had fallen sick. She had lost her husband and was now about to lose her son. *"Now, it happened after these things sometime later that the son of the woman, the mistress who owned the house, fell sick."* (1 Kings 17:17a). A severe domestic calamity seems to have led her to think that as Yahweh had shut up heaven upon a sinful land in consequence of the man who was sleeping under her roof, she was now suffering on a similar account.

Somewhere in the background of this woman's soul, there was, or so it seemed, a dark memory which dwarfed all other remembrances of a transgression or transgressions that stood out in her mind as "her sin" (1 Kings 17:18). What we are referring to we are not told. It may have been connected with the birth of that very son that was now dying. We can only guess. It had possibly been committed long years before and had then occupied her with an acute torment of heart, for conscience is not inoperative even in the hearts of the children of idolisation and heathendom (Romans 2:14-15). But in later life, the keen sense of guilt had become dulled; conscience long outraged had grown dampened and lessened. Occasionally she even lost all recall of her sin for weeks and months together. We all have history we regret, hiding in the corners of our unwanted memories.

How was it to be analysed and rationalised? How could such breathtaking, miraculous, daily provision be so blatantly heaped on her life concurrent with the failing health of all that was left of her much-treasured family? How was the power of God so overwhelmingly present, sustaining the flour and the oil of the widow's home, and yet at the same time ignoring her failing son, leaving him to fade from life altogether. The provision of food demonstrated Yahweh's immanence, closeness, and intimacy with the needs of humanity. The divine neglect and seeming non-interest in the well-being of her son seemed so distant and cold. The dietary provision revealed an omnipresent divine dependability of fatherly attention from Yahweh. The ever-increasing gravity of her son's condition illustrated divine abandonment and negligence and a lack of all those qualities of Yahweh that seemed to be lavishly smothered on her household by the supernatural contents of their daily bread.

The way the author of First Kings tells the story, infers that Elijah knew nothing of the boy's ailment until he had passed away. *"... His illness became very grave and grew worse and worse, and was so strong and severe, that at the end he finally stopped breathing and died."* (1 Kings 17:17b)

It seems to this writer that the child died suddenly, else she would surely have applied to Elijah while he was gradually becoming sicker; but being dead, in her arms, she remonstrates with the prophet being overcome with grief.

No home, large or small, rich or poor, is exempt from the trials and sufferings of life and/or death. If I had a fiver for every occasion I have shared with bereaved (or about to be bereaved) husbands, wives, fathers, mothers, brothers, and sisters who were otherwise living lives of blessing and comfort I would conceivably be as wealthy as Paul McCartney. It happened to Christ Himself who lost his earthly adoptive father. Father in heaven was and forever will be in no way bereft of love, care, or concern for every strike of bereavement and pain. People are usually fully *compos mentis* and then, somewhere along the line, we all must submit to death's clutches be it by a malicious hand, inadvertency, old age, or illness. However, with the same intelligence, the same people seem utterly *non compos mentis* when shrouded with bereavements grief. The universal cry is normally, "Anytime! But not now Lord!" I often hear people say things like, "No parent should have to bury their own child," or "Why should my loved one, full of promise and potential, die so early in life." Grief can be traumatic to the nervous system and temporarily injurious to a person's normal rationale. It is this moment that the news of the boy's demise seems to be "shocking news headlines" to the prophet. He was being fed miraculously, and yet that did not secure him from sickness and death. Just as it was in the desert with Moses and the two million followers.

"She said to Elijah and shouted, "O man of God What do you have against me? What do we have in common, you man of Yahweh? Did you come so you could uncover my guilt? What problem is there between you and me? I thought you were Yahweh's prophet. What have you done to me? You have come to me to bring my iniquity to remembrance and attention. Have you come to remind me of my sins and iniquity and to kill my son? You are responsible for his death." (1 Kings 17:18)

Oh dear! Acute grief is so, so, painful. How regretful outbursts can be when we are unstabilised with the queries raised by the sight of death. How calmly had she spoken of her own and her child's death when she expected to die for want –"*that we may eat and die!*"- when she had first caught sight of the Tishbite. Yet now that her child dies, and not so miserably as by famine, she is extremely disturbed at it. We may speak lightly of an affliction at a distance, but when it *touches us we are troubled. (Job 4:5)*

She calls him *a man of God* and yet quarrels with him as if he had occasioned the death of her child and is ready to wish she had never seen him, forgetting past mercies and miracles. It could be, "What have I done against you?" (so some understand it), "Wherein have I offended you, or been wanting in my duty? *Show me why you confront me.*"

Elijah here clearly teaches us gentleness under provocation. "Are, you come to call my sin to remembrance, and to slay my son?" A remark so uncalled-for and unjust might well have stung the prophet to the quick or prompted a bitter retort. And he would have doubtless done so, had his goodness been anything less than inspired by the Holy Spirit.

Elijah tutors us in the power of a holy life. Somewhere in the background of this woman's life, there was a dark deed, which dwarfed all other memories of wrong-doing, and stood out before her mind as her sin - "my sin" - is what she declares (1 Kings 17:18). What it was we do not know. It may have been connected with the birth of that very son. Perhaps the child's paternity was her problem. She had given hospitality to this stranger from Israel, and the result was that he had brought to Yahweh's mind her sin, of which she herself, too, was no doubt made more conscious of, by the presence of the servant of Yahweh, the God of peace and purity.

She supplied Elijah's need, according to the Word of the Lord at a time in history when the blessing wasn't supposed to be for the

Gentiles. Many tell us that it's not the right time or dispensation for God to act, but the prophet Haggai prophesied that the right time is when the Lord says (Haggai 1:2-11). Even if it isn't the right time for others, it may be the right time for us, for you or for your child. Very little about Elijah was kosher according to the established religion of Israel. Think about it. First, unclean ravens fed him, and then a Gentile widow sustained him. According to the Law, nothing about him was clean. But what made all of this clean and acceptable to God (ravens, Gentile widow, camel's-hair cloak, unclean food, etc.) was the genuine life of God within Elijah.

This passage, which narrates the death of the widow's son and Elijah's subsequent confrontation with her grief, is deeply touching. While traditional interpretations often focus on the miraculous resurrection that follows, several uncommon observations can illuminate deeper layers of meaning within these words in the scrolls.

One striking aspect is the interplay between faith and doubt. The widow, having previously expressed her trust in Elijah's words, now voices her despair: "What do you have against me, man of God? Did you come to remind me of my sin and kill my son?" (1 Kings 17:18, NIV). This moment reveals a raw honesty in her grief, illustrating how faith can coexist with doubt. It invites believing people to reflect on their own experiences of faith during times of crisis, suggesting that vulnerability and questioning are integral to spiritual growth.

The widow's response highlights the power of memory in the grieving process. Her reference to sin suggests that she feels responsible for her son's death, demonstrating how guilt can complicate mourning. This observation prompts a deeper understanding of how personal history and unresolved issues can influence our emotional responses. It encourages us all to consider how their past experiences shape their present faith and reactions to suffering.

Elijah's role as a prophet often emphasizes his authority and power, but this passage reveals a more vulnerable side to him. When confronted with the widow's anguish, Elijah does not respond with immediate answers. Instead, he takes her dead son from her arms and carries him to the upper room (1 Kings 17:19). This action signifies his empathy and willingness to share in her suffering. To be a man of prayer does not happen by accident. That status is built. By recognizing the emotional burden that prophets carry, we gain insight into the human aspects of spiritual leadership, emphasizing the importance of compassion over mere authority.

The setting of this story—the widow's home—becomes a sacred space of transformation. In biblical narratives, homes often serve as sites of divine encounters. Poverty is commonly the home of the great. Elijah's chamber was a small "loft" in that humble cottage. By bringing the boy to the upper chamber, Elijah creates a private space for both mourning and miracles, for wrestling and resurrection. This observation encourages us to consider the significance of our own spaces and how they can become places of healing and encounter with the divine, urging us to cultivate environments conducive to spiritual growth and transformation. Lonely wrestling's are necessary to learn how to do battle without embarrassment. We are often not specific enough in prayer; and not spending enough time in intercession.

In verses 20-21, Elijah's prayer for the boy is pivotal, illustrating the power of pure and authentic intercession. Elijah cried out to Yahweh, and said, *"O Yahweh my God, why have you done such a terrible thing to this widow? Why have you brought further tragedy and catastrophe on this woman who has opened her home to me, who I am staying with, by whom I am, in a sense, sustained, who I sojourn with. Whose witness you are. She has been kind enough to take care of me and now you kill her son."* His prayer turned on the law of hospitality so sacred in the East, *"the widow with whom I lodge."*

"He measured himself upon the child." Humility. He spreads himself on a cadaver. How wonderful that so great a man should spend so much time and thought on that slender frame and be content to bring himself into direct contact with that which the book of Leviticus would not have approved of! It is a touching spectacle.

It is essential to note the intensity of Elijah's plea: *"O Lord my God, let this boy's life return to him!"* The urgency and desperation in his prayer reflect a solid connection to the God he serves.

It must have been a severe trial to Elijah's faith, first to note the gradual diminishing of the brook, then the abject poverty of the woman to whom he was directed; and finally, the illness and death of her child. But through it all, he held fast to the living God. It was still, "O Lord *my* God". Affliction is no proof that we are off the path of duty. The way of obedience is sometimes paved with flints, as every servant of God has discovered. But the difficulties only give room for the exercise of greater faith and reveal more of the delivering power of the Almighty Friend.

"He measured himself three times and cried unto the Lord." Perseverance. He was not soon daunted. It is thus that God tests the genuineness of our desire. These deferred answers lead us to lengths of holy boldness and pertinacity of which we should not otherwise have dreamed but from which we shall never go back. *"Men ought always to pray, and not to faint."*

In that "upper room" he took another and bolder flight and prayed that the *"child's soul come back to him."* Whatever department in the invisible "elsewhere" that receives the souls of the dead, wherever it is heard Elijah's prayer and was commanded to release him. Faith won its victory and had its reward, as *"the soul of the child came back to him, and he revived."* And Elijah took the child and brought him down from the upper room down into the house and gave him to his mother, and Elijah said, *See! Your son lives.*

Elijah teaches us the secret of giving life. It is a characteristic of those who are filled with the Holy Spirit that they carry with them everywhere the Spirit of life, even resurrection-life. We shall not only convince men of sin; but we shall become channels through which the Divine Life may enter them. Thus was it with the prophet. But mark the conditions under which alone we shall be able to fulfil this glorious function.

This is confessedly a miracle - an event altogether out of the ordinary course of nature. Man is the organ of the divine miraculous. In this very chapter there are no less than three miracles wrought by Elijah.

The miraculous resurrection of the widow's son can be seen as a foreshadowing of the greater miracle of resurrection found in the New Testament. This passage prepares the reader for the theme of "life emerging from death", a central tenet of faith. The uncommon observation here is that the miracles of the Old Testament serve as precursors to the New Testament revelation, inviting believers to recognize the continuity of God's redemptive work throughout scripture. This perspective encourages a deeper appreciation for the narrative arc of the Bible, where each miracle points toward a larger story of hope and resurrection.

This narrative from the sacred scrolls offers rich ground for exploration beyond its immediate narrative of loss and restoration. By examining the interplay of faith and doubt, the complexities of grief, the emotional burdens of prophets, the significance of geographical places, the power of intercession, and the foreshadowing of greater miracles, we uncover layers of meaning that resonate with contemporary spiritual journeys. These uncommon observations not only deepen our understanding of the text, but also invite us to engage with our own experiences of faith, suffering, and divine intervention in deeper ways.

And the woman said to Elijah, *"Now, by this, I know that you are a man of God and that the word of Yahweh in your mouth is true."* Thomas Aquinas put it as, "truth is something good, otherwise it would not be desirable; and good is something true, otherwise, it would not be intelligible."

It was with a glad recognition that the mother acknowledged Elijah to be "a man of God"—the prophet of a God greater than any of the gods of her own nation, and the word of the Lord spoken by him to be truth. To her, the incident became the occasion of the birth of a new faith. When Elijah brought the widow lady's son back to life, she wasn't concerned with religious rules or labels. Instead, when her son came back to life, it was infallible proof that she had a genuine man of God under her roof, and the Word of Yahweh in his mouth was true. Assessing the biblical prophets, we see that their primary concern was with those people who were right in front of them.

When the Lord decides it is the right time, some of us will be involved in a head-on collision with the corrupt system of this world. Scripture declares that the day of Yahweh shall begin with gloom and darkness. As long as we seek to solve the problem in any place other than our hearts, we will continue in defeat. We need to understand that the first priority, as far as God is concerned, is to cleanse our hearts. Historians look at all that happened in the early church and try to explain the impotence of the modern church by saying conditions were very different back then. Those who hear directly from the Lord are scarce. We are rarely in danger of examining to excess, especially when the subject is the shape of our own lives and the state of our own hearts.

22

DARKNESS CONFRONTED BY THE LIGHT OF THE PROPHETIC. (JAMES 5:17)

"Elijah was a human being, a man of like passions even as we are. He prayed earnestly and fervently that it would not rain, and it did not rain on the land for three and a half years." James 5:17

The boom of Elijah's entry into the prophetic boxing ring in the context of 1 Kings 17:1-3 may conceivably have been quietly spoken. However, no matter the nature of its audible volume or expression - in the realm of the spirit it was louder than Krakatoa. The ripples of the spoken words gave instructions to the cosmos. Seen and unseen items, be they volitional or abstract, animal, vegetable or mineral; from the sea to the sky; from the winds to the rays of the sun; from every aspect of creation that moves and changes for alterations in climate and temperature; all of these aspects of the planet jumped to obedience. Elijah had spoken. Creation had jumped. Creation reordered itself and, repositioned its elements and eagerly waited, concentrating on the speech of the man from Tishbe. "No rain, till you say so, sir!"

The demons, nearly a millennium later, could clearly and publicly declare, "Jesus I know, and Paul I know." But here, all corners of the working engine of the whole of creation could inwardly cry, "Elijah we know."

The character of the man who fought all powers that are invisible, was so acknowledged by angels and demons of all levels and strengths, that he was known throughout the global universe, and who knows how far beyond. Elijah the Tishbite had ordered "no rain" until he allows it. And creation halted at his word. We are talking of authentic divinely imparted authority.

The cessation was, "ordered," on moral and spiritual grounds. God was being abused by idolators under the influence of demons. Elijah's impact had been so explosive, so bright that the whole nation of Israel was confronted by him. The people, without seeing him, somehow grasped the composure and spiritual stature of the man from Tishbe. He was seen in the national imagination as authoritative and distant, dramatic and theatrical, yet totally authentic. Nevertheless, he was utterly invisible and unseen to the masses. Where had he gone?

While we may all criticize injustices in our society, we forever remain tolerable, yet to Elijah the prophet, "injustice assumed almost cosmic proportions as a taboo that had to be decried and demolished." Elijah's spirit was so sensitive to evil – even what we would refer to as lesser evils. Too often, the population were distracted, confusing the messenger with the message. That's why so many prophets were martyred. The man from Tishbe could not tolerate what the world and other believers tolerated. Heschel used to say something like, "To be a prophet is to be in alignment and agreement with the sensibilities of God and to experience communion with the divine consciousness." That sounds absolutely right when pawing over the full biblical biography of Elijah. The significance of the man from Tishbe and all of Israel's prophets lay not only in what they said but also in what they were. Elijah's task was to convey the divine view to the people and their reigning monarch's, yet as a person he himself was the divine point of view personified. In a single sentence, the message from all the prophets was simple: If you are not loyal to Yahweh, you will be dissipated to the nations and disappear as a historical nation-state. The cognisance of the secret of the revelations to the man from Tishbe was denied and emotionally fled from, as it was with all the prophets. Elijah had clearly upgraded the volume of the prophetic declaration via the cessation of the rain. The entire nation of Israel was aware of who and what was in charge.

We cannot evade the issue of Elijah's prayer life if we are determined to examine every brick in the structure of his life, character and stature. This man prayed like no other. The figure of

Elijah throughout the Bible stands as a potent symbol of prophetic fervour and divine communication, and intimacy. His life, as depicted in the books of Kings and the understated breathtaking statement of James 5:17 reveals elementary yet profound insights into the nature of prayer, the relationship between the individual and God Himself, and the transformative power of faith. We have to explore the multifaceted dimensions of Elijah's prayer life, illuminating what these concepts of dialogue with the Almighty reveal about an effective prayer life, faith, and the role of the prophet in the divine narrative. Yet we cannot take the easy line by introducing – as many do – "but Elijah was a prophet, so we cannot go where he went." A pox on escapism and let us welcome what we can see, whether it scares us, intimidates us, or even if it seems too sacrificial for us.

Elijah's battlefield and warfare unfolds during an incredibly tumultuous period in Israel's history. Elijah's prophetic call to return to Yahweh necessitated a profound and uncommon reliance on prayer as a means of communication with God and a tool for national restoration. Elijah's relationship with God exemplifies a prayer life characterised by fervency and passion, obedience and intensity, and a fathomless understanding of divine sovereignty.

Elijah's recorded prayers reflect a boldness that stems from his unwavering faith in God's power, defying whatever impossibility he was presented with. Faced with militant idolatry, he declares a drought to Ahab and Jezebel's reign, which was a direct thrust to the belly government and their religious fanaticism, taking Baal worship by the throat, which claimed to have dominion over rain and fertility. This act demonstrates the authority that comes from a life steeped in prayer, communion with God and periods of marinading in the Hoy Spirit. His subsequent prayer against death with the widow's son at Zarapheth during the drought (1 Kings 17:7-16) takes us where we haven't been before up to this time in biblical history. He was the first to stare death in the face and order it to vamoose. And it left. These accounts highlight his blatant attitude to battle and war,. to combat with all things that work towards killing, stealing and destroying. 800

years before Jesus spoke the words that revealed the nature of Satan. Elijah had a practical down to earth reliance on God's provision, even in such dreadfully dire circumstances.

Elijah's prayers also clearly reveal a deep intimacy with God. Such intimacy that could only be gained by long, active, purposeful and intentional dialogue within the presence of God. That was the very place he testified of when he laid down the gauntlet with the devil in the text of 1 Kings 17:1. His plea on Mount Carmel (1 Kings 18:36-37) exposes a personal relationship marked by immovable trust and immediacy in God's presence. Elijah intercedes with gusto and energy, not only for himself but for the people of Israel, seeking the nation's return to faithfulness. This dual aspect of prayer—personal and communal—underscores the role of the prophet as both an individual who seeks God and a mediator for the people. This is Elijah at his deepest. This is the peak of the prophetic spectrum.

The incident following the victory at Mount Carmel, where the man from Tishbe flees from Jezebel (1 Kings 19:1-8), reveals a vulnerable aspect of his prayer life. In his total despair and fear of Jezebel, Elijah is actually recorded as praying for death, showing that even the most fervent and powerful men of God can experience moments of doubt and fear. God's response, however, is not condemnation – far from it - but giving Elijah provision - food and encouragement - demonstrating that prayer can be a legitimate and God-sanctioned refuge in times of personal crisis. And few of us face the crisis that Elijah experienced in 1 Kings 19.

Elijah's seven-fold prayer for rain after the drought illustrates the importance of persistence in prayer. In 1 Kings 18:41-45, he sends his servant seven times to look for rain, emphasizing that divine promises often require steadfastness, faith, persistence and repetition. The narrative of the rains teaches that prayer is not merely a one-time event but a continuous dialogue with God, rooted in expectation and trust. In fact it was blatantly hard work to achieve the breakthrough. How many times in our lives can any of us say, authentically, that "prayer today was very hard work"?

Elijah's prayers, as seen in the sacred scrolls, illustrate the dynamic intertwining between divine sovereignty and human agency. His declarations and petitions are met with divine action, affirming that while God is sovereign, He invites human participation in His redemptive plan. This relationship highlights the importance of prayer as a means through which God accomplishes His purposes on earth. It is clear that the more confidence Elijah gained in God's sovereignty, and that once Elijah perceived and knew that Yahweh had a line of action to implement he was free to act. His constant dialogue with the invisible Almighty fed him with his certain activity to follow.

Not throwing out the baby with the bath water, we do need to acknowledge that Elijah was an especially anointed prophet with a specific role to play in Israel's history. Elijah's life exemplifies the unique role of prophets in the biblical narrative. Prophets, especially in the Old Testament, serve as intermediaries, called to communicate God's will to man, and take people's need to the Heavenly throne. Elijah's prayers underscore the intensely heavy burden of prophetic ministry, which often involves standing in the gap for individuals, families, tribes as well as wayward nations, reflecting God's heart for restoration and reconciliation.

Elijah's example teaches that effective prayer is marked by tenacious faith, dogged persistence, and a heart aligned with God's will. His prayers are never mere rituals but profound, heartfelt cries for divine help and intervention, emphasizing that prayer should be more sincere, transparent, persistent, and rooted in a relationship with God. By studying Elijah's prayers, modern believers can draw inspiration and guidance for their own prayer lives, learning to navigate the complexities of faith with courage, sincerity, and unwavering hope in God's promises.

The concept of battling, wrestling and fighting as an accurate description of praying is a vital addition to a believer's arsenal. The narrative of Elijah in the Hebrew Bible in the book of 1 Kings, reveals a prophet engaged in a relentless struggle against the prevailing forces of idolatry and political corruption in ancient Israel. There are invisible forces and powers that set out to destroy the believer's dreams, loved ones, purposes plans and initiative. Elijah's practical and active faith exemplifies spiritual warfare that not only challenges the idolatrous practices of the time but also addresses the broader societal implications of a people turning away from Yahweh. Our exploration of the scriptures here reveals clearly how Elijah's faith was not merely a personal conviction but a call to arms against the forces that sought to undermine the covenant relationship between God and Israel.

To understand Elijah's struggle, it is essential to grasp the sociopolitical and religious context of Israel during the reign of King Ahab and Queen Jezebel. Ahab's marriage to Jezebel, a Phoenician princess, launched Baal worship into Israel, leading to widespread entrenchment, idolatry and immorality. The people of Israel, influenced by the royal family's embrace of these foreign gods, turned away from Yahweh, resulting in a national crisis of faith. Thus came the Divine call for Elijah to man the battlefield. The intertwining of religion and politics during this period created a fertile ground for the proliferation of idolatry, which Elijah was raised to confront.

Elijah's faith was characterized by a proactive engagement with the cultural and political landscape of his time. His confrontation with Ahab in 1 Kings 17:1, where he declares his charge of the nation's geographic climate and declares drought as a divine judgment, marks the beginning of his prophetic warfare. This act was not merely a display of personal faith but a declaration of Yahweh's sovereignty over nature and a direct challenge to the legitimacy of Baal, the storm god worshipped by the Canaanites, who was believed to control rain and fertility.

Elijah's actions can be seen as a strategic move in a larger battle for the hearts and minds of the Israelites. By invoking a drought, he aimed to demonstrate the impotence of Baal and call the people back to faith in Yahweh. This confrontation set the stage for the climactic showdown on Mount Carmel, where Elijah directly challenges the prophets of Baal, showcasing the practical implications of his faith through action.

23

THE CALL TO DEMONIC CONFRONTATION.
(1 KINGS 18:1-15).

The narrative of Elijah in the Hebrew Bible, particularly in the book of 1 Kings, reveals a prophet engaged in a relentless struggle against the prevailing forces of idolatry and political corruption in ancient Israel. Elijah's practical and active faith exemplifies a form of spiritual warfare that not only challenges the idolatrous practices of the time but also addresses the broader societal implications of a people turning away from Yahweh and embracing immoral, idolatrous religion instead. We need to explore how Elijah's faith was not merely a personal conviction but a national call to "arms" against the forces that sought to undermine the covenant relationship between Yahweh, the Living God and Israel.

To understand Elijah's struggle, it is essential to grasp the sociopolitical and religious context of Israel during the reigns of Ahab and Jezebel, the witch queen. Ahab's marriage to Jezebel, a Phoenician princess, brought Baal worship into Israel in a seriously heavy form, leading to widespread idolatry and immorality. The people of Israel, influenced by the royal family's embrace of these foreign gods, turned away from Yahweh, resulting in a national crisis of faith – or should we say, "lack of faith". The intertwining of religion and politics during this period created a fertile ground for the proliferation of idolatrous Godlessness, which Elijah was raised to confront.

Elijah's faith was characterized by a proactive engagement with the cultural and political landscape of his time. His confrontation with Ahab in 1 Kings 17:1, where he declares a drought as a divine judgment, marks the visual and public beginning of his prophetic warfare against the dehumanising cultic practices. This act was not merely a display of personal faith but a declaration of Yahweh's sovereignty over nature and a direct challenge to the legitimacy of Baal, the storm god worshipped by the Canaanites, who was believed to control rain and fertility.

Elijah's actions can be seen as a strategic move in a larger battle for the hearts and minds of the Israelites. By invoking a drought, he aimed to demonstrate the impotence of Baal and call the people back to faith in Yahweh. This confrontation set the stage for the climactic showdown on Mount Carmel, where Elijah directly challenges the prophets of Baal, showcasing the practical implications of his faith through divine supernatural intervention.

The confrontation on Mount Carmel (1 Kings 18) is perhaps the most vivid illustration of Elijah's active faith. In this high-stakes contest (that is more than an understatement), Elijah invites the prophets of Baal to call down fire from heaven to consume their sacrifice. The dramatic failure of the Baal prophets, juxtaposed with Yahweh's immediate response to Elijah's prayer, serves as a powerful testimony to the supremacy of Yahweh over all circumstances and evils. The fire from heaven battlefield is one of the most vivid and visually creating story of the Bible, second only to the crucifixion of Christ. This event was not only a peak of prophetic demonstration to the masses, but also provided a public spectacle that aimed to turn the hearts of the Israelites back to Yahweh.

This moment encapsulates the essence of spiritual warfare: it is a battle for the allegiance of people's hearts, mind and faith. Elijah's challenge was not only against the false prophets but also a confrontation with the broader societal norms that had led Israel astray into an unprecedented darkness that was only superseded by Jezebel's daughter Athaliah, who ruled the southern kingdom of Judah with an iron-fisted, despotic rule, possibly even more dastardly than her mother. The people's ultimate declaration, "The Lord, he is God! The Lord, he is God!" represents a pivotal moment of repentance and recognition of Yahweh's authority, showcasing the transformative power of active faith in the face of idolatry and the population bowing down to the visually manifested truth of Yahweh's omnipotence.

Elijah's journey was fraught with danger and personal sacrifice. Following the victory on Mount Carmel, he faced the wrath of Jezebel, who vowed to kill him (1 Kings 19:1-2). This episode highlights the reality of spiritual warfare. The fight against idolatry and political corruption often comes at a personal cost. Elijah's flight into the wilderness reveals his vulnerability and the psychological toll wrought by the battle on Carmel.

This aspect of Elijah's story underscores a critical issue about faith in action. It is not without struggle. It is never without personal cost and at times, extreme personal sacrifice. The commitment to uphold the truth and challenge prevailing injustices requires resilience and, courage, and intentionality of iron-like determination. Elijah's experience serves as a reminder that true faith involves confronting severe opposition and enduring hardships in the quest for righteousness.

Elijah's practical and active faith serves as a model for contemporary believers navigating a twenty-first-century world often marked by moral ambiguity and spiritual compromise. His example encourages a proactive stance in the face of societal idolatry— whether in the form of materialism, secularism, or other competing ideologies. The call to engage in spiritual warfare today involves not only personal conviction but also collective action.

Moreover, Elijah's story invites believers to examine their own responses to political and cultural pressures. The challenge of maintaining fidelity to God amidst an environment that often contradicts His values is a timeless struggle. Just as Elijah fought against the tide of idolatry in his time, modern believers are called to stand firm in their faith, advocating for truth and justice in a world that frequently prioritizes convenience and compromise.

Elijah's life and ministry illustrate the dynamic interplay between faith and action in the context of spiritual warfare. His confrontations with idolatry and political corruption reveal a model of active faith that is both practical and deeply rooted in a commitment to Yahweh. In a world still grappling with similar challenges, Elijah's example serves as a powerful reminder of the need for courage, resilience, and unwavering devotion to God. Through his story, we are encouraged to engage in the ongoing battle for faithfulness, standing firm against the forces that seek to lead us astray while embodying the transformative power of a faith that acts.

24

THE MINDSET OF AHAB AGAINST ELIJAH'S PARADIGM. (1 KINGS 18:16-19)

In the biblical narrative of 1 Kings concerning the cultural input of Jezebel and Ahab, we see the violent clashing of the contrasting worldviews of Ahab and Jezebel and the the man from Tishbe. This head on clash presents a profound exploration of authority, power, and spirituality that come from opposite sources and inspirations. Ahab & Jezebel were stereotypical despots that we would refer to in the twenty-first century as dictators. Ahab's and Jezebel's worldview was steeped in political pragmatism, materialism, selfishness and extremely self-centred entitlement. Elijah, however, stands as a beacon of prophetic authority rooted in divine allegiance and spiritual fidelity. Understanding this dichotomy with an almost bottomless abyss of difference between them reveals not only the nature of their respective philosophies but also the broader implications for leadership ontologies and faith principles in a fractured world.

King Ahab's reign is marked by a reliance on political alliances and material wealth. He represents a worldview that prioritizes human authority, manipulation of circumstances and people, and the pursuit of power through worldly means. His marriage to Jezebel, a Phoenician princess, serves as a strategic political alliance that brings with it the worship of Baal—a deity that symbolizes agricultural fertility and economic prosperity. Ahab's acceptance of Baal worship reflects a pragmatic approach to governance, where the king's primary concern is, after his own comfort and wealth, the stability of his kingdom at the expense of personal and spiritual integrity.

Ahab's rank materialism is evident in his actions. He builds temples for Baal and promotes the worship of this foreign god among his people, indicating that his philosophy is not one of conviction but rather a means to an end. His leadership is characterized by a willingness to compromise his own values for the sake of political expediency. This approach not only alienates him from the covenantal relationship with Yahweh but also alienates himself from the basic rank and file of his populace and sets the stage for conflict with Elijah.

In stark contrast, Elijah embodies a worldview shaped by Yahweh's word and biblical revelation in the Pentateuch, prophetic authority and spiritual fidelity to the mosaic covenant delivered by Moses. As a prophet, Elijah operates not under the auspices of political power but through divine mandate. His authority comes from God, positioning him as a moral and spiritual counterweight to Ahab's reign. Elijah's philosophy emphasizes the importance of faithfulness to Yahweh and the call to righteousness, regardless of the prevailing political climate.

Elijah's confrontation with Ahab in 1 Kings 18:16-19 illustrates the crux of their differing worldviews. Upon entering the presence of the king, Elijah does not seek permission or favour; instead, he boldly declares the truth of God's word. This act of defiance reveals Elijah's understanding of his role as a prophet. He is to speak truth to power, regardless of the consequences. His authority does not derive from a position of influence or noting alterations with current opinion or public like or dislike but from his unwavering commitment to God's eternal will, as presented by Moses.

The relationship between Elijah and Ahab serves as a fascinating study of authority dynamics. While Ahab holds the title of king, it is Elijah who wields genuine kingly authority due to his prophetic calling. This inversion of power dynamics is significant; it suggests that true authority is not found in titles or positions but in righteousness and trustworthiness to divine truth. Elijah's authority is characterized by his prophetic actions, such as calling for a drought and later challenging the prophets of Baal on Mount Carmel. In these moments, he does not merely critique Ahab's policies but confronts the very essence of the king's allegiance to false gods. Elijah's confidence stems from his conviction that he is acting on behalf of

Yahweh, which grants him the courage to stand before a king with unwavering resolve.

The clash between Ahab and Elijah serves as a microcosm for broader themes on issues of leadership and faith. Ahab's reliance on materialism and political expediency showers moral decay and spiritual desolation all over and throughout the homes and hearts of Israeli people. His worldview ultimately fails to sustain the nation, as it is predicated on alliances with foreign powers and the appeasement of false deities.

Conversely, of course, Elijah's commitment to Yahweh and his prophetic calling highlight the transformative power of spiritual authority. His actions inspire a return to faithfulness among the Israelites, prompting them to reconsider their allegiances and the consequences of their choices. Elijah's leadership is not defined by coercion or manipulation but by a profound sense of duty to God and his people.

The narrative also raises important questions about the role of prophets and spiritual leaders in society. Elijah's example underscores the need for prophetic voices that challenge the status quo and call for accountability among those in power. In a world often dominated by political pragmatism, the prophetic voice serves as a reminder of higher moral standards and the importance of spiritual integrity.

In contemporary society, the lessons drawn from the contrasting worldviews of Ahab and Elijah remain relevant. Leaders who prioritize material gain and political manoeuvring often find themselves disconnected from the very people they are meant to serve. In contrast, those who embrace a prophetic calling grounded in truth and integrity can inspire genuine transformation and foster a deeper sense of community and purpose.

The legacies of both Ahab and Elijah resonate through the ages, presenting us with ageless insights into the nature of authority, leadership, and faith. Ahab's worldview, rooted in materialism and political expediency, ultimately leads to his downfall and the spiritual decline of Israel. Elijah's prophetic authority, however, serves as a beacon of hope, reminding us that true leadership is defined by fidelity to greater truths.

As we reflect on the lives of these two figures, we are invited to consider our own allegiances and the values that shape our decisions. In a world often swayed by the allure of power and material gain, the call to embody the prophetic principles and inputs of Elijah remains as vital as ever. It challenges us to seek authenticity, to stand for truth, and to lead with integrity in all aspects of our lives.

"So Obadiah went to meet Ahab and told him; and Ahab went to meet Elijah." (1 Kings 18:16).

Obadiah was a trusted servant in Ahab's palace. He clearly had great sincere commitment to Yahweh as he hid and fed over a hundred prophets during the three and a half years of the drought and famine. To sustain the living requirements of so many and to keep out of Ahab and Jezebel's radar in their search for Elijah was no mean feat. His loyalty to Yahweh amidst a hostile environment exemplifies the courage required to confront a corrupt culture.

The meeting between Ahab and Elijah represents the tension between the worship of Yahweh and the idolatry of Baal. In all our lives, people often face the challenge of aligning our loyalties consistently.

"When Ahab saw Elijah, Ahab said to him, 'Is it you, you troubler of Israel?'"

Ahab immediately points fingers at Elijah, calling him the "troubler of Israel." The King irresponsibly throws the entire blame for the famine on the shoulders of the Tishbite, completely refusing culpability for any transgression against the Mosaic covenant.

I, personally, find it sometimes incredibly difficult to understand how a king in Israel could reign and yet be so totally ignorant of the role that Yahweh and the Pentateuch played in the history of the people they reigned over. Ahab seemingly has no clue whatsoever as to why the Tishbite closed shop on the land. However, even in this generation, Christians are often blamed as the source of all world troubles, especially wars. We must remember that the truth often exposes darkness, and we should be prepared to face opposition.

"Art thou he that troubleth Israel"

While Ahab accuses Elijah, the truth is that it is Ahab's own actions and the idolatry of Israel that have brought about the drought and turmoil. The real troubler has no concept in the slightest of being the real problem. Are we quick to blame others for the troubles we face rather than recognizing our own failure to follow God?

'I have not troubled Israel, but you have, and your father's house, because you have abandoned the commandments of the Lord and followed the Baals.'"

Elijah responds with clarity and conviction, affirming that the real trouble comes from Ahab's abandonment of God's commandments. He courageously declares the truth while looking into the eyes of Ahab. Yes indeed: As believers, we must be clear about the source of the world's troubles - turning away from God's commands inevitably leads to chaos. Elijah points out the idolatry of following Baal, emphasizing that spiritual compromise leads to national consequences. We need to examine areas in our lives where we may have compromised our faith. Are there "Baal" practices that we need to confront and reject?

"Now therefore send and gather all Israel to me at Mount Carmel, and the 450 prophets of Baal and the 400 prophets of Asherah, who eat at Jezebel's table."

Elijah calls for a public showdown at Mount Carmel, inviting ***all*** of Israel to witness the confrontation between Yahweh and Baal. This is not merely a private dispute but a public declaration of faith. We are also called to be public witnesses of our faith in Christ. Elijah highlights the overwhelming presence of the prophets of Baal and Asherah, reinforcing the seriousness of the challenge. 850 idolatrous priests.

In these verses, we see in the whites of Elijah's eyes great courage in the face of a corrupt authority figure and a wayward nation. He challenges the status quo, inviting Israel to confront its idolatry and return to the true God. Let us not shy away from the call to such a confrontation but rather embrace it as an opportunity to reveal God's glory.

25

THE LEGITIMACY OF TWENTY-FIRST CENTURY PROPHECY.

This volume is written to encourage its readers to aspire to prophesy. The carrot I am using to encourage prophecy to be entered into by all my readers is to model the prophet Elijah as an example to emulate. But in my interaction with folks everywhere I travel, I find many Godly, tutored, Bible believing people , both male and female, that question the legitimacy of prophecy and anything miraculous in this the twenty-first century. So, for people who are reading these pages having concerns about that legitimacy. I ask:

Does the full canon of scripture itself, perceived as prophetic in its value, preclude non-canonical prophecy? Does your full biblical statement of theology preclude or demand the logic that "prophecy has ceased"?

In order for any would-be-prophets or prophetess's to get on the runway in readiness for take-off here is my pennyworth for readiness for flight.

I have, since my conversion to Christ on 21 April 1968 had a passionate and intense love affair with the 66 books of the Bible and the God who bursts out of the reading of its pages. I have a conviction that the unity of the Hebrew Bible and the New Testament when seen in the context of each other, is a soul-blistering blatant miracle that cannot be argued against. The New is in the Old concealed. The Old is in the New revealed. I am sorry if you disagree with me on that, but the more I read, the further I study, the deeper I meditate - the greater the sense of awe in the whole series of documents that makes up the full canon of scripture that overwhelms me with wave after wave, revelation after revelation, understanding on understanding. The book is jaw-droppingly consistent, life-changing and God revealing. It is complete. No book of "Mormon," or writings by Joseph Smith, Mary Baker Eddy, Charles Russell, or anybody else is needed regardless of the Godliness or otherwise of the names held so high by other religious groups.

The Bible is complete. Not to be added to.

So, "why is there prophecy in the church today?" ask the cessationists. How can there be prophets in the church today? If the Bible is complete and I believe it cannot be "added to"? Why do we seek a Word from the Lord? Surely prophecy – if it is truly prophecy inspired by God himself – must be important and added to scripture?!?! I ask why. The Bible itself testifies to prophets and prophecies whose prophetic produce is not considered worthy to be included in the biblical canon at all.

The conservative, non-charismatic, non-Pentecostal section of Christians worldwide will be shouting loud "Amens" at this point, while I ask these questions. Those evangelical sections of the church that preach and teach the scriptures as far as they can dig, will conceivably stop reading this article in a moment when I tell you that over the next few pages, I intend to give you as much of a "biblical rationale" for prophecy today and non-canonical prophecy as I can muster.

There has always been non-canonical prophecy since prophecy began. There is more "directive" prophecy than "doctrinal prophecy" in scripture – especially in the New Testament. It is there! Read, study, and absorb. Some of my statements may be considered weaker than others, but the conglomeration of the many statements I am about to start ploughing through in their combination makes a solid proposition to the purpose of encouraging prophecy today within the church of Christ worldwide.

So, why is there prophecy in the church today? How can there be prophets in the church today? If the Bible is complete and I believe it cannot be "added to," why do we seek a Word from the Lord? Surely prophecy – if it is truly prophecy inspired by God himself – must be world-shakingly important and added to scripture?!?!

The conservative, non-charismatic, non-Pentecostal section of Christians worldwide may be shouting loud "Amens" at this point while I ask these questions. Those evangelical sections of the church that preach and teach the scriptures as far as they can dig, will conceivably stop reading this article in a moment when I tell you that over the next few articles, I intend to give you as much of a "biblical rationale" for prophecy today and non-canonical prophecy as I can muster.

There has always been non-canonical prophecy since prophecy began. There is more "directive" prophecy than "doctrinal prophecy" in scripture – especially in the New Testament. It is there! Read, study, and absorb. Some of my statements may be considered weaker than others, but the conglomeration of the many statements I am about to start ploughing through in their combination make a solid proposition to the purpose of encouraging prophecy today within the church of Christ world-wild.

I am severely taxed by fine Christian writers, teachers, evangelists, and pastors who continue to insist that prophecy (as well as the other biblically listed gifts of the Spirit) have ceased and cannot be genuine in our times (or in any time since the Apostle John went home for his reward). I find myself asking God for patience when talking to those who even suggest that prophets and apostles have ceased as gifts of Christ – even though pastors, teachers and evangelists are included in the same list of gifts that they use as a claim to justify their own role in ministry and prove that the other two are now ceased (see Ephesians 4:11-12).

My nervous system is troubled by Christians who assert that even though they believe that Christ was conceived by the Spirit of God in a virgin's womb, even though they declare boldly that God became man in Christ, even though they teach that Christ raised dead people to life and healed the sick- as well as rising from among the dead Himself, and even though they stand on the fact that Christ sent the Holy Spirit to birth the church in Acts chapter 2, they then boldly declare that, "I don't believe in miracles", or "miracles are not for today!"

God has clearly dealt with mankind in demonstrative miracles, prophecy, wisdom, and invasive inspiration since the fall of man. God is and always has been interventionist with mankind. However, "It has ceased for today," they claim. God give us the patience to challenge these perspectives with common sense and biblical logic as well as rightly understanding scripture.

Since Adam and Eve took of the fruit in the garden of Eden, fallen man has always needed God to speak to them, and God has clearly always wanted to speak to them (see the early dozen or so chapters of Genesis with the narratives concerning Adam, Cain, Noah etc.). When God speaks to mankind, privately or publicly, and the man or woman spoken to then passes on to others what God has spoken, it has been referred to (in English) as prophecy. There have been prophets since Enoch, "the seventh from Adam" – if not before (see Genesis 5:18-24 linked with Hebrews 11:5 and Jude 14).

For those who claim that only the prophetic messages that are recounted in scripture are "true prophecy", I ask: What about the many times in scripture, both Old and New Testaments, where prophecy is referred to, yet the contents of those prophetic messages are not recorded? Surely the very concept of true prophecy recorded as having been spoken in the narrative of scripture, when referencing those spoken prophecies that are not actually verbally recorded in the scriptures, justifies that proposition of the validity of "extra-biblical prophecy", aka "non-canonical prophecy", aka "prophecy beyond the parameters of the accepted text of scripture"! Would you not agree?

For instance, Numbers 11:16-30 has reference to 70 elders outside the Israelite camp prophesying among the people - having received the grace, the gift and the ability to prophesy legitimate divinely inspired prophetic words. Does not the fact that these seventy men who authoritatively and genuinely were Divinely inspired to prophesy with the same Spirit that was on Moses coming upon them, followed by the utter neglect of Moses to tell us what they actually prophesied, suggest that "non-biblical prophecy" is a legitimate orthodox possibility? If it was possible then why is it not possible today?

Enoch prophesied, says Jude 14, and in the real-time of his chronological historical position in scripture, nothing of his prophetic words, or even the fact that he prophesied, are recorded. Biblically, we would not have a clue that Enoch prophesied or was a prophet (was he?) if it was not for the single quotation in the New Testament. Jude grabs one line out of the huge book bearing Enoch's name. The book of Enoch is not accepted as canonical west of the orthodox church, and a western Christian would come under some highly critical scrutiny by textual authorities if he even suggested it was. (I must note that, as far as I know, all Western Christian denominations and traditions accept the Books of Enoch as having *some* historical or theological interest, and even though the Ethiopian Orthodox Church and Eritrean Orthodox Church consider both the Books of Enoch as canonical, i.e. Biblical, most academic authorities tend to belittle its contents – apart from that one single line of a quotation in the early lines of the book of Enoch (1 Enoch 1:9).)

Notwithstanding, keeping myself within the parameters of accepted Western orthodoxy, as I always do (lol), and having a limited view of the value of the books of Enoch, does that necessarily contradict the concept of what was to Jude, a "non-biblical," or "extra-canonical" prophecy being genuine? Jude quotes one line out of a large ocean of prophetic words contained in the Book of Enoch. I am forced to ask if there is a logic to trashing the rest of "the book of Enoch," and not even adding it to some apocryphal list? Whatever - the highway of my thesis in these lines is that there has always been genuine, divinely inspired prophecy outside of that which is contained in the scrolls of the Hebrew Bible and the New Testament.

Why aren't the prophecies and interpretations uttered in the church that Paul founded in Corinth reported in scripture (see 1 Corinthians chapters 12 and 14). The things he writes in first Corinthians have much to say about the manner in which the gifts were used, but not once does he criticise or even ask for the content of what was being prophesied. What do we call that? "Extra-Biblical Prophecy?" "Non-canonical prophecy?" Both those titles are perfectly correct if used, simply because those are the facts of what Paul is referring to in the church in Corinth.

Why aren't all interpreted tongues in scripture recorded? Didn't the apostle write in the scriptures - writings that we evangelicals claim are inerrant and inspired - "Do not despise prophecy?" (1 Thessalonians 5:20-21). If those that deny contemporary prophecy also claim that the New Testament is God-breathed – it suggests that God breathed a line in scripture that is irrelevant for us today. They might claim that the verse is referring to people despising the Old Testament prophets as a justification of the denial of the supernatural, but one does not have to be a Doctor of Divinity to see that such a response is completely overriding the essence of the verse in the full context of the Epistle. The context demands that Paul was referring to what was going on in the churches and not to those that we would refer to as Old Testament prophets.

God still speaks today. Through the scriptures (The Bible), through preaching, and through the gifts of the Spirit, He speaks to individuals about themselves as well as to others. He speaks to churches and church groups across the denominational streams and families.

To take my case further with a query: What about the books that the Bible itself bids us consult that are outside of scripture? At various points in the biblical narrative, we are told to consult other writings to learn more about the issues at hand that are being written about concerning characters and historical accounts and, social contexts etc.. Check these out:

- The Book of the Acts of Solomon (Referred to in I Kings 11:41). Solomon must have appointed a Chronicler to write down a more thorough record of his life, words and actions. So, we have the inspired prophetic Book of Kings (Note that the Hebrew Bible has 1 Kings in the midst of the "Prophets" in their arrangement.), referring us to check the truth and actuality of Solomon's deeds in a "non-canonical" scroll. Surely, this makes "The Book of the Acts of Solomon" to the category of "non-canonical inspired prophecy."

- The Book of the Wars of the LORD (Referred to in Numbers 21:14). This seems to refer to some kind of poetic writing or narration of the wars and victories of the Lord. This reference to an unknown scroll of what is to us, today, without a frame of reference. It is mentioned without any prejudice to the integrity of the holy writings that comprise the Pentateuch. Moses refers to this book as several of the old divines of previous centuries remark, in the same spirit as the apostle Paul referred to some Godless poet in acts 17. However, this is not quite the same. Here, Moses – who we assume to have written this section of Numbers himself, is suggesting that the readers check out the veracity of his recording by looking at the same source Moses had for making a remark about the border between Moab and the Amorites, i.e. the River Arnon. My point is that the inspired scripture refers us to an unknown, non-canonical scroll in order to verify a statement.

I say all this in the same vein that Luke the physician, informs us that *many* wrote a history of the things done and said by Christ whose writings were never received as canonical. See Luke 1:1.

- The Book of Samuel the seer, The records of Nathan the prophet, and The records of Gad the Seer, (Referred to in 1 Chronicles 29:29). The inspired record here bids us study more of the life and activities of David the King. To make the study complete we are given a list of three documents. The book of

Samuel the Seer may or may not be the books of Samuel that are part of the Hebrew Bible, however, even though the prophets Nathan and Gad are both referred to in the biblical narratives, there is no such recorded scroll by the two men of God that are known of. Once again, we have the inspired prophetic word referring us to "non-canonical records" to substantiate our grasp of the life of David.

- The Records of Nathan the Prophet (Referred to in 1 Chronicles 29:29, 2 Chronicles 9:29).

- The Prophecy of Ahijah of Shiloh (Referred to in 2 Chronicles 9:29).

- The Visions of Iddo the Seer against Jeroboam the Son of Nebat (Referred to 2 Chronicles 9:29).

These three volumes are referred to us as substantiates of Solomon's life and activities. This is strange as Solomon seems to the Biblical record to have had no prophetic input from any prophet. The validation of all these three books are stated in Kings and Chronicles concerning King Solomon, accounting further than what is stated in the Hebrew Bible. We are bidden to consult these three scrolls to validate and embellish our knowledge of Solomon's life. Non canonical writings by these three prophets are held up to us as good and informative reads to the understanding of the Hebrew Bible.

There is more.

- The Book of Shemaiah the Prophet and Iddo the Seer Concerning Genealogies (Referred to in 2 Chronicles 12:15). This verse in Chronicles actually states: "As for the events of Rehoboam's reign, from beginning to end, are they not written in the records of Shemaiah the prophet and of Iddo the seer that deal with genealogies?" It therefore seems that Iddo wrote not only during and concerning Solomon's reign (2 Chronicles 9:29), but in his son Rehoboam's reign also. It is as if the

Chronicler (or the editor of the book of Chronicles) is aware of the shortcomings of the narratives concerning Rehoboam in the book that we refer to as 2 Chronicles and therefore calls us to do further research. Non-canonical "inspired prophetic" writings to substantiate that which we refer to as canonical. Once again, "extra-biblical prophecy" is noted and referred to within the scriptures themselves.

- The Book of Chronicles of the Kings of Media and Persia (Referred to in Esther 10:2). Whoa! Now, "the scripture goes too far," some would say. Esther 10:2 actually refers us to the annals of the gentile kings of Media and Persia for us to complete our understanding of the power, might and greatness of Mordecai, Esther's uncle. We may not be comfortable to suggest that the Chronicles of heathen kings were inspired – but we can assert their accuracy and truthfulness concerning Mordecai as explained in the Hebrew Bible's book of Esther.

- The Book of Jasher (Joshua 10:13; 2 Samuel 1:18). In Joshua 10:13 – just in case the reader wanted a second opinion on what the verse says about the sun standing still and the moon stopping – we are given the Book of Jasher as written proof that what the book of Joshua says is true.

These extra-canonical books may or may not be inspired and/or inerrant, but surely, on the grounds of what we claim of the inspiration of the scriptures contained in both the Old and New Testament, it must infer that the books we are encouraged to consult are (or were) faithfully, historically and spiritually correct and true. Is it possible that the Bible, the integrity of which both Christians and Jews hold to such a high level, could refer us to read a book which is not true in its narrative?

In the New Testament. Gifts are mentioned quite often without any comment on the substance or nature of the prophecies. Philip had four daughters that prophesied. That sounds wonderfully spiritual and powerful to me. But how come we are not told what they prophesied? Not a single line is shared with us, and the context of the remark in Acts suggests that they all prophesied regularly and consistently enough for them to be mentioned. That is extra-canonical prophecy, is it not?

Another track that the "non-charismatic", "non-Pentecostal" exponents of the "heresy of modern prophecy" follow is that the doctrinal body of truth is complete in the Bible. Why should God trouble himself to speak outside of the scriptures? I answer as follows:

1. God has always spoken outside of scripture before it was written down and thereafter became part of scripture. To present an example, if the academics are correct, for 60 or so years all the truths that John shares with the world in John's gospel was non-canonical and extra-biblical until the apostle that Jesus loved took quill and pen in order to write it.

2. Contemporary prophecy rarely touches on doctrine, even though underlying the delivery of a prophecy, there is the presupposition that the one delivering the prophecy believes in receiving and speaking prophecy today. Agabus (Acts 11:27-28) predicting a coming famine, and later that the owner of the belt he picked up would be abused and mistreated in Jerusalem (Acts 21:10-12) is not even touching what we would generally refer to as "doctrine." So, playing around with biblical doctrine is not on the agenda at all. God is more than unlikely to say, "please ignore My Word in favour of your modern 21st Century paraphrases." Even basic observation and scanty understanding of how God works in our lives will conform within us of that. (2 Tim 3:16-17)

3. Paul received warnings not to go to Jerusalem because of the trouble that would enshroud him. Extra canonical prophecy there. Why do I say that? Simply because we are not told the contents of what various people said to Paul "in the Spirit".

4. Prophecy is clearly not necessarily if at all, doctrinally based. We believe that the testimony of Christ is the Spirit of testimony, and so all prophecy is Christ-sourced, even when reference to Christ is not actually made.

"Do not quench the Holy Spirit "(5:20) said Paul. The Holy Spirit takes of the things of Christ and makes them real to us. In this sense, prophecy must be Christ-centred and/or Christ-sourced via the Holy Spirit. True Prophecy is Spirit-enabled. A prophetic word is Spirit-empowered. Prophecy is God's revelation. There is clearly a place for extra-biblical prophecy in the church today (1 Corinthians 13:8-12, Acts 2:17-18).

Having said all that in asserting my case for the legitimacy of contemporary prophecy, sadly, much extra bible prophecy is unhelpful and on TV, one thing I have learned about prophecy is God's written Word is indeed inerrant, and His spoken prophetic word may not carry the same weight. There are times when some modern prophetic words seem weightless altogether. However, we test the spirits and refuse to throw the baby out with the bath water. The Word is inerrant, but our interpretation is consistently fallible, hence the need for testing and discerning of those who speak prophetic messages today. (1 John 4:1-6). Just because someone says, "I have a word from the Lord," does not mean they have. Just because somebody got it wrong does not mean the concept of "non-canonical", or "extra-biblical prophecy" is heresy.

Extra-biblical prophecy is *ALWAYS* subject to scripture, without exception. It must always be tested. (1 Thessalonians 5:20). Tested against scripture - our highest authority. However, to prophesy a coming famine can only be tested by the passing of time. A solid prophet from God will speak and gather God's people together. First Corinthians exhorts us all to seek after prophecy. There is a huge difference between a "false prophet" and a "prophet that got something wrong".

26

THE BENCHMARK DEMONSTRATION OF PROPHETIC POWER. (1 KINGS 18:20- 40)

ELIJAH'S BATTLE FOR THE SOUL OF A NATION

Gilead is the highland east of the Jordan River and south of the Sea of Galilee, in the tribal territory of East Manasseh. It was remote from the "city life and social rat race" of Samaria. So, the ruler and the prophet came face to face for an exchange that subsumed the very essence of the agony between them and between their two visions of Israel.

Ahab was not an incompetent, negligent or indolent ruler, unconcerned for the welfare of his realm. He built up its cities, its economy, and its material culture. He brought it to a place of consequence in international affairs and strengthened its military power. He took to the battlefield in person to defend it, and in the end, he was slain fighting its enemies. Perhaps he simply did not perceive the value of its moral well-being. Perhaps he thought it advisable to adapt to the modern mores of the day and accommodate the customs of its region. From such a viewpoint, Elijah could be deemed a reactionary who impeded progress by his insistence on strict adherence to an already ancient Covenant, a fanatic, a meddler in affairs of state. To Elijah, the Covenant was the very essence of Israel's being and the raison-d'etre of their existence, the mould of its identity, and the keystone of its destiny. Without it, wealth and might and fine buildings were hollow and evanescent. Any leader who set it aside for the easier pursuit of superficial successes would lead it to ruin and oblivion.

It is not known when this confrontation came during Ahab's twenty-two years on the throne, but more likely later then early in his days of power. It would take time for tensions to build up as Phoenician cults were established, and Jezebel's crimes took their toll.

He gave his orders to the King, and the King carried them out: *'And now, send; gather to me all Israel to Mount Carmel, and the 450 prophets of the ba'al and the 400 prophets of the asherah, eating at Jezebel's table.' And Ahab sent to all the children of Israel and gathered the prophets together at Mount Carmel* (1 Kings 18:19-20).

The Narrator of the Book of Kings gives more attention to Ahab than to any other ruler of the Northern Kingdom and many of the Southern Kingdom, yet the picture of his character and his personality is not in focus. One thing that does emerge is the domination of his wife Jezebel, daughter of the King of Tyre-Sidon, a very tiny state but one grown very rich through its far-flung maritime trade. The worst of Ahab's doings are ascribed to her instigation: *(1 Kings*21:25-26).

To provide a foreign consort with a shrine for private devotions according to the ways of her native land had a precedent, albeit a disdained one, in the practice of Solomon, but Jezebel's devotions were not private. She maintained in her retinue *450 prophets of the ba'al, and . . . 400 prophets of the asherah eating at Jezebel's table* (18:19) – "the asherah" being not the Canaanite-Phoenician goddess Asherah herself, but rather the sacred trees or cult-objects used in her rites. These prophets, presumably brought from Phoenicia, were far more than would suffice for her spiritual needs and eating at her table signifies more than catering arrangements. They were her henchmen on the mission to foist her native deities on her husband's people. The Israelites who came to the assembly would be the men of standing, the clan and tribal elders acting as representatives of the people as a whole. Elijah addressed himself to them as though in the coming contest, they, not their King, would render the verdict.

Before them on one side stood the 450 prophets of the ba'al. (The prophets of the asherah, it seems, never showed up.) Their Ba'al would not be one of the local Canaanite gods known by that title, but a senior deity of Tyre-Sidon, brought to Israel in Jezebel's trousseau. Several ba'alim were prominent in the pantheon of Tyre-Sidon, and the biblical writers did not bother to distinguish among them or specify which among them Jezebel patronized.

(The common plaint about Elijah's solitude, which he repeats later in I Kings 19:10, raises questions of the whereabouts of the 150 loyal prophets who had been saved by Obadiah.) It seems they did not have the will or spirit to turn up to watch Elijah in action. Elijah then challenged the priests of Baal. Both he and they would place a bull on separate altars but would set no fire; they would call on their gods and he in the name of the Lord. *And it shall be the god who answers with fire, He is God* (18:24). Is it possible to say anything more dramatic?

The priests of Baal called out to their god and danced by their altar (18:26), with no result. *(1 Kings 18:27-29)*. Self-inflicted wounds were also common pagan practices linked to mourning, strictly prohibited to the Israelites in *You shall not gash yourself in mourning for the dead* (Lev. 19:28) and *Priests shall not . . . as a sign of mourning . . . gash their bodies* (Lev. 21:5), and *You are the sons of The Lord your God, you shall not gash yourselves in mourning for the dead* (Deut. 14:1). It is a stretch of our imagination to picture a full 450 men in this chorus line around the altar, but whatever the number their choreography may have been like that described by a Roman account of a religious ceremony in Syria: "They began to howl all out of tune and hurl themselves hither and thither, as though they were mad. They made a thousand gestures . . . They would bend down their necks and spin round so that the hair flew out in a circle. They would bite their own flesh. Finally, everyone took his two-edged weapon and wounded his flesh in diverse places" (Apuleius, *Metamorphoses*, VIII:27).

Elijah's jibes in 1 Kings 18:27 are not necessarily a guide to identification. They may be sardonic references to myths about a particular baal, or they may be a jumble of pagan myths, a mélange of humanlike activities attributed to various anthropomorphic divinities.

Elijah's taunt was at reliance on any god or gods who can be preoccupied, or absent, or dormant, or dependent on the antics of their clergy; a mockery of devotees who must not merely adore them but shore them up with magical rituals, lest they lose the power to perform.

Time ran out for the baal-men. Elijah had given them every advantage: First turn, first choice of sacrificial beast, a good part of the day for their efforts. They had no excuse for the fiasco watched by the assembled Israelites. What on earth were all the viewers doing during the hours of self-flagellation. Now it was the hour of the late afternoon sacrifice [*minhah*], and Elijah came forward. He was playing for the highest of stakes, and he made the conditions so unfavourable for himself that success would be not merely impressive but awesome. And he implored The Lord to vindicate not only His own Majesty but also Elijah's own status as prophet extraordinaire: *(1 Kings* 18:30-35).

There had once been an Israelite altar on Mount Carmel that had either fallen into disrepair through neglect or had been wrecked when – as Elijah was soon to charge – *'the children of Israel. . . have thrown down Your altars'* (19:14). In restoring it, he took care that all the tribes of the sons of Jacob were represented, including those now in the Kingdom of Judah; another instance of the prophetic tradition clinging to the idea of a single peoplehood regardless of political schism. Invoking the memory of their Patriarchs would stir emotion in the assembly, a reminder of an origin and historic identity so distinct from those of the Tyrian-Sidonians toward whom they had been leaning.

Although the trench was no more than twice the width of a furrow for planting seed, the miniature moat combined with the drenching of the altar and the sacrifice would make any combustion more remarkable. At the same time, the water could act as a magnet if there were a streak of heat lightning. Thus far, no word had been spoken about the drought, but there could have been few at the assembly under the long-cloudless sky who were not thinking of it. The precious water streaming from the jars could be both an imitation of the desired rainfall and a display of confidence that the dwindling supply no longer needed to be hoarded. It was also a display of contrast between Elijah who poured water which brings life, and the baal-men who poured blood which brings death. (*1 Kings* 18:36-39).

Elijah now showed no leniency to the defeated Phoenicians, who were quite possibly the very men who had served Jezebel as executioners in the massacre of the prophets of Israel. *And Elijah said to them* [the people], *'Seize the prophets of the baal. Do not let a man of them escape.' And they seized them, and Elijah brought them down to the Kishon stream, and slaughtered them there* (18:40).

With the contest decided and the losers dispatched, rain becomes the explicit subject. Up to this point, Elijah had been in command of the action and the centre of attention. Only now is it noted that King Ahab had been present himself, permitting the man he had addressed as *'You troubler of Israel'* to take charge and even to issue a mass death sentence. The men gathered as witnesses are not mentioned again and had perhaps dispersed, while Ahab and Elijah remained on the mountain, along with the King's charioteer and any other personal attendants he kept with him, and one anonymous man who makes a sudden incongruous appearance as a servant of the solitary and rough-living prophet.

The scene begins with Elijah telling Ahab *'Go up, eat and drink, for there is a sound of abundant rain.' And Ahab went up to eat and drink* (18:41-42). This suggests that the King had been fasting, either with his people or on behalf of them. It was customary for a person or even a community to fast in time of need or peril or distress, or when facing some challenging deed. If Ahab had been fasting throughout the contest on Mount Carmel, it would be as prelude to the hoped for outcome – whether he hoped that the troubler- prophet would fail and be less troublesome thereafter, or that his wife's cohorts would be discredited and excluded from his nation's affairs, or simply that one way or another the drought would at last be broken. The last may be the most plausible, for with the contest over, he was still fasting when he received Elijah's weather forecast. Be that as it may, the forecast cancelled the fast. The sound of abundant rain before any had fallen could be a rustling wind that precedes a cyclonic storm, and while Ahab might now have been taking a picnic repast, Elijah was still in anxious suspense until he was vindicated by a storm cloud blowing in over the Mediterranean. Indeed, he now displayed a nervousness he had never shown during the contest with the baal-men. (1 Kings 18:42-44).

With this reassuring sign, Elijah, whether with unwonted solicitude or a touch of sarcasm, advised Ahab that he should leave for home lest he find himself in an open chariot in a heavy downpour.

At the end of this day, Ahab went not to his royal capital at Samaria but to his private family home in the town of Jezreel, some seventeen or eighteen miles from Mount Carmel. Elijah *ran before Ahab until the approach to Jezreel* (18:46). It was an act of deference to run beside or before the wheels of a royal chariot, but Elijah was no man's lackey. Perhaps in his own moment of triumph, he deigned to allot the head of state this much recognition of his rank. Yet, even for a hardy man on a road mostly downhill, to run that distance in pace with a chariot drawn by two good horses, hints that the charioteer had been told to hold them in.

Ahab may indeed have been in no great hurry to reach his house, where Jezebel was waiting to hear of a victory by her baal-men. Then, her husband finally arrived and delivered his report. *And Ahab told Jezebel all that Elijah had done, and how he had slain all the prophets with the sword. And Jezebel sent a messenger to Elijah, saying, 'Thus do the gods* [to me] *and more – surely about this time tomorrow I will make your life as the life of one of them'* (1 Kings 19:1-2).

(In the Septuagint rendering of this passage, the message begins, "As you are Elijah, I am Jezebel," a wordplay on their own names as epitomes of their causes: "Eliyahu [אליהו]" means "My-God-Is-The-Lord." "Izevel" subsumes "*zevul* [prince]," a title for Baal-Hadad.

That day's blow to Jezebel was heavy but not mortal. She still had her rank and power and could send home to Tyre for more prophets. Yet, this lone wild man could not be permitted to challenge her with impunity or encourage others to defiance. Elijah had won the loyalty of the assemblage at Carmel, men who stood for their households and clans. It remained to be seen how long that loyalty would hold, but at this moment he had the people on his side. Ahab had seen that and could tell her so. To kill him now could provoke such a rage as might shake the throne. That she gave him 24 hours' notice implies that she would prefer his flight to his death, but for that tactic to work, the threat had to carry credibility: That is, Elijah would have to believe that if he did not flee at once, she would indeed murder him. He who dared hurl accusations and commands at the King face-to-face, did not stay to confront the foreign consort. He fled, southward into Judah and even beyond it into the desert of Sinai as far as Mount Horeb, the mountain of the Covenant. The contest for the soul of Israel was not over.

27

CLOSURE TO THE PROPHETIC BAALISTIC CONFLAGRATION – VALIDATING DIVINE VICTORY. (1 Kings 18:40-45)

In the biblical narrative of 1 Kings, the contrasting worldviews of Ahab and Elijah present a profound exploration of authority, power, character and spirituality. Ahab embodies a worldview steeped in political pragmatism, self-interest and materialism, while Elijah stands as a beacon of prophetic authority rooted in divine allegiance and spiritual fidelity. Understanding this dichotomy reveals not only the nature of their respective philosophies but also the broader implications concerning leadership and faith in a fractured world.

Ahab's reign is marked by a reliance on political alliances and material wealth. He represents a worldview that prioritizes human authority, manipulation of circumstances, and the pursuit of power through worldly means. His marriage to Jezebel, a Phoenician, serves as a strategic political alliance that brings with it the worship of Baal—a deity that symbolizes agricultural fertility and economic prosperity, all melded together with immoral sexual activities that were supposed to increase fertility and fecundity. Ahab's acceptance of Baal worship reflects a pragmatic submission to his wife – an approach to governance where the king's primary concern is the contentedness of his deeply discontented queen and, a long way away second, the stability of his kingdom, often at the expense of spiritual integrity.

Ahab's materialism is evident in his actions. He builds temples for Baal and promotes the worship of this foreign god among his people, indicating that his philosophy is not one of conviction but rather a life of expedient means to an end. His leadership is characterized by a willingness to compromise his own values (he must have had some) for the sake of political expediency. This approach not only alienated him from the covenantal relationship with Yahweh but also sets the stage for conflict with all things Godly, personified in the physical existence and presence of the man from Tishbe, Elijah.

In stark contrast, Elijah embodies a worldview shaped by prophetic authority and spiritual fidelity. As a prophet, Elijah operates not under the auspices of political power but through his divine mandate. His authority comes from God. Full stop! This positioned him as a moral and spiritual counterweight to Ahab's reign. Elijah's philosophy emphasizes the importance of faith, and faithfulness to Yahweh and the call to righteousness, regardless of the prevailing political climate.

Elijah's confrontation with Ahab in 1 Kings 18:16-19 illustrates the crux of their differing worldviews. Upon entering the presence of the king, Elijah does not seek permission or favour; instead, he boldly declares the truth of God's word and all changes that were to be made to bring all things in alignment with the will of Yahweh. This act of defiance reveals Elijah's understanding of his role as a prophet. He is to speak truth to power, and speak light to the darkness, regardless of the consequences. His authority does not derive from any earthly position of influence but from his unwavering, solid and complete commitment to God's will

The relationship between Elijah and Ahab serves as a fascinating study of authority dynamics. While Ahab holds the title of king, it is actually Elijah who wields genuine authority that was truly above the king, due to his prophetic calling. This inversion of power dynamics is significant; it suggests that true authority is not found in worldly titles or political positions but in righteousness and fidelity to divine truth.

Elijah's authority is characterized by his God-instructed prophetic actions, such as calling for a drought and later challenging the prophets of Baal on Mount Carmel. In these moments, he does not merely critique Ahab's policies but confronts the very essence and heart of Ahab's allegiance to false gods. Elijah's confidence stems from his conviction that he is acting on behalf of Yahweh, having heard and obeyed what the word of the Lord said to him. It is the imbibed word of Yahweh grants him the courage to stand before a king with unwavering resolvThe clash between Ahab and Elijah serves as a microcosm for broader themes of leadership and faith. Ahab's reliance on materialism and political expediency leads to moral decay and spiritual desolation within Israel. His worldview ultimately fails to sustain the nation, as it is predicated on alliances with foreign powers and the appeasement of false deities. Such a belief system makes one's personal life unsustainable, never mind the national life of the populace.

Conversely, Elijah's commitment to Yahweh and his prophetic calling highlight the transformative power of spiritual authority. His actions inspire a return to covenantal faithfulness among the Israelites, prompting them to reconsider their allegiances and the consequences of their choices. Elijah's leadership is not defined by coercion or manipulation but by a profound sense of duty to God and his people.

The narrative also raises important questions about the role of prophets and spiritual leaders in society. Elijah's example underscores the need for divinely inspired prophetic voices that challenge the status quo of the world and call for accountability amongst those in power. In a world often dominated by political pragmatism, the prophetic voice serves as a reminder of higher moral standards and the importance of spiritual integrity.

In contemporary society, the lessons drawn from the contrasting worldviews of Ahab and Elijah remain relevant. Leaders who prioritize material gain and political manoeuvring often find themselves disconnected from the very people they are meant to serve. In contrast, those who embrace a prophetic calling grounded in truth and integrity can inspire genuine transformation and foster a deeper sense of community and purpose.

The legacies of Ahab and Elijah resonate through the ages, offering timeless insights into the nature of authority, leadership, and faith. Ahab's worldview, rooted in materialism and political expediency, ultimately leads to his downfall and the spiritual decline of Israel. Elijah's prophetic authority, however, serves as a beacon of hope, reminding us that true leadership is defined by fidelity to a greater truth and a higher authority.

As we reflect on the lives of these two figures, we are invited to consider our own allegiances and the values that shape our decisions. In a world often swayed by the allure of power and material gain, the call to embody the prophetic spirit of Elijah remains as vital as ever. It challenges us to seek authenticity, to stand for truth, and to lead with integrity in all aspects of our lives.

Now to the relevant text in the narrative chronology. In 1 Kings 18:40-45, we read about the dramatic conclusion of Elijah's day of confrontation with the prophets of Baal on Mount Carmel. His final act, as instructed by the word of the Lord, to end the day's labour, is somewhat startling. It culminates in the killing (execution) of the 450 priests of Baal. I feel confident in asserting that I am sure the priests of the Asherah were glad they had not attended as they also would have been amongst the line for capital execution. To understand Elijah's actions, we need to examine the context of the narrative and the age in which this took place, the true nature of idolatry and the teachings of Baal worship, and the theological implications of this event.

Elijah, a prophet of Yahweh, lived during a time when Israel was heavily influenced by the worship of Baal, a Canaanite deity associated with fertility and rain. Under Ahab and Jezebel, the worship of Baal had been institutionalized, leading the Israelites away from Yahweh. Elijah's challenge to the foreign priests on Mount Carmel was a pivotal moment in demonstrating to the people of Israel Yahweh's sovereignty over Baal.

After Yahweh answered Elijah's prayer by sending fire to consume his sacrifice, the people of Israel acknowledged Yahweh as the true God. Elijah then ordered the execution of the Baal priests (1 Kings 18:40). In 2025, where modern societies are filled with ideas of multi-faiths and total inclusivity of all being the normal, most commentators softpedal this aspect of Elijah's character and Godliness. However, this act can be understood and even be seen as acceptable through several lenses:

1. It was the Restoration of True Worship.

Elijah's actions were intended to cleanse Israel of idolatry as completely as possible and restore the worship of Yahweh. The execution of the Baal priests symbolized a decisive break from false worship and a call to return to covenant faithfulness. In secular twenty-first century western culture that sounds hardly on any political party's agenda. In eighth century Israel, from the spiritual perspective and the Pentateuch, that was by far the top of governmental priorities.

2. It was Scripturally Accredited Judicial Authority.

In ancient Israel, prophets held significant authority, mediators between God and the people. Elijah's command to execute the priests can be seen as a fulfillment of the law concerning false prophets, which calls for the death penalty for those who lead the people astray from worshipping Yahweh.

If a prophet, or one who foretells by dreams, appears among you and announces to you a sign or wonder, and if the sign or wonder spoken of takes place, and the prophet says, "Let us follow other gods" (gods you have not known) "and let us worship them," you must not listen to the words of that prophet or dreamer. The LORD your God is testing you to find out whether you love him with all your heart and with all your soul. It is the LORD your God you must follow, and him you must revere. Keep his commands and obey him; serve him and hold fast to him. That prophet or dreamer must be put to death for inciting rebellion against the LORD your God, who brought you out of Egypt and redeemed you from the land of slavery. That prophet or dreamer tried to turn you from the way the LORD your God commanded you to follow. You must purge the evil from among you.

Deuteronomy 13:1-5

3. **It was Divine Judgment.**

The execution can also be viewed as an act of divine judgment against the Baal priests for their leading Israel into sin. By participating in and promoting idolatry, they were seen as culpable for the spiritual downfall of the nation, thus justifying their punishment. Although many of them, if not all, were foreign immigrants following on Jezebel's coattails, as living in Israel, they were subject to the precepts of the nations law, no matter how many nationals had submitted to the cult of Baal.

4. **It was a Symbolic Act.**

The act served as a powerful symbol to the Israelites of the utter futility of idol worship and the reality of divine power. By eliminating the prophets of Baal, Elijah aimed to reinforce the message that Yahweh is the only true God, capable of delivering Israel from drought and spiritual desolation. Theologically, this event underscores the seriousness of idolatry in Israel in the biblical narrative.

It also illustrates the concept of covenant faithfulness - Israel's relationship with Yahweh is depicted as one that requires and demands exclusive loyalty. The execution of the Baal priests serves as a stark warning against the consequences of abandoning that relationship. Moreover, it raises questions about the nature of justice and mercy in Old Testament biblical texts. While the execution may seem harsh, especially by modern twenty-first century paradigms and standards, within the context of ancient Israelite society and its understanding of holiness and purity, it was a necessary act to restore righteous worship of God.

This event serves as a critical moment in Israel's history, emphasizing the importance of covenant faithfulness and the dire consequences of turning away from Yahweh.

PART D

THE AFTERMATH OF THE INITIAL PROPHETIC DELIVERY.

28

THE RISE AND FALL OF THE SCHOOLS OF THE PROPHETS.

(Is this how all revolutions ultimately rise and fade into the blandness of the world?)

Within the biblical narrative of both Elijah and Elisha, references to "the sons of the prophets" and/or the "groups of the prophets" are scattered throughout. The phrase "the sons of the prophets" was originally identified and headquartered in the early days of the movement's creation at "the Naioth". This word is the anglicisation of the Hebrew word for "dwelling" or "home." The Naioth was in the town known as Ramah (abbreviated from Ramathaim-Zophim). The Naioth was the home of the great prophet Samuel (1 Samuel 19:18-24), where the original fellowship, or "school of the prophets" assembled to worship, pray, and ask God for wisdom and to strut their divinely inspired "thing." Naioth could accurately be referred to as the birthplace of Prophecy in Israel.

The entire text of the Hebrew Bible, of course, was, in essence, written by prophets. Modern scholars, however, tend to hang on to Deuteronomy 18:15-18 as the founding Mosaic utterance that legitimised the eruption into existence of the "schools of the prophets" in later years and their sustained existence through generations. It was a God-inspired idea that nobody was skilled enough to bring to reality until the prophet Samuel was at his prophetic peak.

[15] The Lord your God will raise up for you a prophet like me from among you, from your fellow Israelites. You must listen to him. [16] For this is what you asked of the Lord your God at Horeb on the day of the assembly when you said, "Let us not hear the voice of the Lord our God nor see this great fire anymore, or we will die." [17] The Lord said to me: "What they say is good. [18] I will

raise up for them a prophet like you from among their fellow Israelites, and I will put my words in his mouth. He will tell them everything I command him.

(Deuteronomy 18:15-18. NIV)

From Moses (who wrote the text of Deuteronomy) to Samuel, Israel passed through a few generations of blindness to the Spirit of God. It was a period equivalent to Europe's Dark Ages. In the context of the possessed Promised Land of Israel, Samuel was the last of the Judges and the first of the prophets. Samuel himself was a watershed, the founder of a new age, the gatekeeper that closed the door on the theocracy and opened the door to monarchy. His genius was far beyond people's normal perception of the man as a biblical key figure. He anointed the first king, and then after Saul's rejection, anointed David. Centuries later, Prophetic writers compared Samuel with Moses (Jeremiah 15:1. Psalm 99:6). The birth of the prophetic schools is mentioned in an almost "by the way" spontaneous moment after Samuel had poured oil on Saul's head and was prophesying what would happen to the newly chosen monarch on his way home. In the midst of the giving of his directions, he states,

"... afterward you will come to the hill of God where the Philistine garrison is; and it shall be, as soon as you have come there to the city, that you will meet a group of prophets coming down from the high place with harp, tambourine, flute, and a lyre before them, and they will be prophesying. Then the Spirit of the Lord will come upon you mightily, and you shall prophesy with them and be changed into another man."

(1 Samuel 10:5-6).

The group he referred to was based in Bethel it seems. From the overall reading of the Hebrew Bible, and reading the output of Hebrew scholars, these prophetic groups were attributed to Samuel as founder. These schools form the first generation of the prophetic order had continuous existence vaguely traced through to the exile in 587BC. It has to be seen through the generations that there were periods when the prophetic groups seemed rather rag-tag, and more of a religious guild than groups of men earnestly seeking the how's and wherefores of Prophecy. The impact of these schools permeates the entire Old Testament history and all the Hebrew writings up to the fall of Jerusalem and the Babylonian exile, with even traces of prophetic groups afterwards.

In the same scroll recording Samuel and the groups, in the same later strand of history, we read that the young man David was spending a historic two weeks with Samuel. This is David having been anointed by Samuel when he was probably 12 years old, having time with the elderly Samuel shortly prior to becoming king. Angry King Saul, desperately wanting to stop David's ascension to the throne, sent groups of soldiers on three different occasions to bring David back to him as a prisoner. But something phenomenal took place. The text of the manuscripts tells the story:

"It was told Saul, saying, "Behold, David is at the Naioth in Ramah." Then Saul sent messengers to take David, but when they saw the company of the prophets prophesying, with Samuel standing and presiding over them, the Spirit of God came upon the messengers of Saul; and they also prophesied. When it was told Saul, he sent other messengers, and they also prophesied. So, Saul sent messengers again the third time, and they too prophesied."

[19] Word came to Saul: "David is in Naioth at Ramah"; [20] so he sent men to capture him. But when they saw a group of prophets prophesying, with Samuel standing there as their leader, the Spirit of God came on Saul's men, and they also prophesied. [21] Saul was told about it, and he sent more men, and they prophesied too. Saul sent men a third time, and they also prophesied. [22] Finally, he himself left for Ramah and went to the great cistern at Seku. And he asked, "Where are Samuel and David?" "Over in Naioth at Ramah," they said. [23] So Saul went to Naioth at Ramah. But the Spirit of God came even on him, and he

walked along prophesying until he came to Naioth. ²⁴ He stripped off his garments, and he too prophesied in Samuel's presence. He lay naked all that day and all that night. This is why people say, "Is Saul also among the prophets?"

1 Samuel 19:19-24 NIV

We are compelled to add that the Spirit of God was moving through means of music. Quantitive numbers of group members are not mentioned at all till years later.

Thus, we have a clear, verbally drawn picture of the majestic elderly man, Samuel, presiding as the master of the class while the company of prophetic "students" prophesied out loud. Saul was knocked to the floor when he arrived at the "hill of God" in 1 Samuel 10. So, it is somewhat logical to conclude that with harp, tambourine, flute, and a lyre music, the spirit of God came upon Saul also as he approached Samuel. As the three groups of soldiers were smitten by the Spirit of God and never returned to the king who had commanded them to go, so, finally, as it had been years earlier, Saul rides into Samuel's ambience and atmosphere again and is smitten down by the Spirit of God.

The School of the Prophets that started at the Naioth had brought into Israel's social fabric a group that was to seek after and look into the whys and wherefores of prophecy and the person of God Himself. Thus, we are aware at this stage of observation, of at least two school bases, one in Bethel and one in the Naioth, in Ramah, under the masterful supervision of Samuel.

The statement of 1 Samuel 10:5-6 awakens us to something new in God's economy for the nation of Israel. Prophecy, dreams and visions were extremely rare in the days of Samuel's youth (1 Samuel 3:1). The son of Hannah was later acknowledged as *the* prophet (cum king, priest and ruler) in charge of the nation. Then, of a sudden, in his mature years we are struck by this phrase; "… a group of prophets …" It is a striking introduction of future things to follow.

Let me shock many Christian and Hebrew scholars of the Old Testament (The Hebrew Bible) by stating as we start, that, to be strictly honest, there is no such phraseology as, *"Schools of the prophets"* used anywhere in the scripture. That statement is an absolute truth. Good translations deliver the phrase as "Sons of the Prophets, "Groups of the prophets", "Assembly of the prophets" or "Companies of the prophets." In the Hebrew, the word used in 1 Samuel 19:20 is "ahaqah" which means to assemble a company of people for whatever the cause of the gathering is about. So, from this "assembly of the prophets" the world of Biblical readers, scholars and preachers arrive at the conceptual idea of the "Schools of the Prophets." I merely want to make this point to distract people and scholars from the presupposed western or modern concept of "a school." I strongly carry this requirement to qualify what these gatherings and semi-permanent groups of prophets were all about.

These companies of prophets were the fruit of a genius-like insight to the workings of the Spirit of God. It is a concept that was created by the mastermind and creativity of the prophet Samuel. It seemed that men (and women?) who desired to be prophets gathered to learn the dynamics of receiving the word of God by the Spirit of God and to learn the ways of God also, seeking to be trained in divine matters by a senior prophet if there was one contemporary with their generation. They sought God and were anointed by the Spirit of God, as were people throughout the history of Israel. Certain men in most ages and all strata of Hebrew society were hungry for God and were themselves pursued by the Spirit of God.

Samuel had a lot of things militantly raging against him throughout his lifetime. He lived in days of moral, spiritual and educational darkness. He was brought up by Eli, who had a shocking record of a deep lack of parental skills and a profound deficit of spiritual insight. Samuel had two of the most godless men of his generation as foster brothers. These two men were so wicked the text of the Bible actually says that God wanted to kill them. Whoa! Get your head around that one.

To be frank, since Israel had left Egypt and sought to settle in Israel, Samuel was living in what was, conceivably the most chaotic and darkest days of the history of the nation of Israel thus far.

God was not in the picture for the vast majority of Israel. Occult-filled nations with demon-led religious practices had a heavy influence on the Children of Israel. The ten nations that surrounded their geographical position almost took over the spiritual life of Israel. The nation was leaderless, and what leaders they had were by most people's standards a bit south of pathetic and even further south in their weakness of character. The days were like night with thick, smothering, gloopy spiritual darkness.

In the midst of this darkness, Samuel was conceived and gestated by a dear godly woman, Hannah, who had been, prior to Samuel's conception, childless. His mother had prayed for a son, and when Eli had spoken to her, whether Eli thoughtlessly spoke to hide his embarrassment for accusing the prayerful woman of being drunk, or whether he was wilfully and consciously prophesying over the woman, I truly am not sure. But he stated in prophetic words, *"The Lord grant you what you have asked for",* not knowing what it was she had asked for. She had actually told Yahweh that if He gave her a son, she would give him back to God.

If a woman made such a vow in a similar context in the twenty-first century, I believe she would have been put into some secured mental home. But the vow meant that once baby Samuel was weaned off his mother's milk, he was taken off to the extremely old man Eli, placed in his care along with Eli's sons, two of the most godless men in Israel. And on top of all that, we are nowhere told that "Mrs Eli" was alive as aged Eli took charge of the child. Oh dear! Some could make a valid case to prove that this was child abuse in our generation. Logically, using empirical logic, the child had no chance.

However, what Samuel had going for him that was positive, far outweighed what was confronting him negatively. Yes! He had a godly and devoted mother who weaned him with deep love, and thereafter visited him once a year, having drowned Samuel's circumstance with prayer. Such a mother was undoubtedly a priceless encouragement and motivational factor in Samuel's life, footing everything he did while she lived. Most of all, we must take note, that from an early age, Samuel had a deeply personal acquaintance with Yahweh, God Almighty. As the old philosophical Christian cliché says, "One man with God is in the majority."

The listed characteristics of Samuel are endearing to say the least. He worshipped God as a child. He grew in favour with both God and man. He was loyal and committed to the old man, Eli. He wore a linen Ephod as he worked with Eli – the Ephod being a contemporary priest's outfit. He must surely have known that prophecy had been the means that gave Hannah the assurance she would have a child.

We are not told in the Bible when or how Samuel initiated the initial grouping of the prophets, and he seems to have based them all in comparatively short distances from his hometown from the beginning. Then later, in his lifetime, there was a kind of, "Central Office," set up at the Naioth in Ramah – full titled town of Ramathaim-Zophim. It was "Prophetic Headquarters" if you will.

What were the spiritual grounds of such a venture? What was the criteria for enrolment to the groups? Did they have any curriculum? What was the goal of these fellowships of kindred hearts?

In their gatherings, there seemed to be a general spirit of prophecy that would come upon all present. Needless to say, when the spirit fell on Saul his murderous thoughts toward David must have receded into the ether. I say this because when it occurred to Saul, David was present with Samuel.

There were dark days when there was no open vision prior to Samuel's birth. There were no prophets, no seers, no dreams or visionary insights in the hegemony that was the tribes of Israel. (I was on the cusp of writing "nation State of Israel, but they were far short of being a unified state at the closing days of the Judges.) In the Bible, before the days of Samuel, the word "prophet" very rarely occurs".

When the prophets gathered and worshipped, there occurred supernatural phenomena as they played musical instruments, danced, sang and prophesied, It quite clearly seems that people were "felled" when they came near to Samuel during these meetings of music and celebration. The so called "Schools of the prophets" had arrived.

DEFINING THE MEETINGS CONTENTS.

The group, the family, the party or whatever title was used was ***not an academic*** or syllabussed curriculum as we would know it, but experiential and a tutoring of what to do and how to handle oneself when under the anointing.

It was a bringing of the hungry into the "nabi" spirit and watching responses and character. Prophets were, are and always have been God's communication channels to people and the world. Jesus Christ is the prototype of all that prophesy and what the prophet is. Prophecy is the voice of the Holy Spirit. Prophets, and prophecy are undoubtedly special to the heart of God as with 2 Chron 20:20 and the divine explanation of each prophet's calling. Prophets are forth telling as well as foretelling, as well as history interpreting.

The prophetic schools were clearly seen to be the hothouses of prophetic iron sharpening prophetic iron. They were fertile wombs gestating divine guidance for the nation through several centuries of tumultuous history that was to follow. The fruit that blossomed from the offspring of these wombs was far reaching and deeply searching. It doesn't seem correct to refer to the prophets as a "guild", as most of them were "loners" who did not seem to relate to other prophetic persons as far as the biblical narrative reveals or withholds. So we shall simply refer to them as prophetic groups. These groups brought to birth the sum and substance of the divine guidance of the Hebrew people, which included the various characters and spiritual giants that fed Israel and Judah for centuries following Samuel's demise. Those groups that were initiated by the prophet Samuel were raw, estranged and fringed to society and were at first deeply influential and very dynamic. Birthed apart from, and clearly not part of, the institutionalised Mosaic sacrificial system as contained in the Pentateuch, they started, as it were, quite literally in the hometown of Samuel. It is clear that the groups were not part of the priestly institutions of Yahweh worship – although we need to add that several of the high-profile canonical prophets were indeed of the priestly Levitical line:

Jeremiah was a descendant of the priestly line of Abiathar, which can be traced back to Aaron. Jeremiah's priestly heritage is mentioned in his book (Jeremiah 1:1). Ezekiel was a priest and a prophet, specifically identified as the son of Buzi, a priest (Ezekiel 1:3). He was taken into exile in Babylon and prophesied there. Zechariah is also considered a prophet of the Lord and is identified as the son of Berechiah and grandson of Iddo, who was a priest (Zechariah 1:1). Malachi, while not explicitly detailed in his writings, some traditions and interpretations suggest that he may have had Levitical ties, as his name is associated with the priestly context.

IMMEDIATELY POST SAMUEL.

It was the separation of these organisms of spiritual life and power from what was nationally institutionalised religion that was their very strength. While Samuel was perceived as the "Grandmaster" of all that was prophetic during his lifetime, immediately after his demise, the groups seem to continue with a much lower profile. Probably, the characters concerned were finding their own new level without the kudos of having Samuel as their chief. Individuals like Gad and Nathan, who spoke into David's life with remarkable courage and frankness undoubtedly came out of the schools of the prophets and very possibly were introduced to David during David's brief time with Samuel at Naioth.

THROUGH TO ELIJAHS AND ELISHA'S DAY

From the death of Samuel through to the reign of Ahab and Jezebel, the schools of the prophets are simply not mentioned. In scripture we read of the existence of these schools next in the narratives of Elijah and Elisha. Thereafter, we are left to draw our own conclusions. Scholars join the dots of the groups from Samuel's day through to Elijah and Elisha's day.

ISAIAH'S AND JEREMIAH'S DAY

We then move on to Isaiah's disciples and the prophecies concerning drunken and debauched "prophets" in both Isaiah's and Jeremiah's day. Isaiah's disciples are never linked by academics as part of the scattered schools of the prophets. It seems logical, piecing the times that groups of prophets are referred to in the Old Testament scrolls, that the sharp and spiritual nature of the groups soaked into Israel's religious wallpaper.

JEREMIAH

By the time Jeremiah was prophetically in harness, in his heartbreaking twenty-third chapter, the great prophet is seemingly in tears as he tells us that his heart is broken because of the prophets of his era (23:9). His explanation suggests that his emotions were high because they claimed to handle the holy word of God yet were living unholy lives. Jeremiah responded to God, and his word as Isaiah did with great fear and trembling. In Jeremiah 23:29-32, Yahweh speaks through the prophet saying:

> *"Is not my word like fire,"* declares the LORD, *"and like a hammer that breaks a rock in pieces? Therefore,"* declares the LORD, *"I am against the prophets who steal from one another words supposedly from me. Yes,"* declares the LORD, *"I am against the prophets who wag their own tongues and yet declare, 'The LORD declares.' Indeed, I am against those who prophesy false dreams,"* declares the LORD. *They tell them and lead my*

people astray with their reckless lies, yet I did not send or appoint them. They do not benefit these people in the least," declares the LORD

(NIV) Jeremiah 23:29-32

My mental response to this passage is this. The men that Jeremiah is referring to simply cannot be labelled or given the title "Prophet." They are neither prophesying, nor teaching. They are lying and plagiarising each other whenever they believe somebody has said something that seems wise and prophetic.

But God rubbishes their words and their conduct. It is not of God, and therefore is not prophecy. So, how is it possible that Yahweh refers to them as prophets. And note it is clearly in the plural, suggesting to this writer that they were accumulated groups of, if not schools of the prophets. My own answer is simply that they were known as prophets in the public conception of things. They were accepted as prophets in the religious circles of the day. They were Temple prophets. They were the sad vestiges of the schools of the prophets that had become religious and "respectable" (I use the term loosely). They were religious officials. They each had a job without either calling or anointing. They were people who simply fancied themselves as a prophet. It was a good, respectable job for some. "Nice work if you can get it," sort of thing.

THE PLATEAUING OF THE SCHOOLS OF THE PROPHETS

The wild, revolutionary worshipping groups that were the offshoot of Samuel, and then fathered generations later under Elijah and Elisha, were only effective on their contemporary culture and politics. The story of calling fire from heaven was through the life of Elijah living at the peak of the prophetic spectrum. The prophets of the schools were in hiding, filled with fear because of the prophets that Jezebel had killed. Jezebel was clearly after anybody who belittled or relegated Baal.

The account from 1 Kings 22 when Jehoshaphat (King of Judea) and Ahab (king of Israel) were going to battle together reveals something of an indictment against the schools also, although it has to be noted that Elijah was still active when the battle for Ramoth-Gilead took place, so perhaps we shouldn't read too much into the absence of the schools when Jehoshaphat asks for somebody with a word from Yahweh. The very next verse tells us that Ahab had 400 prophets before him. In the presence of both kings, they ask the prophets if it is in God's plan for them to fight and regain Ramoth Gilead. As one would expect, if 400 men, all known as prophets, were asked a question of direction, they would all agree. Methinks one "loudmouth" among the 400 would speak up, and the other 399 would follow the loudmouth. So, predictably, it was a unanimous thumbs up for challenging the Syrians concerning the ownership of Ramoth-Gilead. Ahab is delighted.

Jehoshaphat, however, responds with a question that calls any reader to shout, "Ouch!" In my paraphrase, Jehoshaphat says, "That's wonderful, King Ahab! Really good! But is there not a prophet of Yahweh we could consult?" This query is a phenomenon. Jehoshaphat's statement presupposes that the 400 hailed by Ahab were not prophets of Yahweh, but perhaps of Baal. Clearly the account of Elijah calling fire from heaven in recent years gone by– a moment at which Ahab was present, did not have the impact on King Ahab *and his wife* as it has had on Christians for the last two thousand years. Ahab was still immersed in Baal idolatry. (Or was he meekly submitting to his Baal-worshipping wife?)

The extrapolation that I am suggesting is somewhat vindicated by what happens next. Ahab is forced to call a "prophet of Yahweh" named Micaiah. He knows what the 400 have said. Ahab's messenger who went to call Micaiah to the summit meeting, advised him to say the same as the other 400, and so told him what they had said.

One needs to look deeply to understand what happens. The King who speaks to him seems to be Jehoshaphat (The text does not tell us which king is speaking). Micaiah says, "Attack and be victorious. Yahweh will give Ramoth Gilead into the hands of the king." Wonderful. However, it seems clear to me that Micaiah was talking to Jehoshaphat and not to Ahab. I surmise this as a fact because Ahab was very annoyed, and says, like a spoilt child, to Jehoshaphat, "Didn't I tell you that he never prophesies anything good about me, but only bad?" This could only mean that Micaiah was addressing the king of Judah, ignoring the presence of Ahab the king of Israel.

Micaiah then tells an amazing story of how he was present when Yahweh sent a deceiving spirit to convince all the 400 prophets of Baal that Ahab would be victorious. The vivid word picture sees the man who was probably the leader of the 400 slap the face of Micaiah with the cynical and sarcastic remark, "Which way was the Spirit going when he told me to slap your face?" Micaiah told the big mouth that he would know the answer to his own question when he later goes to hide in his private room. Ahab ordered Micaiah to be put in prison, promising to deal with him when he returns from the fight. Micaiah answers Ahab with, "If you ever return safely, Yahweh has not spoken through me. Mark my words, all you people," addressing the 400 prophets of Baal.

THE SAD DECLINE OF THE PROPHETIC GROUPS IN JERUSALEM.

The thought that academics have applied to this subject leaves many of them wondering if any of the writing prophets came out of one of the prophetic schools. I am beginning to perceive that the revolutionary schools of the prophets died the death simply because they incredibly evolved to become part of the institution of formalised, dead "Yahweh worship" in Israel and Judah, and the greatest number of the schools were in the territory of the Northern Kingdom, meaning that much of the structure of the schools dissipated with the fall of Israel to the might of Assyria. I am becoming more and more convinced that these radical schools of raw spirituality and nation-directing prophetic output went out like a damp squid as they were, frankly, assimilated into the religious formalism of Hebrew religious culture.

They were similar to the radical ranting of Arthur Scargill in the UK, who entered public life in the mid-1980s as a far-left communist and who now luxuriates in his millionaire's home in upper-class London. In the days of the infamous miner's strike in Britain, the only thing that struck me about him was the awe and wonder of his seemingly rock-solid beliefs. Not that I believed them, but I was convinced he did. Yet time proved that he really did not believe any such thing. As it was with Scargill, so it was with many of the attendees of the schools of the prophets in Old Testament pre-587 B.C. days. The radical "far out" extreme schools of prophets, I fear, turned out to be like a wet kipper handshake as they soaked into the landscape of dead religiosity that was the very terminal Hebrew disease that was epidemically raging in the days of the pre-exilic writing prophets. The dynamic, thriving, revolutionary beast became a dead dog on the streets. Isaiah, who seemingly always stood alone apart from his disciples, separated himself from what were seemingly "temple prophets." Isaiah's reference to their pride and arrogance, while they were being known generally as both drunkards and prophets, were spoken against by the Spirit of God in Isaiah 28:7. A generation after Isaiah, the prophet Jeremiah speaks as the very voice of God in Jerusalem and cries:

> *[11] "Both prophet and priest are godless; even in my temple I find their wickedness," declares the LORD.*
> *[12] "Therefore their path will become slippery; they will be banished to darkness and there they will fall. I will bring disaster on them in the year they are punished," declares the LORD.*
>
> *[13] "Among the prophets of Samaria I saw this repulsive thing: They prophesied by Baal and led my people Israel astray.*
>
> *[14] And among the prophets of Jerusalem I have seen something horrible: They commit adultery and live a lie. They strengthen the*

hands of evildoers, so that not one of them turns from their wickedness. They are all like Sodom to me; the people of Jerusalem are like Gomorrah." ^{15} Therefore this is what the LORD *Almighty says concerning the prophets: "I will make them eat bitter food and drink poisoned water, because from the prophets of Jerusalem ungodliness has spread throughout the land." ^{16} This is what the* LORD *Almighty says: "Do not listen to what the prophets are prophesying to you; they fill you with false hopes. They speak visions from their own minds, not from the mouth of the* LORD. *(NIV)*

Jeremiah 23:11-16

It seems clear to this writer that these were men who had a job title as "Prophet" and a job description that comprised of them being commissioned to speak the word of God at all times, but clearly did not know how to, or perhaps more so that they did not want to. These men were cursed for defaming the high office and function of a prophet of Yahweh and were about to pay the price for their blasphemous, destructive ways.

The prophetic movement initiated by Samuel was by its very nature "charismatic" with its frenzy of music and dance that were indulged into the point where the Spirit of God brought the word to the prophetic scholars. I can only conclude that some strange mentality concerning the Holy Spirit and human spirituality in general led people to believe that the music and the dance and the frenzy were necessary to enter the realm of the Spirit. Perhaps in those days this was true. The enduement of divine power and the vindicated and verified words from God gave the group the authority to speak to those who were in high priestly authority or even the social hierarchy. The deadly disease within the religious practice of the Levitical priesthood was, strangely, the power that turned the schools into a kind of official institution that was carnally standardized and regulated by the officials of state and religion. They, therefore became tamed and were made mute and were as non-inspired as it was once inspired. It obviously became a place for personal battles of egocentric people. In Jeremiah 6: 11-13 Yahweh confides to the prophet that this is exactly what was happening amongst the "professional prophets" in Jerusalem.

The moment, whenever it was, that the wild and dangerous prophets became a distinct professional class was the day that the death sentence was announced on the schools of the prophets. It was clearly this evolutionary process of survival of the most prophetically unfit that killed the schools off and did great damage to the general knowledge of prophets and prophecy in both Isaiah's and Jeremiah's day and the years in between. This process was affecting the schools of the prophets even in days as early as in the prophet Elijah. It seems that while Jezebel ruled and Ahab waspishly had his tantrums concerning his authority, there were 7000 of God's true prophets that were actually in action. Only Elijah was authentically free, doing what prophets do. Somehow, after Elijah had called the fire down, the schools of the prophets seem to have come out of hiding and had gone back to their institutions. However, when the institutional prophets prophetically knew that Elijah was about to be translated to heaven and even told Elisha so, they all stayed in their official country seats and did not even trouble themselves to follow and to see Elijah fly home, apart from the school that was near to the site of Elijah's ascension. Something has never seemed right to me in that story – a story I have fascinatedly read over and over again for the last 57-plus years.

The people in the schools at the beginning were clearly the exceptional and the radical. When the mundane and commonplace finally got around to accepting the schools of the prophets, the exceptional ceased to be exceptional. From that moment on, Yahweh sought a new prophetic expression apart from the schools. The product was the likes of Isaiah, Joel, Amos, etc., and all the men we refer to as "the writing prophets".

If one was to scour the biblical statements to see to what level the "institutional schools of the prophets" had dropped to, one needs to be prepared to be shocked. These men who were, in presumption, to humanly control what they said was God's word were blatantly poking out the eyes of their own understanding as to the very nature of the God they were serving, or, if *not* serving, in whose name they were speaking. They were using God's word for their own ends and if not strictly for themselves, for other human ends (Jeremiah 23:14,17 and 6:13). Their so-called prophetic words were mingled and mixed like some pharmaceutical concoction, with lies and mysteriously cryptic and dark dreams that even fooled themselves (Jeremiah 5:31, 23:26 onwards). It would seem that they also used prophecy as if they were some democratically appointed figures looking for popular acclaim by telling them out-and-out lies in the name of Yahweh (Jeremiah 14:13. 23:14). This kind of thing was even seen by Ezekiel when in Babylon (Ezekiel 13:1-6). It must have been gratifying for such false "prophets" to know that the common people were so ignorant of the books of Moses that they were not aware that when any man, claiming to be a prophet spoke, he was by God's own statute made captive to that word which he had spoken, whatever it was, and was threatened with death if anything was added or his words were proved to be false (Deuteronomy 18:20). If that fact was part of the general knowledge of the Hebrew nation, many a so-called prophet would have been stoned to death early in their career.

In general, the liquid life of the schools of the prophets solidified into religious congealed death.

"Her leaders pronounce judgment for a bribe, her priests instruct for a price and her prophets divine for money. Yet they lean on the Lord saying, "Is not the Lord in our midst? Calamity will not come upon us." (Micah 3:11).

"…they continually mocked the messengers of God, despised His words and scoffed at His prophets, until the wrath of the Lord arose against His people, until there was no remedy." (2 Chronicles 36:16)

For the Lord has poured over you a spirit of deep sleep. He has shut your eyes, the prophets, and He has covered your heads, the seers. (Isaiah 29:10)

We are talking, of course, of what happens to any revivalist movement in the course of its history. I use the word "revivalist" very loosely, whether referring to spiritual, political or social movements. Behind the initial burst of life, radicalism and exceptional leaders and new groups - with the fresh thoughts and philosophies, lurks the horrific yet expected danger that the exceptional and "far out extremes" will be transformed and diluted into the commonplace, mediocre and mainstream. That gloriously violent jump into something new and hitherto unknown, the defiance of all established custom, becomes diluted and runs out of steam and is thereafter replaced by the harmless choice of nothing more than a straightforward new profession. A routine day in a well-used office takes the place of wild days of new experimentation and hacking one's way through the jungle of opposition. Those that once opposed the movement are now part of it having not moved an inch towards the movement in their thinking. Group conformism and the technique of public speaking takes the place for the wild preparation of the prophetic atmosphere and the receiving of an anointing from above, together with an inner compulsion to prophecy. The whole thing becomes dominated by human thought and committees after having been birthed in wild individuality and deep relationships with the Almighty.

God's answer was to raise up individuals and not schools and groups. Thus, we have our heroes like Isaiah.

THE FINAL DEMISE OF THE GROUPS AND "SCHOOLS" OF PROPHETS

After ploughing through the book of Jeremiah, we learn that right up to the Babylonian breaching of Jerusalem's walls, there were false prophets peddling their wares.

"The prophets are as wind, and the word is not in them. Thus, it will be done to them!" (Jeremiah 5:13) "The prophets prophesy falsely, and the priests' rule on their own authority; And My people love it so!" Jeremiah 5:31

"Therefore, thus says the Lord of hosts concerning the prophets 'Behold, I am going to feed them wormwood And make them drink poisonous water, for from the prophets of Jerusalem Pollution has gone forth into all the land.'" Jeremiah 23:15

Jeremiah 23:21. "I did not send these prophets, But they ran. I did not speak to them, But they prophesied."

Jeremiah 23:31. "Behold, I am against the prophets," declares the Lord, "who use their tongues and declare, 'The Lord declares.'

Jeremiah 27:18. "But if they are prophets, and if the word of the Lord is with them, let them now entreat the Lord of hosts that the vessels which are left in the house of the Lord, in the house of the king of Judah and in Jerusalem may not go to Babylon."

Jeremiah 29:8. "For thus says the Lord of hosts, the God of Israel, 'Do not let your prophets who are in your midst and your diviners, deceive you, and do not listen to the dreams which they dream."

THE INSTITUTIONALISATION AND NOMINALITY OF THE SCHOOLS OF THE PROPHETS

The groups made prophetic things a profession. The profession of prophecy became a guild. The guild became tribalism. The tribes were paid for "the word of God", and the kings and the people asked for words that the tribal members could not deliver. Where money is involved, anybody could apply for a job and become part of the group. There were always prophets in harness throughout Hebrew history through to the 587 BC exile, but there were "loners" apart from the "prophetic groups" that weren't prophets. We don't even have any evidence that contemporaries like Isaiah, Amos, and Micah ever grouped or shared with each other.

Like the Lutherans, Methodists, Congregationalists, Baptists, Evangelicals and Pentecostals, followed by the Charismatics in the church history of the last 3 or 4 centuries, movements that explode as radical spiritual revolutionists for Christ, within a generation or two having been perceived as counter culturalists leading people into a "new world" of sorts, become integrated with the culture that they came to birth defying. Methodists, in Wesley's time, were seen as what we would today refer to as "para-church" and were so successful and thorough in their proselytising that within 80-90 years, they were indeed part of the religious wallpaper of Britain. The revolution has, over the centuries, slowed down to a steady progression that begins to blend in with the entire Christian scenario. In other words, the revolutionary Methodist army of Christ became integrated into the society which they started off wanting to change.

The schools of the prophets who were at first living in a sort of campus outside of society, became institutionalised and part of the dead religious culture. In fact, after the demise of Elisha, we read nothing about "schools of the prophets," but there are lots of statements, both poetic and prose, about how many of them were drunks (Jeremiah 13:13), liars (Isaiah 9:15. Jeremiah5:31) deceitful (Jeremiah 8:10.), saying things that people would pay to hear (Isaiah 30:10. Jeremiah 6:13. Micah 3:11). There is much spoken by the pre-exilic prophets that reveal plainly that a vast number of "prophets" lived as an integral part of the sinful society, with all its evil goings on. This was the society that the original tenets of the prophetic schools were striking at. Prophets had sadly become institutionalised in the context of Judah. Society had been ravaged and removed in the Northern kingdom.

2 Kings 17:13 informs us that many paid and institutionalised prophets were not prophets at all, while the true prophets spoke against idolatry. This spiritual and moral fall of the sons of the

prophets was the very reason given for Israel's deportation, says this verse of scripture.

The LORD warned Israel and Judah through all his prophets and seers: "Turn from your evil ways. Observe my commands and decrees, in accordance with the entire Law that I commanded your ancestors to obey and that I delivered to you through my servants the prophets. **2 Kings 17:13**

The unknown issue is whether or not the schools of the prophets totally disintegrated in 722 BC with the exiling of the Northern kingdom, or did they simply move down to Jerusalem, where many prophets seemed to make a living as "professional prophets"?

The biblical scrolls are silent after Samuel, concerning the numbers within the groups of prophets, until we arrive at 1 Kings 18:4. "… when Jezebel destroyed the prophets of the Lord, Obadiah took a hundred prophets and hid them by fifties in a cave and provided them with bread and water." Queen Jezebel had an unlisted number of prophets put to death. How many survivors were left is not stated. We are told, however, that a man named Obadiah sheltered some prophets. This man, Ahab's right-hand servant, later informs Elijah, "… I hid a hundred prophets of the Lord by fifties in a cave, and provided them with bread and water?" (1 Kings 18:13)

Later when Elisha was following Elijah, immediately prior to his rapture, the group of prophets said they had, "50 strong men" (2 Kings 2:16). These passages of scripture show that the groups/sons of the prophets were not only living in bands in different locations, but that these groups comprised considerable numbers. In the days of Elisha (post Elijah), a man brought food that Elisha suggested being placed before the sons of the prophets, to which the man responded with "What! Should I set this before 100 men?"

THE VARIOUS GROUPS OF PROPHETS THAT AROSE IN THE EARLY DAYS

Where were these schools of the prophets? How many were there? As to their locations or campuses, we know of several.

1. **Ramah** was Samuel's home. It was the base within Samuel's regular circuit. "His settled home was at Ramahthaim-Zophar, and there he judged Israel: building an altar to Yahweh." (1 Samuel 7:17). It has to be noted that Ramah as a centre for the bands of prophets is not mentioned after Samuel's death. Whether or not it continued at the Naioth after the great man's departure is up for open discussion.

2. **Gilgal** also had a campus for the prophetic bands. In 1 Samuel 10:8, Samuel's words to Saul were, "You shall go down before me to Gilgal". The resulting prophesying of Saul "among the prophets" in the geolocation of Gibeah suggests that, in Samuel's day at least, a school of the prophets existed. The fact that Samuel paid annual visits to Gilgal in his circuit as judge, leader and prophet adds weight to that suggestion. Only in the days of Elijah and Elisha is the Gilgal campus referred to again, and that is around a century and a half later. (2 Kings 2:1) The much-discussed final walk together of Elijah as master and Elisha as mentoree began from Gilgal. This writer would suggest the idea that before his departure, Elijah was visiting certain campuses to deliver final lectures, lessons or whatever it was that Elijah ministered within the schools. They visited 2 other schools on this "final" walk. (2 Kings 2:2,4 and 5) Elisha revisited Gilgal several years later (2 Kings 4:38). While healing a poisoned pot of food, we are told that there were at least 100 "scholars" at the Gilgal school

3. **Bethel**. We are not specifically told that there was a campus here in Samuel's day (1 Samuel 10:3), but it was clearly a religious centre, be it for idolatry as well as for true worship. In the days of

"Jeroboam the son of Nebat," an old prophet lived there while longing for things to be in the days of his youth. (1 Kings 13:11) Referring again to Elijah's last day before translation, the master and future prophet passed through Bethel. Elisha "went up from there to Bethel". (2 Kings 2:23)

4. **Jericho** also held campus for a prophetic school. This was the third stopping place for Elijah and Elisha on that destined world-changing walk. Before the invention of telescopic glasses, or binoculars, crossings of the Jordan, and indeed the viewing of Elijah's ascension to the glories of God were made from the site of their base. (2 Kings 2:4-7). Fifty of the group watched the two walk down to the river and beyond to the eastern bank. We are clear that there was an established school of the prophets at Jericho. The expansion of the group at Jericho may be soundly concluded from 2 Kings 6:1-2 where we are told that they had grown in numbers beyond the capacity of their "present building". The days of Elisha were obviously days of considerable growth. The fame of Elisha brought out the desire for the word of God among the youngsters of Israel. We are not told of any females at the schools apart from the wives of one or two of the prophets. Elisha clearly spent lots of time with the people at the prophetic schools.

5. **Carmel.** Again, this assertion is extrapolated rather than specifically stated. In 1 Kings 2, we find that Elisha, on his return from the Jordan and Jericho, "went up from there to Bethel" (2 Kings 2:23) and "from there he went to Mount Carmel" (2 Kings 2:25). Added to that, when the Shunamite's son had died, "she went and came to the man of God, Elisha, at Mount Carmel." (2 Kings 4:25). Summarily, this must have been one of his regular visits, because it was "neither new-moon, nor sabbath." (2 Kings 4:23). That comment made by the Shunamite's husband suggests also that Elisha held special gatherings at places other than the schools on those special occasions of the calendar. One scholar suggests that a campus at Carmel may have been chosen as a

centre for the sons of the prophets in remembrance of the mighty battle between Elijah and the 400 prophets of Baal at the site (1 Kings 18). Sounds like an intelligent proposition.

6. **Mizpah.** 1 Samuel 7:16 says, "He used to go annually on a circuit to Bethel, Gilgal, and Mizpah, and he judged Israel in all these places." Perhaps this suggestion stretches things a little. Nothing but this verse validates my inclusion of this location as a possible base for one of the schools of the prophets.

7. **Samaria.** 2 Kings 2:23 states, "And he went up from thence unto Bethel: ..." and verse 25 adds, "And he went from thence to mount Carmel, and from thence he returned to Samaria." At Jericho, Bethel, and undoubtedly Carmel, Elisha had already visited the schools of the prophets. Samaria was, at least, part of his life and his home (2 Kings 6:32). Samuel had opened his initial and greatest school in his home at the Naioth in Ramah, so it is logical to see how straightforward it would be for Elisha to have a home at Samaria opening his doors for prospective future prophets and aspiring men of God. We discover in 1 Kings 18:4, during the persecutions of the prophets by Jezebel, that, "... when Jezebel cut off the prophets of the LORD, Obadiah took a hundred prophets, and hid them by fifty in a cave, and fed them with bread and water." Years later, at this same place, when Ahab of Israel and Jehoshaphat of Judah were making war with Ramoth-Gilead (1 Kings 22:1-6), "the king of Israel gathered the prophets together, about 400 men." These passages in their combination, reveal that there were large numbers of prophets at Samaria. Thus, this writer extrapolates that such a number were members of a school under the direct authority of Elisha, whose residence was in Samaria itself.

The fact that the schools dwelt apart and in their own buildings is qualified by other passages of scripture.

a. I read, in 1 Samuel 19:18-19, that when David fled to Ramah, "David fled, ... and came to Samuel at Ramah (the town or city) and told him all that Saul had done to him. And he and Samuel went and dwelt in the Naioth (the college campus). And it was told Saul, saying, Behold, David is at Naioth (the college campus and home of Samuel) in Ramah (the town)."

b. 2 Kings 6:1-2. "And the sons of the prophets said unto Elisha ... the place where we dwell with you is too small for us. Let us go ... unto Jordan, and take every man a beam, and let us make us a place there, where we may dwell." This suggests that the college campus at Jericho relocated slightly, moving closer to the Jordan Riverbank.

c. 2 Kings 4:38-41. "Elisha came again to Gilgal: ... and the sons of the prophets were sitting before him: and he said unto his servant, Set on the great pot, and seethe pottage for the sons of the prophets." The school lived and ate together.

We conclude from these three passages that in various locations, prophets were living in community. Some, within the groups were married.

THE "TEACHING" FACULTIES OF THE SCHOOLS OF THE PROPHETS

We know nothing beyond three great prophets, who were, by default, the teachers at the schools of the prophets. Samuel, Elijah and Elisha.

(A) **Samuel**. "... They saw the group of prophets prophesying, and Samuel standing and presiding over them, the Spirit of God came on the messengers of Saul; and they also prophesied." If they had anybody else as teacher, we know nothing. Samuel went from year to year in circuit to Bethel, to Gilgal and to Mizpah, and he judged Israel in those places. Whether all other locations were offshoots of Ramah at the

Naioth, or whether there were other prophets, we are sadly unable to affirm or deny.

(B) **Elijah.** It was only in Elijah's last days that we have evidence of Elijah's relationship to the schools. 2 Kings 2:1-8 tells us that he was at Gilgal, Bethel and Jericho. Yahweh had sent him to these places, evidently to inform them of his forthcoming ascension. Or perhaps Elijah was simply making one of his circuitous visits and the prophetic scholars had received by the Spirit that Elijah was about to be taken from them.

(C) **Elisha.** Elisha was acknowledged by all as Elijah's successor. The text suggests that the prophet spent most of his prophetic life, post Elijah, at the various schools of the prophets. If Elisha lived emulating his former master, this would vindicate the writer's thought that Elijah spent more time at the schools than the biblical scrolls tell us off. Reading through every reference to Elisha's life, we see him staying at Jericho, Bethel, Carmel and Samaria (2 Kings 2). Gilgal (2 Kings 4:38), then Carmel again (2 Kings 4:25), and Jericho once more (2 Kings 6:1-7). He obviously cared for the families of the prophets (2 Kings 4:1-7). While carrying the burden and responsibility of the entire kingdom of Israel, he was pastorally vigilant over hundreds of prophets.

The respect given to these three prophets is shown in the terminology of honour and esteem they were shown. "Father" -1 Samuel 10:10, 2 Kings 3:12. "Master" -2 Kings 2:3, 5, 16, 2 Kings 6:5. "Man of God" – 2 Kings 4:40. See in comparison 2 Kings 2:15, 2 Kings 4:38.

CURRICULUM?

Intelligent research and extrapolation leads us to suggest that:

1. **TORAH.** The Law must have been taught, for nearly all prophet's directive words were based on the Mosaic statements of law and

Levitical ceremonies. For prophets to speak of the uniqueness of Israel in relationship to Yahweh and for Elijah to have a solid reason why Naboth was right to attempt to keep his land and why Ahab was unlawfully wanting to buy Naboth's garden, required sound knowledge of the law from the Pentateuch.

2. **PROPHESYING: ITS PRACTICE AND GROUNDS.** This issue cannot be overstated. When newly anointed Saul initially met the bands of prophets coming down from the hill of God, they were prophesying. (1 Samuel 10:5) When he met them in Gilgal, the Spirit of God came upon him, and he himself prophesied. When the three military detachments came to Ramah in order to arrest David, they all prophesied when they engaged with Samuel, presiding over the active worship, singing, dancing and prophesying of the group. The dancing and the euphoria were undoubtedly a physically active and exhausting style of worship. Saul was so exhausted he lay down and slept (or prophesied) a day and a night.

3. **MUSIC.** 1 Samuel 10:5 gives us insight into the use of music. Psaltery, timbrel, pipe and harp indicate that the music could have been quite lively. "Happy Clappy" even. Music was utilised in Elisha's prophetic ministry (2 Kings 3:15). Only a few years after Samuel's death, David and his captains separated certain sons of Asaph (Heman and Jeduthun) for them to prophesy with Harps, psalteries and cymbals (1 Chronicles 25:1-7). There is scholarly debate as to whether that phrase means that they sang prophetically while using the aforementioned instruments to back the singing or whether the prophetic content was manifested in the playing of the harps, psalteries, and cymbals. The latter idea seems remarkably creative and artistic and would demand of a supernatural clarity in the instrument playing for the "plain people on the street" to understand what prophetic word was being played. It was so important as to their form of music that there were 288 men to do the job adequately in David's day before the Temple was built (1 Chronicles 25:7). Note that David was present

with Samuel for two weeks in Samuel's lifetime. It is evident that music was an important and large part of the King's worship and prophetic training, and the inter-relationship of the two were well within the reach and hearing of the sons of the prophets. "Without doubt, these sons of the prophets composed sacred poetry and music and used them widely in their praise and worship."

4. **CURRENT ISRAELI AFFAIRS.** Perhaps the student prophets were instructed in the religious and political matters of the times in which they lived. They learned of the wisdom of their master and were clearly abreast of all that was going on in the various king's courts in the area. (2 Kings 4:38)". (Prof Ira M. Price MA) "It is clear after a thorough read of the Hebrew Bible, that many a Hebrew prophet was correcting or even initiating political personnel and direction."

5. **ON THE GROUND.** The "sons of the prophets" (students) at the "schools of the prophets" were expected at these schools to:

    i. **Study and Worship.** (1 Samuel 10:10-13.1 Samuel 19:18-24) The insights and motivations of Samuel must have been a major tuition aspect of the school groups of the prophets. David lived with Samuel for only a couple of weeks where the great prophet would have imparted to David a whole paradigm of what and how to rule, worship and the importance of a relevant contemporary word from God.

    ii. **Run errands and Messages** for the Senior Prophet. Read 2 Kings 9:1-12. In the case of anointing Jehu to be king, Elisha sent a young man, "even the young man, the prophet" (2 Kings 9:4)

    iii. **Regular duties of a prophet.** 1 Kings 20: 29-34 and especially verse 35. "A certain man of the sons of the prophets" had his own anointing and word from God to deliver.

6. **MEANS OF INCOME.** It would seem that the charity of the public of Israel was a sustaining resource of the schools of the prophets. 2 Kings 4 is a powerful insight. The poverty of one of the wives of the prophets (1-7), the charity of the Shunamite woman (8-11) and the gratis food harvested from the fields (4:39) reveal the normal course of things, I believe. The dearth around Gilgal may have induced the farmer to aid Elisha and these sons of the prophets, but the aid is received as a matter of course and justifies the supposition that this was not unusual. The claims that Gehazi falsely made towards Naaman, even though he was a "foreigner" from a different culture, endorse the scenario I am suggesting here. Naaman was only too willing to give to the upkeep of the prophet.

29

THE EXHAUSTED PROPHET FLEES WANTING TO DIE. (1 Kings 19:1-9)

This passage of the Elijah narrative presents a pivotal and extremely moving moment in the life of the man from Tishbe. It hits us head-on, revealing the naked horror of the profound psychological, spiritual and physical drain he was immersed into, following the incredible confrontation with the prophets of Baal on Mount Carmel. This passage reveals not only Elijah's physical exhaustion but also his emotional and spiritual desolation in the face of a death threat from Jezebel. The raw reality of Elijah's situation allows everybody to see what a stretch and fatiguing job of work he put himself through on carmel. And if we can for a moment forget the debate on the morality of slaying 450 men, think of the physical effort and the Trauma of being the executioner of 450 human beings. Elijah was "done" before Jezebel's message had arrived. Through this, we gain insight into the complexities of prophetic ministry, the human condition, and God's sustaining grace.

To understand the gravity of the Tishbite's situation, it is needful to consider the broader context of his action. Elijah had just experienced an incredibly awe-inspiring supernatural victory over the demons of Baalism and the prophets of Baal (1 Kings 18). Elijah's lengthy preparation of the altar and the sacrifice in the build-up to the fall of the fire from heaven. God demonstrated His power through fire from heaven, licking up even the huge amount of water on the sacrifice and around the altar. The exhaustion was total, impacting body, soul and spirit.

Things, however, were swiftly overshadowed by Jezebel's vengeful threat: *"May the gods deal with me, be it ever so severely, if by this time tomorrow I do not make your life like that of one of them"* (1 Kings 19:2). This murderous declaration not only signifies a personal vendetta, but also reflects the ongoing spiritual battle between Yahweh and the pagan worship of Baal that Jezebel fervently promoted.

1 Kings 19:3 sees Elijah's immediate reaction to Jezebel's threat: *"Elijah was afraid and ran for his life."* This response is telling of his mental state. Despite witnessing God's miraculous power and the public defeat of Baal, despite experiencing Yahweh's protection for the entire three and a half years of maintaining silence and secrecy, Elijah succumbs to fear - a very destructive human emotion. His flight to Beersheba, where he leaves his servant behind, indicates a desire for solitude and not wanting to see or talk to people. Perhaps the response spurted from feelings of isolation and despair, uselessness and helplessness. The prophet's exhaustion becomes increasingly evident as he journeys into the wilderness, where he ultimately collapses under a broom tree.

The Tishbite's fear is compounded by feelings of inadequacy and doubt. He expresses a sense of failure, lamenting, "I have had enough, Lord. Take my life; I am no better than my ancestors" (1 Kings 19:4.). This plea reveals deep-seated hopelessness - Elijah feels he simply cannot continue, overwhelmed by the weight of his prophetic calling and the seemingly insurmountable opposition he faces, as well as just being drained throughout the experience on Carmel. His decision to flee rather than confront Jezebel highlights a significant moment of vulnerability for a prophet who had previously displayed unwavering courage.

In verses 5-8, we witness a remarkable shift. As Elijah rests under the broom tree, an angel of the Lord appears from "elsewhere," providing sustenance in the form of food and drink. God was on his case. He had Elijah's file on His desk. This divine intervention was pivotal. It signifies God's awareness of Elijah's physical and emotional state. The angel's instructions to eat and drink emphasize the importance of physical care, suggesting that spiritual battles cannot be fought effectively without addressing our physical needs.

Elijah's subsequent journey of forty days and nights to Horeb (Mount Sinai) mirrors the Israelites' own forty-year journey in the wilderness, representing a time of reflection and renewal. At Horeb, Elijah seeks refuge in a cave, where he experiences a profound encounter with God. Here, God asks, "What are you doing here, Elijah?" (1 Kings 19:9, NIV). This question is not merely a logistical inquiry; it invites Elijah to reflect on his circumstances and emotions, encouraging a deeper engagement with his fears and doubts.

Elijah's response reveals his sense of isolation, loneliness and a feeling of loss. We see his sense of desolation and defeat contradicting what his faith had always told him: "I have been very zealous for the Lord God Almighty. The Israelites have rejected your covenant, torn down your altars, and put your prophets to death" (1 Kings 19:10.). He is wondering what life is all about. He is in distress because he didn't stay long enough to discover the results of repentance amongst those who were present at Carmel. His lament underscores a perceived failure—he believes his efforts have been in vain, and he is the last of the prophets, facing annihilation. This moment of vulnerability is significant; it highlights a common theme in the lives of many leaders and prophets who grapple with the weight of their responsibilities.

God's reply to Elijah is instructive. Rather than providing immediate reassurance or a direct answer, God instructs Elijah to go out and stand on the mountain in the presence of the Lord. The subsequent elements - wind, earthquake, and fire—represent powerful manifestations of God's presence, yet it is in the "gentle whisper" that Elijah truly encounters the divine (1 Kings 19:11-12). This gentle whisper symbolizes how God often operates in subtlety rather than grandiosity, reminding Elijah that His presence is not always synonymous with overwhelming power.

1 Kings 19:1-9 serves as a poignant exploration of the exhaustion and despair that can accompany prophetic ministry. The public sees a confident, fresh, man of strength and confidence. Nobody sees the

brokenness before God on his knees and/or his prostration in prayer. Elijah's flight from Jezebel reflects a profound human struggle with fear, isolation, and feelings of inadequacy. Yet, through divine intervention, God addresses both Elijah's physical and spiritual needs, leading him toward renewal and purpose.

This invites us to recognize the importance of self-care, the reality of spiritual battles, and the assurance that God meets us in our moments of vulnerability. Ultimately, it reinforces the notion that even the most faithful servants of God can experience deep despair, yet divine grace and presence are ever available, offering hope and restoration in times of need.

30

THE WORD OF THE LORD CAME AGAIN.
(1 Kings 19:10-18)

The phrase "The Word of the Lord came again" resonates and repeats deeply within the biblical account of Elijah. This phrase not only marks significant moments in Elijah's journey but also encapsulates profound theological, psychological, and existential themes that speak to the human experience. The repeated use of this phrase throughout the Elijah biblical biography - approximately eight times - serves as a literary and spiritual motif that invites reflection on divine communication, prophetic authority, personal renewal, and the ongoing relationship between God and His servants.

The phrase "The Word of the Lord came again" (a different translation of the statement) underlines the nature of divine revelation in the life of the prophet of God. Throughout the scriptures, the recurring theme of God speaking to His chosen individuals signifies not just a one-time communication but an ongoing dialogue. In 1 Kings 19, after Elijah's dramatic encounter with the prophets of Baal and his subsequent flight from Jezebel, the phrase serves as a pivotal transition point. It is an indication that despite his despair and sense of isolation, God is still actively engaging with Elijah.

"The word of the Lord came to him"	1 Kings 17:2
"The word of the Lord came to him"	1 Kings 17:8
"The word of the Lord came to Elijah"	1 Kings 18:1
"The word of the Lord came to him"	1 Kings 19:5
"The word of the Lord came to Elijah"	1 Kings 21:17
"The word of the Lord came to Elijah the Tishbite"	1 Kings 21:28

"The angel of the Lord came to Elijah" 2 Kings 1:3

"The angel of the Lord said unto Elijah" 2 Kings 1:15

This divine communication reflects the broader theological principle that God is actively involved in the lives of His people and His prophets. The phrase signifies assurance and reaffirmation of purpose, emphasizing that God does not abandon His messengers, even in moments of doubt and fear – doubt and fear-induced because of the servant's body, soul and spirit being over-taxed in serving his Lord and King. This is crucial for understanding the nature of prophetic ministry: it is not merely about delivering messages but about cultivating an ever-deepening relationship with the Divine.

Note that Elijah's narrative is marked by extreme highs and equally extreme lows - culminating in the extreme triumph over the prophets of Baal with undoubted popular adulation that the Bible does not refer to. This was followed by descending into an abyss of despair after Jezebel's threats. The phrase "The Word of the Lord came" again is particularly significant within this psychological context. Elijah's experience reflects the profound human struggle with anxiety, fear, and feelings of inadequacy, especially after a moment of victory, followed by a death threat from Jezebel.

When God speaks to Elijah after his flight to Mount Horeb, it is a moment of restoration. The repetition of divine communication serves as a reminder that God understands Elijah's emotional and spiritual turmoil. It is in these unshielded moments that God's voice becomes crucial; it is not a voice of condemnation but one of reassurance and purpose. The significance of the phrase lies in its ability to convey God's empathy, suggesting that even the most faithful servants will experience moments of doubt and despair.

The repeated assertion that "The Word of the Lord came," also highlights the authority and responsibility inherent in prophetic ministry. When God speaks to Elijah, it signifies not only personal guidance but also the restoration of his prophetic mission. Elijah is instructed to anoint Hazael as king over Aram, Jehu as king over Israel, and Elisha as his own successor.

This moment is pivotal; it shifts Elijah's focus from his personal crisis to the broader implications of his prophetic role. This encapsulates the notion that prophetic authority is not merely about individual experiences but about personal responsibility.

Elijah's mission extends beyond his own struggles; it involves the fate of nations and the spiritual direction of Israel. The Word of the Lord serves as a catalyst for action, emphasizing that divine communication comes with the expectation of response. Thus, the phrase implies a call to re-engage with the world, to act decisively in accordance with God's will, and to fulfil one's divinely appointed role.

The implications of "The Word of the Lord came again" extend beyond Elijah's individual narrative, suggesting a broader theological and communal context. The multiple instances of divine communication throughout the narrative of the man from Tishbe reflect the continuity of God's relationship with His people. Each time God speaks, it reinforces the covenantal bond and the ongoing nature of His promises.

This continuity is significant in understanding the historical and communal ramifications of prophetic ministry. The repeated phrase invites the reader to consider how God's Word has been a guiding force throughout Israel's history. It emphasizes that prophets are not isolated figures; they are part of a larger narrative that includes the community of believers. By re-establishing communication with Elijah, God reaffirms His commitment to Israel, reinforcing the idea that divine guidance is available to all who seek it.

The phrase also invites philosophical reflection on the nature of faith. In moments of despair, such as those experienced by Elijah, faith can feel tenuous or even absent. Yet, when "The Word of the Lord came again," it signifies a renewal of faith and a re-establishment of hope. This interplay between doubt and divine communication highlights the complexities of belief in the face of adversity.

The philosophical implications extend to the understanding of how individuals navigate their spiritual journeys. The phrase suggests that faith is not a static condition but a dynamic process characterized by ebbs and flows in the midst of overall growth and development. Just as Elijah experienced profound lows following his triumph, individuals today may encounter spiritual crises that challenge their beliefs as Elijah's were challenged under the broom tree. God's persistent communication serves as a reminder that faith can be rekindled, that divine guidance is always available, and that hope can emerge from despair.

The phrase "The Word of the Lord came again" is rich with significance, ramifications, and corollaries that resonate across time and context. It encapsulates the nature of divine communication, the psychological landscape of prophetic ministry, the authority and responsibility of the prophet, and the communal and philosophical dimensions of faith. In the life of Elijah, this phrase serves as a poignant reminder that God is continually present, actively engaging with His people, and offering hope and restoration, even in the darkest moments.

As contemporary readers engage with this narrative, I invite them to reflect on their own experiences of divine communication and the ways in which they respond to God's call. The enduring relevance of this phrase lies in its ability to inspire hope, reaffirm purpose, and encourage a deeper understanding of the relationship between the Divine and humanity. In a world marked by uncertainty and despair, the assurance that "The Word of the Lord came again" resonates as a powerful affirmation of faith, renewal, and divine presence.

31

THE RECOMMISSIONING TO ANOINT TWO KINGS, AND A KINGLY PROPHET.
(1 KINGS 19:15-17)

In 1 Kings 19:15-17, we encounter yet another profound moment in the life of the man from Tishbe. He is instructed by Yahweh to anoint and appoint a new king of Syria, a new king of Israel to replace Ahab, and a new prophet in Israel to replace himself. When thinking things through of all that Elijah did in his life, God recommissioned Elijah and gave him an assignment which was, in essence, even more influential than the assignment that led to the clash on Mount Carmel. What God assigned to Elijah was influencing the surrounding nations more than the drought and the battle for the fire from heaven sent by Yahweh.

God's purpose was to elevate Elijah to put men in offices that would really finish the job that Carmel's fire started but left unfinished. The king of Syria was a key role enactor for God's kingdom's sake. Nothing is mentioned again about Jezebel's "hit-man-contract". When Elijah went back looking for Elisha, whether he was still fearful of Jezebel or not -we are not told.

After fleeing from Jezebel and experiencing profound depression and despair, God reestablishes Elijah's purpose through a divine commissioning that involves these three anointings. Each anointing not only signifies a new direction in Elijah's prophetic ministry but also reveals deeper theological truths about God's sovereignty, judgment, and the continuation of His covenant promises. In exploring these anointings and their significance, we are invited into a richer understanding of God's work in our lives and the call to fulfil His purposes.

"The Lord said to him, "Go back the way you came, and go to the Desert of Damascus. When you get there, anoint Hazael king over Aram. Also, anoint Jehu son of Nimshi king over Israel. And anoint Elisha son of Shaphat from Abel Meholah to succeed you as prophet. Jehu will put to death any who escape the sword of Hazael, and Elisha will put to death any who escape the sword of Jehu.""

1. The First Anointing: Hazael

God commands Elijah to anoint Hazael as king over Aram (Syria). This is significant for several reasons. First, Hazael represents God's sovereign plan to use foreign nations as instruments of judgment against Israel. By appointing Hazael, God demonstrates that His authority truly extends beyond Israel's borders. This foreign king would execute divine judgment, fulfilling God's promise of retribution against idolatry and unfaithfulness that was, until recently, totally rampant in Israel. The anointing of Hazael reflects God's willingness to use even ungodly gentile rulers for His purposes. It serves as a reminder that God is not limited to human expectations or religious boundaries. He can raise up leaders - even those outside the covenant community - to accomplish His will. This challenges our understanding of who is "*qualified*" to be used by God.

2. The Second Anointing: Jehu

Next, Elijah is instructed to anoint Jehu, the son of Nimshi, as king over Israel. Like Hazael, Jehu's anointing serves a dual purpose. He is to execute judgment on the house of Ahab, thereby purging Israel of the Baal worship that Jezebel had propagated. Jehu is described as a fierce leader, and his reign will be marked by violence against those who have led Israel astray. In verse 17, God states, "Jehu will put to death any who escape the sword of Hazael." This layered approach to slaying illustrates a systematic dismantling of idolatry and corruption in Israel. It shows that God's judgment will be thorough and relentless. It also indicates that the prophetic word has consequences. Those who reject God's call will face inevitable judgment through the hands of appointed leaders.

Jehu's anointing highlights the complexity of divine justice. God's judgment is not capricious; it unfolds through a series of ordained actions and actors, emphasizing the interconnectedness of His plans. This layered execution of judgment suggests that God's ultimate purpose is restoration, albeit through sometimes severe measures.

3. The Third Anointing: Elisha

Finally, Elijah is commanded to anoint Elisha of Abel-Meholah, his successor, who will carry on the prophetic ministry after Elijah's departure. Whether Elijah was aware at this point that he was not to die at all is an unknown factor. On the day that Elijah did go up in the whirlwind, it is clear that Elijah, Elisha and all the constituent members of the schools of the prophets had an understanding of Elijah's departure, but at this point of time we are not informed what was known and what wasn't. This anointing signifies the continuation of God's covenant relationship with His people. The anointed prophet for the nation fully signified that God was building social installations of powerful prophets and kings intended to stop another foreign wife to a Hebrew King from running rampant with idolatrous religions to lead the nation away from God. Elisha represents hope and renewal, a counterbalance to the impending judgment. Where Hazael and Jehu symbolize God's judgment, Elisha embodies God's mercy and the promise of restoration.

The promised anointing of Elisha serves as a reminder that God's work is always generational. While judgment may come, God is also preparing a remnant to carry forth His purposes.

In the Old Testament, the anointing of leaders and prophets is a significant theme that underscores God's sovereign choice in appointing individuals for specific roles and tasks.

Elijah was assigned to anoint three people. But what actually took place? Elijah only anointed one of the three. We will explore the anointing of Hazael, Jehu, and Elisha, focusing on the relevant verses and the reasons behind their anointings.

Hazael: Anointed King of Syria.

Hazael, a significant figure in the history of Israel and Syria, was anointed as king over Aram (Syria) during a pivotal moment in Israel's history. This event is recorded in 2 Kings 8:7-13. The prophet Elisha was commanded by God to anoint Hazael. The context of this anointing is rooted in Israel's ongoing rebellion against God and the impending judgment that would come through foreign nations. The relevant verses state:

"Then Elisha went to Damascus. Now Ben-Hadad king of Aram was sick; and it was told him, saying, 'The man of God has come here.' And the king said to Hazael, 'Take a gift in your hand and go to meet the man of God, and inquire of the Lord by him, saying, "Will I recover from this sickness?"' ... And Elisha said to him, 'Go, say to him, "You shall certainly recover." However, the Lord has shown me that he will certainly die.' ... And he said, 'The Lord has shown me that you will be king over Syria.'" (2 Kings 8:7-10, 13, NKJV)

Elisha's anointing of Hazael was significant because it foreshadowed the judgment that would come upon Israel through Hazael's reign. Hazael would become an instrument of God's judgment against Israel due to their idolatry and sin.

Jehu: Anointed King of Israel

Jehu's anointing as king of Israel was another critical moment in the biblical narrative, signifying a dramatic shift in leadership. This anointing is found in 2 Kings 9:1-13. It is important, I think, to note that **the prophet Elisha sent a messenger to anoint Jehu** in the midst of an ongoing crisis in Israel, particularly concerning the wicked reign of King Ahab and his descendants. The relevant verses include:

"And Elisha the prophet called one of the sons of the prophets, and said to him, 'Get yourself ready, take this flask of oil in your hand, and go to Ramoth Gilead. When you arrive there, look there for Jehu the son of Jehoshaphat, the son of Nimshi; and go in and make him arise up from among his associates, and take him to an inner room. Then take the flask of oil, and pour it on his head, and say, "Thus says the Lord: I have anointed you king over Israel."'" (2 Kings 9:1-3, NKJV)

Jehu's anointing was significant for several reasons. First, it was a divine mandate to eradicate the house of Ahab, which had led Israel into idolatry and moral decay. Jehu was charged with the task of purging Baal worship from Israel, fulfilling God's judgment against Ahab's lineage.

Elisha: Anointed as Prophet

Elisha, the disciple of Elijah, was anointed as a prophet to succeed Elijah and continue the prophetic ministry in Israel. His anointing is recorded in 1 Kings 19:15-16. God instructed Elijah to anoint Elisha, emphasizing the continuity of divine guidance and prophetic leadership. The pertinent verses state:

"Then the Lord said to him: 'Go, return on your way to the Wilderness of Damascus; and when you arrive, anoint Hazael as king over Syria. Also you shall anoint Jehu the son of Nimshi as king over Israel. And Elisha the son of Shaphat of Abel Meholah you shall anoint as prophet in your place.'" (1 Kings 19:15-16, NKJV)

Elisha's anointing was crucial for several reasons. It marked the transition of prophetic authority from Elijah to Elisha, ensuring that God's message would continue to be proclaimed in a time of moral and spiritual decline. Elisha would go on to perform many miracles and serve as a key figure in confronting Israel's apostasy.

The anointing of Hazael, Jehu, and Elisha in the Old Testament illustrates God's active role in shaping the leadership of His people, and other nations around the land. Hazael was chosen to bring judgment upon Israel through his kingship over Syria, Jehu was appointed to cleanse Israel of Baal worship and end Ahab's dynasty, and Elisha was tasked with continuing the prophetic ministry. Each anointing reflects God's sovereignty and purpose in guiding His people through turbulent times, demonstrating that even in judgment, God is at work for His ultimate plan of redemption and restoration.

Elijah's decision to pass on the anointing of Hazael and Jehu to Elisha, as instructed by God, can be understood through several key points:

1. Divine Command:

God specifically instructed Elijah to anoint Hazael as king over Aram (Syria) and Jehu as king over Israel, as well as to appoint Elisha as his successor (1 Kings 19:15-16). This divine mandate indicates that these anointings were part of God's plan for the future of Israel and its leadership. As Elijah would be anointing Elisha, we can only conclude that the "organic" relationship betwixt Elijah and Elisha meant that any "outstanding" commissioned jobs that Elijah did not do were then automatically passed on to Elisha.

2. Continuity of Prophetic Ministry:

By anointing Elisha as his successor, Elijah ensured the continuation of the prophetic ministry. Elisha would carry forward the mission of confronting idolatry and calling the people back to God. This was crucial, especially given the moral and spiritual decline in Israel during that period.

3. Judgment Against Idolatry:

The anointings of Hazael and Jehu were part of God's judgment against the house of Ahab and the idol worship that had permeated Israel. Hazael would bring judgment upon the nations, and Jehu would purge the worship of Baal from Israel (2 Kings 9). By entrusting these tasks to Elisha, Elijah played a critical role in God's plan to restore Israel.

4. Symbolism of Succession:

The act of anointing signifies the transfer of authority and responsibility. Elisha's appointment was not just about leadership; it was about empowering him to carry out God's will. Elijah's obedience in following through with God's command exemplifies the importance of prophetic succession in Israel's history.

Elijah's actions reflect his faithfulness to God's command, the importance of prophetic continuity, and the unfolding of God's judgment and restoration plan for Israel. By passing on these responsibilities to Elisha, Elijah ensured that God's purposes would be fulfilled even after his own ministry concluded.

32

ELIJAH GOES LOOKING FOR ELISHA
(1 KINGS 19:19-21)

Without Sat Navs, and Tom Toms in Elijah's day I would love to know how Elijah knew how to handle his search. Had he already heard of or been to Abel Meholah. Or had he heard of Elisha already. If not – what? Did he just go around asking? However, sure enough, however, he found out. Elijah came over a hill and saw a busy man ploughing his field and was directed to the man named Elisha. Elijah wasn't much into interviews or staff assessments. So, he simply threw his cape – his mantle, over Elisha's shoulders and walked off. As far as we are told, not a word was transpired between them, apart from Elisha asking for time to party and say good-bye to his family.

By Elisha's fair-sized family farewell party we now home in on another pivotal moment in Elijah's life. One that carries profound implications not only for him personally but also for the broader prophetic tradition in Israel and for the future of the nation itself. These statements in the scrolls depict God's instructions to the Tishbite to anoint Hazael as king over Aram, Jehu as king over Israel, and, of course, Elisha as his prophetic successor and erstwhile servant. This moment is rich with practicalities, significance, ramifications, and corollaries that extend far beyond the text itself, influencing the trajectory of Israel's spiritual and political landscape for the future.

The practical aspects of Elijah's task reflect a structured approach to prophetic ministry that emphasizes divine authority and intentionality. Anointing, a sacred ritual in ancient Israel, signifies the selection and empowerment of leaders. By instructing Elijah to anoint Hazael and Jehu, God is not only designating future rulers but also re-establishing divine order in a nation plagued by idolatry and moral decay. Kings, prophets and priests were the three posts and positions in society and before God that were, by Levitical statutes, in need of personal anointing with oil in order to substantiate the position.

Elijah's actions seem to be imbued with urgency and purpose. He is called to undertake significant tasks that require both physical and spiritual readiness. This reflects a larger principle within the prophetic ministry, namely, the necessity for prophets to act decisively in accordance with divine command. However, we are privy to see that the anointing of the two kings were both left to the Elijah's successor, and Jehu's anointing was also left to one of his assistant prophets.

The act of anointing is not merely ceremonial. It is a means of transferring authority and initiating change. The act of anointing is acknowledged as a divine impartation. By involving Elijah in this process, God affirms the importance of human agency in enacting divine will.

For Elijah, this moment represents a crucial turning point in his prophetic journey. After experiencing profound despair and isolation following his confrontation with the prophets of Baal and the threats from Jezebel, Elijah's encounter with God at Mount Horeb reinvigorates his sense of purpose. The anointing of Elisha, in particular, signifies a restoration of Elijah's prophetic mission.

This restoration is significant on multiple levels. First, it acknowledges Elijah's ongoing role as a prophet despite his previous doubts and fears. By providing him with a successor, God reassures Elijah that his work will continue beyond his personal struggles. This transition also allows Elijah to pass on his prophetic mantle, ensuring that the voice of Yahweh remains present in Israel.

Moreover, the designation of Elisha as Elijah's successor embodies a deeper theological principle that God's work is ongoing and even more multifaceted. The prophetic mission is not confined to a single individual but is a communal effort that spans generations. Elijah's acceptance of this new role reinforces the idea that prophetic authority is not static; it evolves and adapts over time.

The ramifications of this moment extend beyond Elijah to all the Hebrew prophets of his generation and in the future. The anointing of Hazael and Jehu marks a significant shift in leadership dynamics within Israel. Both figures would play crucial roles in the political landscape, with Hazael consolidating power in Aram (Syria) and Jehu ultimately purging Baal worship from Israel.

For the other prophets, this moment serves as a clarion call to reaffirm their commitment to Yahweh amidst a corrupting culture. The actions taken by Elijah under divine command demonstrate that prophetic voices are essential for maintaining spiritual integrity in the nation. The subsequent rise of Jehu, who would eradicate the worship of Baal, illustrates the power of prophetic action to influence political realities.

Furthermore, Elijah's relationship with Elisha establishes a model for mentorship and continuity in prophetic ministry. This mentorship highlights the importance of training and empowering future leaders to carry on the work of the prophetic. The establishment of a prophetic school, as suggested elsewhere in this volume, becomes a corollary that ensures the sustainability of prophetic witness in Israel.

In a nation marked by idolatry and moral decay, these actions represent a divine initiative to reclaim Israel for Yahweh. The appointment of Hazael and Jehu suggests that God is working through both foreign and domestic leaders to bring about His purposes. This complexity highlights a theological principle: that God can use diverse means and individuals to fulfil His divine plan.

The execution of judgment upon the house of Ahab through Jehu is a critical aspect of this narrative. Jehu's violent but necessary purge of Baal worship indicates a decisive break from the past. While the means may be troubling by modern ethical standards, it underscores the seriousness of idolatry and the lengths to which God will go to restore faithfulness among His people.

Moreover, the role of Elisha as Elijah's successor signifies the continuity of prophetic ministry, ensuring that Israel will not be left without a voice to call them back to covenant faithfulness. Elisha's ministry would later be characterized by miracles and signs that reaffirmed Yahweh's presence among His people. This continuity suggests that despite human failures, God's purposes will prevail, offering hope for the future of Israel.

The events of 1 Kings 19:16-21 encapsulate a moment of significance for Elijah, the Hebrew prophets of his generation, and the future of Israel. The practicalities of anointing signify a structured approach to leadership and prophetic authority, while the significance to Elijah personally reflects a restoration of purpose and renewal. The ramifications for other prophets highlight the call to uphold spiritual integrity amidst societal corruption, and the corollaries for Israel's future reveal a divine commitment to reclaim and restore His people.

As contemporary readers engage with this narrative, they are clearly subliminally invited to reflect on the enduring relevance of prophetic authority and the importance of mentorship and continuity in spiritual leadership. The legacy of Elijah, Elisha, Hazael, and Jehu serves as a powerful reminder that divine purposes are fulfilled through human action and that the call to faithfulness remains ever-present, even in the face of adversity. This narrative ultimately challenges us to consider our own roles in advocating for justice, truth, and spiritual integrity in our communities, echoing the timeless call of the prophets throughout history.

33

ELISHA WHO? FROM WHERE?

A Deeper Look

So, as Elijah's removal from office is now being placed on the table for consideration, we have to ask, as the news sifted out to the people on the street, was it known widely the way Elijah was to leave this world, or was he plainly expected just to die. And as Elijah was getting to be seen continuously walking around with this "Elisha-servant" person, they must have been asking, who is Elijah's friend.

At first glance, the ministry of the prophet Elisha may seem underwhelming compared to his predecessor, Elijah. Unlike Nathan, who boldly confronted David, or Elijah, who fiercely opposed Ahab, Elisha appears much more subdued. Yet, a careful examination reveals a significant impact: 9 of the 25 chapters of 2 Kings focus on Elisha, while the remaining chapters detail the reigns of numerous kings over centuries.

The author of Kings, likely from a prophetic tradition (possibly Jeremiah), emphasizes Elisha's achievements over the fleeting nature of kingship. Although the narratives may seem disjointed at first, they collectively reflect Elisha's unwavering commitment to eradicating Baal worship in Israel.

Elisha's journey begins as a disciple of Elijah, ploughing with 12 oxen in Abel-Meholah. After being called, he readily follows Elijah, indicating his readiness to serve. The transition from disciple to leader is marked dramatically when Elijah is taken up to heaven in a fiery chariot. Elisha's leadership among the Bnei Nevi'im (disciples of prophets) is solidified as he dons Elijah's mantle and performs miracles, such as purifying the waters in Jericho and dealing with mocking children.

In contrast to Elijah's solitary nature, Elisha actively engages with the Bnei Nevi'im, eating with them and expanding their community. This group, established under Samuel, played a crucial role in nurturing faith in Israel through music and prophecy, aiming to draw people away from idol worship.

Elijah's life was marked by solitariness and isolation, culminating in his flight from Jezebel following his triumph on Mount Carmel. Despite his significant victory, he faced despair, leading him to question his efficacy. Conversely, Elisha thrived in his ministry, becoming a revered figure sought by kings like Jehoram and Jehoshaphat for guidance. While Elijah struggled for recognition, Elisha's reputation as a miracle worker and "man of God" grew, reflecting his successful engagement with both royalty and common people.

After Elijah's ascension, he was canonized as a harbinger of redemption, particularly in the prophecy of Malachi, who foretold Elijah's return before the "great and terrible day of the Lord." In this way, Elijah became an eternal figure, while Elisha was the man of his time.

The discovery of the Moabite Stone in 1868 provides historical context for Elisha's influence. The stone narrates King Mesha of Moab's rebellion against Israel, which parallels events in 2 Kings 3. When Jehoram of Israel sought Elisha's counsel during a military crisis, Elisha prophesied water for the troops and victory over Moab. This demonstrates Elisha's central role in Israelite history, contributing to the narrative of their military endeavours.

The respectful approach of kings toward Elisha contrasts sharply with the treatment of Micaiah during Ahab's reign, highlighting Elisha's elevated status. Unlike Micaiah, who was imprisoned for speaking truth, Elisha was sought after for his wisdom and spiritual authority, emphasizing that true prophetic power surpasses worldly authority.

Interestingly, Elisha's prophecy regarding victory was ultimately unfulfilled, as divine wrath fell upon Israel, leaving the reasons ambiguous. This irony underscores the complexities of prophetic ministry, where expectations may not align with outcomes. Elisha's fame extended beyond Israel, largely due to a young Israelite girl who informed Naaman, a Syrian commander, of Elisha's healing abilities. This narrative not only highlights Elisha's miraculous powers but also emphasizes the role of ordinary individuals in spreading God's work.

Elisha's life and ministry reveal a remarkable legacy that transcends his immediate context. While he may not exhibit the dramatic confrontations of Elijah or Nathan, his dedication to eliminating Baal worship and nurturing prophetic communities was profound. Through his actions and the respect he garnered, Elisha embodies the call to faithfulness amidst challenges, illustrating that God's work often unfolds through quiet yet impactful leadership. In reflecting on Elisha's journey, we are reminded of the importance of perseverance, collaboration, and the transformative power of faith, urging us to recognize and embrace our own roles in God's ongoing narrative.

Jewish tradition generally holds that Elisha lived for a total of 50 years after he began his prophetic ministry. While the Hebrew Bible does not explicitly state Elisha's age at the time of his death, it is often interpreted that he died at the age of somewhere around 80.

Other Jewish traditions count the years from Ahab's years on the throne – as Ahab was still ruling when Elijah was raptured, and Elisha commenced his prophetic service, and the –through to Joash's death (sometimes spelt Jehoash) from which they calculate Elisha died at 110. The case to prove that Elisha died at age 110 originates from certain Jewish traditions and interpretations rather than explicit biblical evidence. Understanding this claim involves examining how Jewish scholars and texts have historically interpreted the life and times of Elisha.

1. Biblical Account: The Hebrew Bible, specifically the Books of Kings, provides an account of Elisha's prophetic ministry but does not specify his age at any stage of his narrative. The narrative focuses on his actions, miracles, and interactions with the kings of Israel rather than personal details like his age.

2. Rabbinic Literature: Over the centuries, Jewish scholars have sought to fill in gaps left by the biblical text. The Talmud and various midrashim (interpretive stories and commentaries) often expand on biblical narratives, adding details that are not present in the original texts. These sources sometimes attribute symbolic ages to biblical figures, reflecting an idealized lifespan rather than historical fact.

3. Age of 110 in Tradition: The age of 110 is significant in Jewish tradition. It is often seen as a symbol of a full, blessed life. For example, Joseph in the Bible is said to have lived to 110 (Genesis 50:26), which is considered a sign of divine favour. This symbolic use of age can influence interpretations of other figures like Elisha.

34

BENHADAD THREATENS AHAB AND ISRAEL - A PROPHET SPEAKS.
(1 KINGS 20:1-41)

1 Kings 20:1-41 is rich but often overlooked because Elijah is not mentioned in it. Political intrigue, divine interventions, and prophetic authority make for a juicy plot and exciting occurrences. Set against the backdrop of Israel's tumultuous history during the reign of Ahab (circa 874-853 BC), this chapter illustrates the complexities of leadership, the intricacies of warfare, and the profound implications of divine sovereignty. The events unfold as King Ben-Hadad of Aram (Syria) lays siege to Samaria, demanding tribute from Ahab, thus setting the stage for a dramatic confrontation that reveals not only the nature of power but also the enduring faithfulness of God to His people.

To fully appreciate the significance of 1 Kings 20, one must first understand the historical context. Ahab, known for his marriage to Jezebel and his promotion of Baal worship, ruled a politically fragile Israel. His reign was characterized by both military conflicts and internal strife, particularly as he attempted to navigate alliances with neighbouring states. The state of Aram, under King Ben-Hadad, was one of Israel's primary adversaries, and the tensions between these two kingdoms often manifested in military confrontations.

The year 853 BCE is significant as it marks the Battle of Qarqar, where a coalition of kings, including Ahab, faced off against Ben-Hadad. This context enriches our understanding of the events in 1 Kings 20, as it illustrates the geopolitical landscape and the stakes involved in the conflict. Ahab's vulnerability, compounded by his reliance on foreign alliances, sets the stage for the dramatic encounters that follow.

The narrative begins with Ben-Hadad's demands, which escalate from tribute to outright threats of violence. In verses 1-6, Ben-Hadad sends messengers to Ahab, demanding not only wealth but also the personal possessions of Ahab's household, including his wives – one of which was Jezebel. This brazen display of power is met with a calculated response from Ahab. Instead of yielding immediately, Ahab seeks counsel and ultimately agrees to negotiate.

A pivotal moment occurs when Ahab's advisors remind him that the king of Israel cannot simply capitulate. The significance of this moment lies in the interplay between human agency and divine sovereignty. Ahab, despite his flaws and previous failings, is given the opportunity to assert his authority and rally his people. This underscores a theme prevalent in the narrative: that God often uses flawed leaders to accomplish His purposes.

As the siege intensifies, God intervenes through an unnamed prophet of God, who delivers a message of hope and victory to Ahab. This prophetic message (verses 13-14) indicates that the battle is not solely about military might; it is also a demonstration of God's sovereignty over the nations. Ahab is reminded that victory will come not through his own strength but through divine intervention. This moment serves as a reminder that God's plans often transcend human understanding and capabilities.

The ensuing battle, described in verses 15-21, illustrates the remarkable effectiveness of divine strategy. Despite being outnumbered, Ahab's forces secure a decisive victory against Ben-Hadad's army. The narrative emphasizes the miraculous nature of this victory, reinforcing the idea that it is God who orchestrates the outcomes of battles. The defeat of Ben-Hadad serves as a testament to God's faithfulness to Israel despite Ahab's earlier transgressions.

However, the aftermath is equally significant. Ben-Hadad, realizing the gravity of his defeat, seeks to negotiate peace. His subsequent appeal for mercy reveals the vulnerability of even the most powerful rulers in the face of divine authority. Ahab's decision to spare Ben-Hadad's life, while politically expedient, raises moral questions. Is it justifiable for a king to show mercy to an enemy? This act foreshadows future consequences, as it illustrates the complexities of leadership and the potential for miscalculated compassion.

The narrative takes a critical turn in verses 35-43 when a prophet confronts Ahab, delivering a stark warning about his choice to spare Ben-Hadad. The prophet uses a dramatic parable to illustrate the consequences of Ahab's actions. The emphasis on justice - where a man who spares a life must pay a price - underscores a central theme in the biblical narrative: the principle of retribution and accountability.

The prophet's message serves as a prophetic lens through which Ahab's character and decisions are evaluated. The question arises: Can a king who compromises his integrity expect to lead effectively? The sparing of Ben-Hadad becomes emblematic of Ahab's broader failure to uphold his covenantal responsibilities. This moment foreshadows Ahab's eventual downfall, illustrating the interconnection between personal choices, divine justice, and national destiny.

The narrative of 1 Kings 20 offers profound theological insights that resonate with contemporary audiences. At its core, the text emphasizes the sovereignty of God over human affairs. The victories and defeats of nations are not merely the results of military strategy but are intricately woven into the fabric of divine purpose. This understanding challenges modern readers to consider the implications of their own leadership decisions and the extent to which they acknowledge a higher authority in their lives.

Moreover, the character of Ahab serves as a cautionary tale. His initial willingness to negotiate reflects a pragmatic approach to leadership, yet his later choices reveal the dangers of compromising one's principles. Ahab's story invites reflection on the moral complexities faced by leaders today. In a world often marked by political expediency, where difficult decisions must be made, the narrative challenges leaders to consider the long-term ramifications of their actions.

In 1 Kings 20:1-41, the intricate interplay of human agency, divine intervention, and prophetic authority unfolds against a backdrop of political tension and moral complexity. The chapter serves as a powerful reminder of the significance of faithfulness to God's covenant, the consequences of leadership choices, and the enduring nature of divine sovereignty.

As contemporary readers engage with this narrative, they are encouraged to reflect on their own roles within their communities and the ethical considerations that accompany leadership. The legacy of Ahab and the prophetic voices that guided him continue to resonate, urging individuals to seek wisdom, uphold justice, and remain steadfast in their commitment to a higher purpose. In doing so, they can contribute to a legacy that honours the divine sovereignty at work in their lives and in the world around them.

35

ELIJAH (WITH ELISHA?) AND NABOTH'S VINEYARD (1 KINGS 21)

Here we have a profound and multifaceted narrative centred around Ahab, Jezebel, and Naboth, a humble vineyard owner in Jezreel who had the misfortune to own his family vineyard home in such a beautiful view that the king and his evil wife built one of their homes leaning against his wall. There was no fault in Naboth apart from the fact that he would not sell his heritage going back to the days of Joshua, and that was not a fault, but a show of a man who treasured the statements of Moses and the centuries where the point made by God was for each Jewish family to hold their property in perpetuity. We shall highlight this a little later. This chapter (21) is rich with themes of greed, injustice, the abuse of power, and the consequences of sin. It serves as a powerful reminder of God's justice and the moral responsibilities that accompany authority. Power and authority truly break down a lot of personnel character in that position.

The events of 1 Kings 21 occur during the reign of Ahab (874-853 BC). Ahab's rule is marked by his alliance with Jezebel, a Phoenician princess who promoted the worship of Baal in Israel, leading the nation further away from Yahweh. This chapter provides insight into the moral decay of Ahab's reign and serves as a poignant critique of how power can corrupt.

Including Elijah, there are just four characters in this narrative. I am sure there is a silent fifth character because Elisha was now trailing around with the man from Tishbe. The active voices are Ahab: King of Israel, who represents moral compromise and injustice. Jezebel: Ahab's wife, whose ruthless ambition and manipulation drive the plot. Naboth: A righteous man whose vineyard symbolizes integrity and the inheritance of God's people. Elijah: The prophet who serves as God's voice of judgment against Ahab and Jezebel.

1. AHAB'S COVETING AND NABOTH'S REFUSAL
(1 Kings 21:1-4)

The chapter opens with Ahab expressing his desire for Naboth's vineyard, which is located next to the king's palace. Ahab's request reflects his pretensive entitlement and desire for more than what God has provided. Naboth's refusal, grounded in the law of Moses (Leviticus 25:23-24), emphasizes the importance of land as a divine inheritance, which cannot be sold permanently. Ahab's desire for Naboth's vineyard screams to us of the destructive nature of covetousness. The commandment "You shall not covet" (Exodus 20:17) is directly violated by Ahab's actions. This sets a precedent for examining our own hearts for desires that lead us away from God's will. Ahab went home to whinge and whine that he could not take Naboth's property legally.

2. JEZEBEL'S MANIPULATION (1 Kings 21:5-10)

Jezebel's intervention reveals her cunning and ruthless nature. She chastises Ahab for his weakness and takes matters into her own hands. By crafting false accusations against Naboth and orchestrating his execution, she embodies the most extreme abuse of power. And in so doing she incriminates her husband and the people she paid to lie about Naboth's good character. Her actions demonstrate a stark contrast to the character of Naboth, who remains faithful to God's laws even unto death.

This highlights the dangers of manipulation and deceit in positions of power. Jezebel personifies a system that prioritizes ambition over justice and integrity. Her actions serve as a cautionary tale about the consequences of using power for personal gain.

3. THE AFTERMATH OF NABOTH'S DEATH
(1 Kings 21:11-16)

After Naboth is unjustly killed, Ahab seizes the vineyard, believing he has finally acquired what he coveted. This moment encapsulates the tragic outcome of unchecked ambition and the perversion of justice. Ahab's actions not only reflect moral failure but also a blatant disregard for God's commandments, as well as abuse of plain and simple humanity. The ease with which Ahab takes possession of Naboth's vineyard illustrates the corrupting influence of power. The tragic irony is that Ahab truly believes he has triumphed and that his ownership of Naboth's property has no negatives about the transaction. Yet this triumph is built on injustice, selfishness, and childish "want", and bloodshed. This highlights the biblical principle that sin may provide temporary pleasure, but its consequences are ultimately destructive.

4. God's judgement through Elijah (1 Kings 21:17)

In response to Naboth's murder, God sends Elijah to confront Ahab. Elijah's message is direct and unambiguous: Ahab's actions have provoked God's wrath, and he will face dire consequences. The prophetic pronouncement includes the foretelling of Ahab's downfall and the judgment that will befall Jezebel. The arrival of Elijah signifies God's unwavering commitment to justice. Prophets serve as God's mouthpieces, calling out sin and offering a path to repentance. This interaction is a reminder that God does not ignore injustice; He addresses it and holds leaders accountable.

5. Ahab's Response and Repentance (1 Kings 21:25-29)

Ahab's character takes an unexpected turn in this section. Upon hearing God's judgment through Elijah, he humbles himself, tears his clothes, fasts, and wears sackcloth. God acknowledges Ahab's repentance and mitigates the judgment, stating that the calamity will not occur during Ahab's lifetime, although it will befall his descendants. Ahab's response illustrates the possibility of repentance, even for those who have sinned grievously. This moment reveals God's mercy, demonstrating that genuine contrition can alter the course of divine judgment. It emphasizes the biblical concept that while sin has consequences, God's grace is always available for those who turn back to Him.

As insights into Elijah's prophetic work on the Naboth episode we need to observe:

1. The supernatural prophetic gift of a word of knowledge to the Prophet. As far as Ahab knew, his transaction was to a degree know only to a handful of people. How did Elijah know what had gone on? God told him. How did Elijah know about Ahab's repentance? That has the same answer.

2, The Nature of Power and Responsibility. The chapter underscores the moral responsibilities that accompany leadership. Without moral restraint instigated by Gods law and its accompanying sanctions, Ahab and his wife could have continued and gone unchecked. Indeed, without moral restraint, all people in high office can abuse the privileges of their position continually. Ahab and Jezebel's actions illustrate how power can corrupt and lead to injustice. Leaders are called to uphold righteousness and act in accordance with God's will.

2. Divine Justice: God's judgment on Ahab and Jezebel reinforces the biblical principle that God *will* address sin. The narrative demonstrates the certainty of divine justice and the importance of accountability for actions taken against His commandments.

3. The Role of the Prophet: Elijah's role emphasizes the importance of prophetic voices in society. Prophets are called to challenge injustice and remind leaders of their obligations to God and the people. This highlights the need for courageous voices that speak truth to power.

4. Repentance and Grace: Ahab's moment of repentance reveals that no one is beyond redemption. This theme of grace serves as a powerful reminder that turning back to God can change the trajectory of one's life, regardless of past sins. God's response to repentance was the same in Old Testament days, just as it is in the new.

5. Self-Examination of Desires: Reflect on personal desires and ambitions. Are there areas in life where greed or covetousness may lead to decisions that compromise integrity? Developing a heart of contentment is crucial in avoiding the pitfalls exemplified by Ahab.

6. Understanding Authority: Recognize the weight of responsibility that comes with positions of influence, whether in the workplace, church, or community. Leaders must strive to act justly, uphold truth, and be mindful of the impact of their decisions on others.

7. The Importance of Prophetic Voices: Encourage and support those who act as prophets in contemporary society—individuals who challenge injustice and advocate for the marginalized. Engage with and listen to voices that call us back to God's standards.

8. Embrace Repentance: Foster a culture of repentance both personally and within any community. Repentance will always be needed with any group of people in church, in work, in play, at parties, even. Encourage openness about failures and the importance of seeking forgiveness, knowing that God's grace is available to all who turn back to Him.

9. Advocate for Justice: Stand against injustice in all its forms. Just as God responded to the cries of the oppressed, believers are called to advocate for righteousness and justice in society.

1 Kings 21 encapsulates the themes of power, justice, and repentance. Ahab, Jezebel, and Naboth provide a cautionary tale about the dangers of unchecked ambition and the moral responsibilities of leadership. Through Elijah's prophetic personage, we see clearly God's commitment to justice and the transformative power of repentance. God give us all grace to embody integrity, advocate for justice, and remain open to the transformative grace of God in our lives and communities.

36

THE REMOVAL OF ELIJAH. THE SUCCESSION OF ELISHA (2 KINGS 2:1-18)

> "When, by th' Almighty's dread command
> Elijah, call'd from Israel's land,
> Rose in the sacred flame,
> His Mantle good Elisha caught,
> And, with the Prophet's spirit fraught,
> Her second hope became."

Opening lines of "Elijah's mantle" by George Canning.

Elijah's Departure and Elisha's Succession: Examining the Prophetic Transition in 2 Kings 2:1-18

The text of the biblical scrolls of Elijah's departure from this world and the prophetic succession of Elisha, as recorded in 2 Kings 2:1-18, marks an amazing epic moment in the history of Israel's prophetic saga. This passage not only captures the unique and dramatic ascension of Elijah, but also serves as a profound commentary on the continuity of God's mission through Elijah and Elisha in particular and prophetic leadership in general. The visual impressions of Elijah's departure supplied by the normal scanty and minimal biblical texts are striking. How can such few words paint such a full and, energetic and detailed graphic? The implications of this transition reverberate throughout the biblical narrative, emphasizing the enduring significance of prophetic authority, mentorship, and the ongoing relationship between God and His people. The relationship that obviously existed between the man from Tishbe and the farmer from Abel Meholah is completely omitted in the biblical text, though it undoubtedly carried a rich mentor/mentoree significance. Wouldn't we love to know the details there.

The imagery surrounding Elijah's departure is both vivid and symbolic, and is difficult to imagine the scene without the glorious colouring of chariots and horses of fire. As the story line unfolds, we see Elijah and Elisha striding together from Gilgal to the Jordan River. Each location at which they stopped carries historical and spiritual weight: Gilgal, a site of Israel's renewal after crossing the Jordan, is a place of beginnings, while the Jordan River symbolizes both separation and transition.

The schools of the prophets, Elisha and Elijah himself, were all aware that "Today is the day" their master Elijah was to be taken. What on earth does a giant of the faith talk about when he is aware he is to be taken before the day is finished? What sort of dialogue transpired between the master and his successor?

1. The Chariot of Fire: The climax of Elijah's departure occurs when he is taken up into heaven by a whirlwind accompanied by a chariot and horses of fire (2 Kings 2:11). This dramatic, mind-blowing visual evokes feelings of deep awe and knee bending reverence. The chariot of fire serves as both a vehicle of divine presence and a symbol of God's power. This image is not merely spectacular; it signifies the divine endorsement of Elijah's prophetic life and ministry and his unique relationship with God. The fiery chariot contrasts sharply with the earthly concerns of Ahab and Jezebel, illustrating the transcendence of divine authority over human power.

2. The Whirlwind: The whirlwind itself encapsulates chaos and divine mystery. In the ancient Near Eastern context, whirlwinds were often associated with theophany - manifestations of God's presence. Elijah's ascent in a whirlwind conveys the idea that he is not merely leaving the physical realm but is being gathered – scooped up if you will - into the divine presence. This moment serves as a powerful reminder of the transient nature of human life and the eternal reality of God's kingdom. This account also assures humanity of the fact that there is "life and energy" beyond walking in this life and activity beyond.

Unlike most biblical figures who face death in a conventional manner, Elijah's ascension is unique. His departure challenges conventional notions of mortality and illustrates a profound truth: faithful service to God can result in extraordinary experiences. This raises questions about the nature of faithfulness and the potential for divine encounters in the lives of those who remain obedient.

3. Elisha's Reaction: The visual impression culminates in Elisha's response. As he witnesses Elijah being taken up, he cries out, "My father, my father! The chariots of Israel and its horsemen!" (2 Kings 2:12). This poignant declaration reflects both grief and recognition of Elijah's role as a protector and guide. Elisha's use of "father" underscores the deep mentorship and bond between the two prophets, highlighting the emotional weight of this transition. The cry of Elisha also indicates that he saw Elijah rise, the sight of which, was the condition that necessitated and qualified the double anointing to be descending on Elisha.

The Importance of Prophetic Succession

The transition from Elijah to Elisha is emblematic of the theme of prophetic succession in the Hebrew Bible. The prophetic office is crucial not only for delivering God's word but also for guiding the nation of Israel through turbulent times. The way in which Elisha inherits Elijah's mantle carries significant implications for understanding the nature of prophetic ministry.

a. Mentorship and Spiritual Legacy: The relationship between Elijah and Elisha is characterized by mentorship, where the older prophet prepares his successor for the monumental task ahead. Elisha's faithful companionship during Elijah's final days illustrates the importance of spiritual formation and the passing of wisdom. This theme is relevant not only in the context of prophetic ministry but also in contemporary faith communities, where mentorship plays a critical role in shaping future leaders.

The Pentecostal explosion of life that commenced in the early 1900s was driven by many remarkable leaders of apostolic and prophetic stature, even though such titles were never used. Because of passionate conviction that the second coming of Christ was logically imminent. Mentoring and thoughts of succession in leadership roles was sadly neglected. Discipling, mentoring, and leadership training is now in depth being pressed much to the betterment of the body of Christ worldwide.

b. The Mantle of Prophetic Authority, both literally and allegorically, descended on Elisha after Elijah's ascension. Elisha picks up Elijah's cloak - cum mantle, which had fallen from him. This action symbolizes the transfer of prophetic authority and responsibility. The mantle represents not only the physical embodiment of Elijah's ministry but also the spiritual anointing that empowers Elisha to continue the work of God. The act of putting on the mantle signifies Elisha's acceptance of the prophetic call and the challenges that lie ahead.

The response of the prophetic community in the aftermath of Elijah's ascension adds another layer to the narrative. The "sons of the prophets" witness the event and express their recognition of Elisha's new role (2 Kings 2:15). This communal acknowledgement reinforces the idea that prophetic ministry is not solely an individual endeavour; it is a collective responsibility. The community's recognition of Elisha's authority is essential for legitimizing his role and ensuring the continuity of prophetic witness in Israel. It is unsure exactly what the watching school of the prophets nearby actually saw. They wanted to check whether or not he had landed somewhere. They pleaded with Elisha to search around to see if he had landed anywhere. They pressed Elisha until he conceded to allow search parties to look for their erstwhile master.

c. Continuity of God's Mission: The succession from Elijah to Elisha underscores the continuity of God's mission despite the transition of human leaders. Elisha is not merely a replacement for Elijah; he is called to carry forward the prophetic mandate in a new context. This continuity is vital for understanding how God's purposes endure through generations, reminding believers that divine work transcends individual lives.

Upon receiving Elijah's mantle, Elisha faces an immediate test of faith and authority. The first miracle he performs is parting the Jordan River (2 Kings 2:14), mirroring Elijah's previous actions. This miraculous act serves not only to confirm Elisha's prophetic authority but also to remind the community of Israel that God's power continues to work through His chosen servants. It highlights the importance of demonstrating faith in action and the need for confidence in the face of seemingly insurmountable challenges.

The visual impressions of Elijah's ascension evoke awe and reverence, highlighting the divine authority that undergirds prophetic leadership. Elisha's acceptance of the mantle signifies not only a continuation of Elijah's work but also a fresh opportunity for God to speak and act through His chosen servant.

As contemporary Christians reflect on this narrative, we are encouraged to consider the implications of prophetic ministry in our own lives. The call to be a voice for God, to mentor others, and to recognize the ongoing nature of God's work in the world remains as relevant today as it was in ancient Israel. Elijah and Elisha's story invites us to embrace our roles within the prophetic community and to seek divine guidance as we navigate the challenges and opportunities of faithfulness in a complex world.

37

TWICE AS MUCH OF YOUR SPIRIT.
(2 Kings 2:9-10)

Elisha's request for a double portion of Elijah's spirit in 2 Kings 2:9-10 captures an incredible moment in biblical history, overloaded with theological implications and insights into the dynamics of prophetic succession. We are compulsorily compelled in our spirits to explore the context, significance, and implications of this request, reflecting on the relationship between Elijah and Elisha, the role of prophets in ancient Israel, and the theological themes that emerge from this poignant interaction. Elisha's request is breathtaking. I have always wondered if it was a spontaneous thought of Elisha or whether it was a question he was expecting and so rehearsed his response.

The events surrounding 2 Kings 2 occur at the end of an amazing "Elijahn era" that was about to transform into an even longer "Elishan era" – not that anybody had a clue that Elisha was about to live until he was possibly 110. Israel's history, forever characterized by political instability, idolatry, and moral decay, had been brought back from the brink of destruction and dissolution by the man from Tishbe, Elijah. He was indeed one of the foremost prophets of Israel ever and played a crucial role in confronting the moral failings of the nation under Ahab and Jezebel, who were still alive and kicking even though both had had their idolatrous wings severely clipped, and Ahab had undoubtedly reigned in a little due to his repentance for having Naboth murdered. Elijah's ministry was marked by miraculous acts, prophetic confrontations, and a staunch commitment to Yahweh in the face of Baal worship.

Elisha, a farmer called to be Elijah's successor, represents the next generation of prophetic leadership. His calling is initiated in 1 Kings 19:19-21, where he is anointed by Elijah to take on the mantle of prophetic ministry succeeding from the very hand of Elijah. The relationship between Elijah and Elisha is characterized by mentorship, with Elisha closely following Elijah and witnessing his latter prophetic deeds from the Naboth narrative and onwards.

The transition from one prophet to another is a recurring theme in the biblical narrative. For example, Moses to Joshua, Elijah to Elisha, Paul to Timothy.

The specific verses in question, 2 Kings 2:9-10, read:

"When they had crossed, Elijah said to Elisha, 'Tell me, what can I do for you before I am taken from you?' 'Let me inherit a double portion of your spirit,' Elisha replied. 'You have asked a difficult thing,' Elijah said. 'Yet if you see me when I am taken from you, it will be yours—otherwise, it will not.'"

Elisha's request for a "double portion" is multifaceted. Traditionally, a double portion refers to the inheritance right of a firstborn son, who would receive twice as much as the other sons. In this context, Elisha's request indicates not only a desire for power and authority but also an acknowledgement of the weighty responsibilities that come with prophetic leadership. He seeks not just to replicate Elijah's ministry but to exceed it, reflecting an understanding of the challenges that lie ahead in guiding Israel.

Elisha asked Elijah for twice as much as his spirit; Elijah said it was a difficult request (2 Kgs 2.9). Elijah did eight miracles, and Elisha did sixteen. Elisha's miracles not only double Elijah's but seem to parallel and multiply them in their themes, elements, and language. Themes repeat themselves self-referentially, referring to Elijah's miracles. The patterns give us the sense that we can register the miracles and the terms and figures of their implicit intertextual allusions, but perhaps we will not understand them. Throughout the cycle of miracles of Elijah and Elisha are the three keys of the *Midrash. Teh. 78.5:*

1. The keys of the womb- to cure the barren,

2. The keys of the grave - to make the dead live

3. The keys of the rains - to bring rain.

Or life, death, and the sustaining of life. Elijah stops the rain, multiplies the oil, brings a boy to life, brings down rain, brings down fire on the altar and on Ahab's soldiers and splits the Jordan. Elisha replicates each of these acts.

Elijah's response is significant. He acknowledges the difficulty of Elisha's request, suggesting that it is not simply an issue of authority or power but also one of spiritual readiness and divine appointment. The conditional nature of his response—*"if you see me when I am taken from you"*—implies that spiritual insight and awareness are crucial for receiving this double portion. This moment encapsulates the essence of prophetic ministry: it requires not only a calling but also a keen spiritual perception to recognize and accept God's work in one's life.

Elisha's request and Elijah's response bring to the forefront the nature of prophetic leadership in Israel. Prophets are not merely spokespersons for God; they are individuals who embody God's presence and mission in their communities. The request for a double portion signifies a desire for an intimate connection with God's spirit, as well as a commitment to the prophetic vocation.

Elisha's aspiration to exceed Elijah's ministry also highlights the expectation of growth and development in spiritual leadership. Each generation of leaders is called to build upon the foundation laid by their predecessors, seeking greater depth and breadth in their relationship with God.

The relationship between Elijah and Elisha serves as a powerful model for mentorship in spiritual contexts. Elijah's willingness to mentor Elisha reflects the importance of investing in the next generation of leaders. The double portion request symbolizes the transfer of spiritual authority and the continuation of God's work through human agents.

Furthermore, the conditional aspect of Elijah's response emphasizes the necessity of spiritual vigilance and attentiveness to God's movements. It serves as a reminder that receiving God's blessings requires an active engagement with Him, marked by faithfulness and discernment.

In a broader theological context, this narrative challenges contemporary believers to consider how they engage with spiritual legacy, mentorship, and the pursuit of a deeper relationship with God. The request for a double portion resonates across generations, calling all believers to aspire to greater faithfulness, effectiveness, and impact in their spiritual journeys.

PART E

LEGACY AND REFLECTION

38

RESURRECTION IN THE OLD TESTAMENT

The concept of resurrection in the Old Testament is a nuanced theme that hints at the hope of life beyond death but is cryptically hidden in Messianic prophecies scattered about the Hebrew Bible. While the explicit doctrine of resurrection as it is understood in later Christian revelation, belief and teaching is not fully developed in the Old Testament, various passages and narratives provide significant insights into the nature of life, death, and the promise of future restoration to life, i.e., resurrection. I want to briefly show and explore key examples of resurrection in the Old Testament and examine the implications of these narratives for future hope.

1. The Widow of Zarephath's Son (1 Kings 17:17-24): One of the earliest instances of resurrection in the Old Testament occurs in the story of the man from Tishbe, Elijah, while he was lodged with the lady we know as "the widow of Zarephath". (Her name is not given in the Bible) When the widow's son falls ill and dies, Elijah, moved by compassion, prays fervently and stretches himself out on the child three times. God hears Elijah's prayer, and the boy is brought back to life. This narrative not only showcases God's power over life and death but also highlights the prophet's role as an intermediary between God and humanity. The act of resurrection here serves as a testament to God's mercy. The account puts the subject of resurrection clearly on the table of possibility.

2. The Shunammite Woman's Son (2 Kings 4:32-37): In a similar vein, Elisha raises the son of a Shunammite woman, again, unnamed. After the child dies, the mother seeks out Elisha, expressing her unwavering faith that he could help. Elisha enters the house, prays, and performs a series of actions that culminate in the boy's revival. This miracle reinforces the idea that God's power can restore life, and it highlights the faith of the mother, suggesting that belief in divine intervention is crucial in the face of despair. So we have yet another practical historical example intended to raise faith after negotiating the story with a faithful heart looking to receive God's word about the subject of people rising from the dead.

3. Ezekiel's Vision of the Valley of Dry Bones (Ezekiel 37:1-14): Perhaps one of the most vivid illustrations of resurrection is found in Ezekiel's vision of the Valley of Dry Bones. God asks Ezekiel if the bones can live, to which Ezekiel replies, *"O Lord God, you know."* God commands Ezekiel to prophesy to the bones, and they come together, receiving flesh and breath. This vision serves as a metaphor for the restoration of Israel, promising that just as the bones are revived, so too will God restore His people from exile. The resurrection imagery here extends beyond individual revival to encompass national renewal, symbolizing hope for a future where God's people will be revitalized and reunited as one single nation and not divided as Judah and Israel.

4. Job's Hope of Resurrection (Job 19:25-27): In the midst of his suffering, Job expresses a profound hope in his Redeemer, declaring, *"For I know that my Redeemer lives, and at the last he will stand upon the earth."* Job's confident assertion suggests a belief in a future resurrection, as he anticipates standing before God after his earthly life. This passage provides a deeply personal and existential perspective on resurrection, emphasizing the relationship between faith and hope in the face of mortality.

The examples of resurrection in the Old Testament not only depict God's power over death but also lay the groundwork for future promises. These narratives contribute to the broader theological understanding of resurrection within the Judeo-Christian tradition.

5. The Restoration of Israel: The resurrection motifs in the Old Testament often correlate with the theme of restoration for Israel. The dry bones in Ezekiel's vision symbolise the hope that God will bring His people back to life spiritually and physically, especially after the trauma of exile. This promise of restoration suggests that physical resurrection is intertwined with spiritual renewal, emphasising God's covenant faithfulness.

6. The Messianic Hope: The prophetic writings, particularly those of Isaiah and Daniel, allude to a future resurrection associated with the coming of the Messiah. Isaiah 26:19 states, *"Your dead shall live; their bodies shall rise."* This verse reflects a growing expectation of life after death, which would find its fulfilment in the New Testament teachings about the resurrection of Christ and the hope of eternal life for believers.

7. Theological Foundations: The Old Testament lays the groundwork for the understanding of resurrection as a divine act that transcends human limitations. The miracles of Elijah and Elisha, along with Job's affirmation of hope, contribute to a theology that affirms that death is not the end of existence but a transition to a new phase of life. This theological perspective shapes the later understanding of resurrection in both Judaism and Christianity.

Resurrection in the Old Testament serves as a rich and multifaceted theme that reveals God's power over life and death, offering hope for individual and collective restoration. Through the narratives of Elijah and Elisha, the prophetic vision of Ezekiel, and Job's declaration of faith, the Old Testament illustrates a burgeoning understanding of life after death. These examples not only provide a glimpse into the nature of divine intervention but also set the stage for the future promises of resurrection, culminating in the New Testament revelation of Christ's resurrection and the hope of eternal life for believers. The Old Testament's engagement with resurrection invites readers of the scrolls to contemplate the profound mystery of life, death, and the enduring promise of renewal by faith that resonates throughout scripture.

39

THE REVOLUTION THAT WAS THE HEBREW PROPHETS.

If it was not for the prophet Samuel's input into the life of the entire Hebrew people of his generation, the twelve tribes could have dissipated into a bland, dilapidated sort of existence that simply blended in with the idolatrous ethnic groups that lived all around them (1 Samuel 3:20). Samuel was God's prophet, chosen, anointed and, in the deepest meaning possible, a man of God. This writer esteems Samuel on par with Moses as far as the impact on future generations were concerned.

Prophets sustained the life and Direction of Israel

Samuel was the first prophet in Israel who addressed the whole nation. God initiated prophets and their prophecies to address Israel throughout their own generations as well as impacting future generations. Samuel was the prototype of them all, and that is why Peter infers that Samuel was the first in Acts 3:24. From then on, prophets and prophecy was in the warp and woof of Israel's timeline. Whether Israel was in blessing or in poverty, in revival or backslidden, Israel was drip-fed on prophets and prophecy. God always had something to say. As it was, so it is today.

Samuel, the prototype prophet, cum teacher, cum apostle, cum evangelist, cum father of the nation, singlehandedly brought Israel out of the darkness of the days of anarchy and the Judges into the light, and the prosperous days of the monarchy with David and Solomon. It was his whole life's calling and project.

If it wasn't for Samuel listening to and acting on a word from God, when Saul had died at the battle of Gilboa the Philistines would have utterly routed the nation of Israel after having routed their armed forces in battle. Who knows? Logically and practically speaking, they might have been close to annihilation and slavery.

The day Samuel poured his ram's horn full of oil over David's head, David became a different person. From then on he was killing lions, bears and giant Philistines, learning how to handle people by what he learned from leading sheep. There was nothing special about the oil that was poured on his head *per se*. The precious oil was merely a symbol of the reality of what was happening. This young lad, whom I fancy to have been around 12 years old, was destined to be king. All that was needed for him to reign was supernaturally poured on David by God at that moment. He had to grow up into a character that could handle all the gifts and abilities that God had given him at that same moment when Samuel prophesied to him and poured the oil on his head. It was, as all prophecy is, a matter of the word and the Spirit working together. As Samuel anointed David with oil, at that very moment God anointed David with something that only heaven knows about. And this all started when a prophet ignored his own physical vision when he saw the huge strapping sons of Jesse and listened to the word of God prophesying over a twelve-year-old shepherd boy. That is how important prophets were and still are.

It was Samuel who initiated the schools of the prophets. When Samuel was a mere lad there was no prophecy, no open vision, and prophets were sparse, rare and low-key in Israel. Samuel set the bar high as becoming the definitive description of a prophet of God and then introduced others to moving in the realm of the Spirit.

Prophets sustained both sections of the divided kingdom

There are quite a few moments throughout the history of Israel and Judah where, if it had not been for the voice of a prophet, utter catastrophe or even annihilation could have taken place. I believe in the sovereignty of God most passionately. I also believe that the Old Testament Hebrew Prophets issued their produce from His sovereignty. When these men spoke, it was the sovereign Yahweh speaking.

If it wasn't for the prophet Gad, there is a strong probability Saul would have caught and killed David before he was ever crowned king (1 Samuel 22:5.) That is what one prophet accomplished with the word from God for that moment.

If it wasn't for the prophet Nathan, David would not have received the promise that he would have a descendant who would sit on his throne forever (2 Samuel 7). That promise sustained not only David but the faithful of Israel through the centuries. One prophet with one glorious prophecy!

If it wasn't for Ahijah, the prophet who anointed Jeroboam, the son of Nebat, to become king over the ten northern tribes of the Hebrews, Rehoboam, Solomon's brash, headstrong son and heir, would have singlehandedly destroyed the spirit of the Hebrew people. It would have been slavery under a Hebrew king (1 Kings 11:29-39. 2 Chronicles 10:15). How incredibly influential was that prophet with his word, that was not his word, but God's. One prophet, one message, leading to a redirection of history! Such large doors swinging on such a small hinge!

If it wasn't for Ahijah in his old age and blindness, Jeroboam, the son of Nebat, would never have had judgment spoken over him that was to put another dynasty on the throne of Israel (1 Kings 14:1-18). One aged blind prophet changed the historical timeline of Israel for a second time. Oh! The power of a single prophetic message at the right time, in the right place, spoken to the right person.

If it wasn't for Shemaiah the prophet, speaking to Rehoboam and the nation of Judah (comprising Judah and Benjamin) as they were about to declare war with a fight to the death with Israel (comprising the ten northern tribes) (2 Chronicles 11:1-5), who on earth can possibly guess what terrible things would have happened? Carnage and death throughout the entire Hebrew people, with animosity, hatred, and mutual military belligerence for generations, is all I can imagine that would have been the result if Shemaiah had not spoken. The anger and ill feelings at that moment was so deep, that annihilation for their fellow Hebrews was clearly in the air. One prophet again literally saved the nation and changed history.

If it wasn't for that same prophet Shemaiah speaking to King Rehoboam and the princes of Judah when Pharaoh Shishak came to rape Judah and Jerusalem, Egypt would have utterly ravaged the City of David and the surrounding state. Because the king and his cronies listened to Shemaiah and publicly repented of not having followed Yahweh in their leadership, partial deliverance was granted to Judah (2 Chronicles 12:5). All because of the courage of a single prophet to stand up and reprove the king and his government. That took incredible courage. That took the certainty of a word from God.

If it wasn't for the prophet Azariah, speaking to King Asa about the godlessness of the nation of Judah (2 Chronicles 15:1-12), the dark ages that lay before them would have been nothing but a deep swamp of misery. Azariah's word brought repentance and a new and national covenant to serve Yahweh. One prophet brought Judah to its knees before God. and ushered in days of blessing, radically changing the course of the nation's history at that point of time.

If it wasn't for Jehu the prophet (not the Jehu who later became king of Israel) that wicked king Baasha of Israel would have assumed his godless lifestyle was all in the will of God. Baasha's son Elah was assassinated by a man called Zimri, who took the throne. And just as Jehu the prophet had prophesied, Zimri had all and sundry related to Baasha murdered. (1 Kings 16:7) Even though Jehu, by the Spirit of the Lord, could see the demonic things that were coming, by the prophetic word he spoke and it all came to pass. The prophets see and say the bad things as well as the good. Again, a single prophet was predicting and explaining the historical narrative of Israel before it happened. My grasp of prophecy would teach that if a prophecy of this kind had not been spoken, what was spoken would never have come to pass. The word of God is an event. It was imperative for the prophetic word to be spoken out loud in the earth. Jehu's words came to pass as all true predictive prophecy does.

If it wasn't for Elijah confronting idolatry by the word of the Lord, Israel would have been lost to Baal worship and missed their destiny even earlier than they did. What Elijah did in calling down fire from heaven was completely according to the word of God that had come to him (1 Kings 18:36). His actions were prophetic and done at the impulse of the word of God. One man; one prophet; a man of like passions such as we; and such a man as this was called "prophet" and was given a message that again, changed history.

If it wasn't for Elisha telling the king of Israel what the king of Syria was up to, Israel may have been wiped off the map by their northern neighbours (2 Kings 6:8-23). Every plan for battle and the destruction of Israel that the king of Syria concocted was revealed from heaven in detail to Elisha, who, in turn, reported those plans to the king of Israel. The Syrian king was positive he had a traitor in court until he learned of the anointing that sat on Elisha. Israel was saved from annihilation by Elisha's prophecies of those days. But there was more. Because of his powerful prophetic gift, Elisha was personally attacked by the entire Syrian army. But by another of Elisha's prophetic words, the Syrian forces were all struck blind. Elisha had them all fed and led back to their homeland. Needless to say, Syria did not attack Israel again for quite some time. One prophet of the Lord had changed the course of current affairs and international relations. A prophet of God is not a man to trifle with.

If it wasn't for Elisha instructing one of his disciples to anoint Jehu, son of Nimshi as king over Israel, the nation's history would have been utterly different. (2 Kings 9:1-13)

If it wasn't for Jonah declaring God's word to Assyria, the entire military strategy programme of Assyria during those days would probably have been more successful against Judah and Jerusalem than it actually was. Jonah's prophecy and the humble response of the Assyrians would have undoubtedly altered their attitude to Israel and Judah for a generation or two. Again, the destructive forces of an alien nation were delayed by the strength and courage of a prophet with a word from God (Jonah).

The priceless value of true divinely inspired prophecy to both Judah and Israel is as awe-inspiring as the priceless value of the prophets themselves, especially the writing prophets. The prophet and the prophetic words that are present on nearly every page of the Old Testament reveal their immense importance to the God-guided history of God's nation. Israel's existence, both biblically and thereafter, is a fact of history that was actually directed and fed by prophecy and God's prophets every step of the way.

The Prophetic Revolution

The prophetic revolution that was initiated by Samuel and, to a degree was perpetuated by the presence of the schools of the prophets that he created was a moving animal in gestation until the likes of Elijah and Elisha burst forth. These two men were incredibly separate, different and alone. None of the schools of the prophets supported Elisha in his battles. In fact, the schools all seemed to be in hiding whilst Elijah's intense confrontation with the demons that drove Jezebel and Ahab. They were all out of their caves and watching Elijah at a distance after the fire from heaven event. Elisha, no matter how singular he was in his dealings with the world, seems to have had some kind of intimacy with the scattered schools.

By the time Isaiah comes to the fore there are institutionalised groups of prophets that did not have the character, morality or behavioural routines of the likes of Elijah, Elisha and the writing prophets. Isaiah, Amos, Hosea, Micah and Jonah were all alive around the same generation. Each one of these writing prophets seems alone, wilfully isolated and utterly different. It is with the writing prophets, the so-called classical prophets, that the prophet and his prophecy reach its peak of influence and power.

The writing prophets stand out from any crowd of believers. Even though we only have the writings they left for posterity, each one of these extraordinary men of God seems radically different than the one before or the one after. The choice of words, the sentence construct, their characteristics and their language flow are all astonishingly unique. And each one was vitally important to the Hebrew people. It is no wonder that the Hebrew scribes treasured and revered the very scrolls of their writings.

40

DESTINY AND FATE.

The concepts of "destiny" and "fate" are often used interchangeably in everyday language in 2025, yet in the context of biblical theology and spirituality, they carry totally distinct meanings and implications. Understanding these differences is crucial for grasping the biblical perspective on human purpose, divine sovereignty, and individual agency. I want, here, to present the differences between a biblical pursuit of a God-intended destiny and the notion of fate.

Let me define the two words and their meaning.

Destiny: In a biblical context, destiny refers to the purpose or calling that God has designed for an individual or a community. It encompasses the unique plans and intentions that God has for each person, informed by His love, wisdom, and sovereignty. Pursuing one's destiny involves aligning oneself with God's will and actively engaging in the journey that leads to fulfilling that purpose.

Fate: Fate often connotes a predetermined outcome that is fixed and unchangeable, governed by impersonal forces or a cosmic order. In many philosophical and religious traditions, fate suggests that events are destined to happen regardless of human actions or decisions, implying a sense of inevitability and lack of control.

One of my neighbours, who would not wear a facemask during the COVID lockdown, regularly told me, "Well, if I die, it must be my time." The media, in general, and TV drama and film scripts are strewn with similar lines that say, "God's got this." "It'll be alright", "Don't worry, everything is gonna be OK!"." These words, when taken seriously, conclude that we are all fated to a future that is already determined for us. I believe there is a bit of tosh here.

To believe this stroke drags us into spiritual slumber like the ancient confidence in the "law of the Medes and the Persians," with the same mental gymnastics somersault, the (anti-Daniel) minions of Persia easily persuaded King Darius to commit an atrocity by arguing, "Now, O king, establish the injunction and sign the document so that it may never be changed, in accordance with the law of Medes and Persians, which guarantees that it may not ever be altered or revoked." (Daniel 6:8) This thought, similarly antiquated and fashionable, is an ambition for and conviction in a world that is steady, secure, static, conventional, and maintaining a happy status quo that will exist forever.

2. Agency and Responsibility

Biblical Destiny: The biblical pursuit of destiny emphasizes human agency and responsibility. Scripture repeatedly highlights the importance of individual choices, faith, and obedience in fulfilling God's intended purposes. For example, Jeremiah 29:11 states, *"For I know the plans I have for you,"* affirming that God has specific intentions for individuals, yet these plans require active engagement and faithfulness from those called.

Fate: Fate, on the other hand, often implies a lack of agency. If one believes in fate, they may feel that their life is governed by external forces beyond their control. This perspective can lead to fatalism, where individuals may resign themselves to outcomes without taking responsibility for their choices or actions. In this view, personal effort and moral decisions may seem irrelevant since the outcome is already determined.

To believe this stroke drags us all into spiritual slumber like the ancient confidence in the "law of the Medes and the Persians," with the same mental gymnastics somersault, the (anti-Daniel) minions of Persia easily persuaded King Darius to commit an atrocity by arguing, "Now, O king, establish the injunction and sign the document so that it may never be changed, in accordance with the law of Medes and

Persians, which guarantees that it may not ever be altered or revoked." (Daniel 6:8) This thought, similarly antiquated and fashionable, is an ambition for, and conviction in a world that is steady, secure, static, conventional, and maintaining a happy status quo that will exist forever.

This sense of simultaneous fate, chance and fortune, when spoken, seems to me to surreptitiously believe that life is in God's (or "fate's") hands and, therefore, circumstances are all to be wonderfully received and accepted because "He's got the whole world in his hands." In fact, however, it is a statement of despair and resignation, without hope or expectation for anything new. It is a thoughtless remark used by many to avoid any serious "God talk". The paradigms of TV series and Hollywood movies, as well as the statement of my neighbour together, suggest a sense of helplessness at the mercy of circumstances that are beyond our control. We are helpless in the clutch of blind, arbitrary fate. This sort of thinking is often spoken lightly by people, but it is seriously a philosophy of death and apathy.

It amounts to an utter loss of agency when being an agent is understood as the capacity to act to open new futures for self, neighbour, and the world. When one truly unredeemably loses agency, one is nothing but a passive, helpless recipient of whatever comes. Whether what comes is from God, the devil or from elsewhere, who gives a fig if we are all helpless to respond and alter anything? This mindset is a refusal to take any initiative or responsibility beyond the present status quo. Let's just all relax and let the current take us over the Niagara to wherever the falls take us and finish up.

3. Divine Sovereignty and Human Free Will

Destiny as God-Intended: The biblical understanding of destiny involves a harmonious relationship between divine sovereignty and human free will. God is sovereign and omniscient, knowing the end from the beginning (Isaiah 46:10). However, His sovereignty does not negate human free will; rather, it works in conjunction with it. For instance, the story of Joseph in Genesis illustrates how God's sovereign plan unfolds through human actions, choices, and even suffering, resulting in a greater purpose (Genesis 50:20).

Fate as Determined: In contrast, fate suggests a deterministic worldview where outcomes are fixed and unalterable. This perspective often does not account for the complexities of human decision-making or the moral dimensions of life. In fatalism, the belief that one cannot change one's fate can lead to despair or apathy, as individuals may feel powerless against the predetermined course of events.

Psalm 115. Talking about philosophies, actions and mindsets that bring a blanket loss of agency or the wilful allowance of anything to come and get you.

Our God is in the heavens;
he does whatever he pleases. (Verse 3)

Yahweh is alive, active, and free to do whatever He wishes. What a succinct affirmation of the Living God. By contrast, the Psalm lingers in a detailed characterization of idols that are quite unlike Yahweh:

Their idols (of the nations) are of silver and gold,
the work of human hands.
They have mouths, but cannot speak;
They have eyes, but do not see.
They have ears but do not hear;
They have noses, but do not smell.
They have hands, but do not feel;
They have feet, but do not walk;
they make no sound in their throats. (Verses 4-7)

The idols are inanimate and powerless; they can do nothing. They cannot even clear their throats! "Ahem!" However, the point to notice is the derivative statement of verse 8:

Those who make them are like them;
so are all who trust in them. (Verse 8)

Aha! Those who worship and trust in dumb, deaf, and daft powerless idols become like the idols they worship – that is inanimate, purposeless, and stupid, unable to act as an agent to better their future. They remain, like a block of wood or a fancy stone, lifeless waiting their fate in the fire or stuffed into any built construction. The idols have no agency; those who worship them arrive at the same constituency. I do not conclude that my neighbour is a worshipper of idols. But I do conclude that he has willingly signed on for a world in which she is neither permitted nor expected to exercise any kind of agency. She understands herself to have no role to play in the shaping of the future that is to come upon him, and/or all of us.

I fear, moreover, that the Church's singular insistence upon grace from God has become "cheap" in the sense that it seems not to consist in a call to, or offer of, agency. God is not after Pew warmers, but world mind changers.

In Psalm 115 we see that worshipping idols leads people to become like idols. Worshipping the God who freely does what he pleases – with the implied message; "become free like the God of freedom." The covenantal-prophetic statement of the Old Testament, to which Jesus is an heir, is an invitation to agency in the world as a part of the human role in the covenant with Yahweh.

4. Purpose and Meaning

Biblical Destiny: Pursuing a God-intended destiny imbues life with purpose and meaning. It encourages individuals to seek alignment with God's will through prayer, study of Scripture, and community engagement. This pursuit involves discovering one's gifts, talents, and calling, which can lead to a fulfilling life that contributes positively to society and reflects God's glory. Hebrews 12:1-2 encourages believers to "run with endurance the race that is set before us," emphasizing the active pursuit of God's purposes.

Fate: The concept of fate can lead to a more nihilistic worldview, where life may seem devoid of purpose. If everything is predetermined, the search for meaning may diminish, as individuals might believe their lives are merely the result of chance or fatalistic forces. This view can foster a sense of hopelessness, as the notion of fate often lacks the redemptive and transformative power found in the pursuit of destiny.

5. Biblical Examples

Examples of Destiny:

Moses: Called by God to lead the Israelites out of Egypt, Moses' journey illustrates the pursuit of a God-intended destiny involving both divine calling and human response.

Esther: Her story reflects the idea of being placed in a specific position *"for such a time as this"* (Esther 4:14), emphasizing the importance of actively fulfilling one's role in God's plan.

Examples of Fate:

- While the Bible does not explicitly endorse the idea of fate as understood in a deterministic sense, certain narratives can illustrate the consequences of choices that lead to seemingly inevitable outcomes. For instance, the tragic fate of King Saul, who, due to his disobedience to God, faced dire consequences, illustrates how a series of choices can lead to a predetermined end.

So, the biblical pursuit of a God-intended destiny is characterized by an understanding of divine purpose, human agency, and the belief that individuals can actively engage in fulfilling God's plans through their choices and actions. In contrast, fate suggests a predetermined and unchangeable outcome that often leads to a sense of powerlessness and lack of purpose. By embracing a biblical understanding of destiny, individuals are encouraged to seek God's will, exercise their free will, and find meaning in the journey of life, ultimately reflecting the divine image and contributing to the broader narrative of God's redemptive plan.

As the book of Deuteronomy makes clear, being responsive to God's "Statutes, commandments, and ordinances" requires energetic interpretive engagement and decision-making about the concrete shape of loyalty, fidelity, integrity, and purity in the context of human relationships. Thus, the covenant explanation of Deuteronomy posits Israel as a community at work and interacting to assist in the generating of an improved and better future.

41

DOES ONE HAVE TO BE ECCENTRIC AND/OR LOSE COMMONLY ACCEPTED NORMALCY, OR OTHODOXY IN ORDER to CHANGE THE WORLD?

Most Christian denominations, movements and streams have a statement of orthodoxy. They cling to a "This is what we believe," document. In these constitutional statements, one has access to a list of aspects of their own denominational flavour, all listed as essential, factoring in the ministers and members that belong to each body, movement, or denomination of Christians. It is a kind of "This is our identity. Believe these points, or go elsewhere" kind of thing. These variant tenets for group orthodoxy commonly sanitise God and the Biblical narrative to their own standard of spiritual normalcy, minimising issues that are not considered vital to the faith unless or until somebody makes a major issue of those minimised issues within the body of the group. Redactions are especially majored on in many Christian Old Testament rationalisations. It is my theory that conventional ministerial training tends to develop an aversion of what is theologically termed "not our ethos," in whatever each denomination is administrating in their theological training. This aversion leads to rejection of anything defined as "not of our ethos" because of where it may supposedly, hypothetically lead. "If it's not a stated tenet of our faith, it needs to be avoided in case it interferes with our identity and stature amongst other groups."

Why do so many Christians want to sanitise God, the death and resurrection of Christ, as well as the Bible into a set of static statements that reduce their faith to a boring set of dead motionless canons? Orthodoxy is an Anglicised Greek word. It was utilised as a Latin word and strictly means "true teaching", or "correct worship." Orthodoxy refers to humanly authorised and/or generally accepted theology, theory, doctrine, or practice. Today it carries conservatism, traditionalism, conformism, and the like. Non-conformist Christianity holds firmly to its own conformist Orthodoxy. All groups come into being with revolutionary fire burning in their spirits. All groups, however, blend into the national wallpaper as groups settle and get larger. Pioneering groups become settlers within a generation or two. Now, there is an oxymoron if ever there was one. These "strange doctrines" that everybody has (but not "us" – whoever "us" may be) are explained to us quite clearly in denominational colleges and seminaries. However, my world-shaking observation is, that not being part of the other denominations and streams, I discover that all that I was taught of the cults and deviations are just not consistent from what the cults and deviations teach and believe. Not only have I discovered that much of what I was taught concerning Mormonism, Jehovah's witnesses, Christadelphians, etc., was inaccurate, but methinks those various cults and deviations must be horrified and thinking us as totally mocking them, as I think and feel when evangelical cessationists teach against Pentecostals and Charismatics, "because they believe this …" and then I hear 1 hour, and sometimes 2 hour talks of what we Pentecostals believe and get up to. I seriously am caught between raucous laughter and violent anger when I, fifty-six years a Pentecostal have never seen or heard of their long list of complaints about what we believe. Methinks that wisdom calls us to shut our mouths and just pray for each other. It seems that nearly all Christian people believe that their group is orthodox, while all others are just a little strange. Poor them!

Orthodoxy is a formulation and organising of truth that fully intends to silence and/or eliminate all or any alternatives. Orthodoxy exists with the assumption that it holds a body of truth that cannot be added to nor subtracted from. Orthodoxy carries certitudes that, by their very nature breed legalism and pervert faith's work in believer's hearts and minds. For these reasons, it is true that the denominations, streams, and movements are the very Guardians of the status quo. Apart from clear absolutes of integrity and, purity of heart, and the power of Christ, there are a few aspects of the Christian faith that maintain a status Quo.

ECCENTRIC UNORTHODOXY IS THE NORM THROUGHOUT THE BIBLE FOR PIONEERS.

The perceived eccentricity of major achievers and powerful ministers of the Word can be attributed to several factors.

Passion and Commitment lead many to be considered eccentric.....: Their strong devotion to their faith and mission may lead them to express themselves in unique ways that may seem unconventional to others.

Visionary Thinking can scare the average members of any group. Many successful ministers operate outside traditional norms, driven by a vision that others may not immediately understand or accede to. This forward-thinking mindset can come across as eccentric.

Different cultures have varying definitions of what is considered "normal." What seems eccentric in one context may be celebrated in another.

Many powerful ministers possess charismatic traits that can lead them to adopt distinctive styles of preaching and leadership, which might be perceived as odd or unconventional. I am referring to personal charisma here when I use the word charismatic.

Some people and/or leaders may have extravagantly striking and interesting personal experiences. Their life stories, including struggles, triumphs, and divine encounters, can shape their personalities and behaviours in ways that might appear to the majority of "normal" members of a group as eccentric.

The creative expression found in one person's ministry - through music, art, or innovative outreach - can lead to unconventional methods that stand out as eccentric.

Some may consciously reject societal expectations, choosing instead to live and minister in ways that align with their beliefs and values, which can seem eccentric to the broader public.

Overall, pastors, leaders, members or groups with unique approaches and perspectives often stem from a deep-rooted commitment to their faith and mission, which may not always align with mainstream societal norms.

The Bible is full of narratives and biographies of people whose belief systems and experiences were not consistent with any statements of orthodoxy of their time. The apostle John, for instance, spoke of the Seven Spirits of God. It is in the scriptures, so we accept it as a wonderful mystery. However, I am sure he would have been rejected in many churches today if he had introduced the concept to us for the first time in our generation. "We believe in God the Father, Son and Holy Spirit. The idea of seven spirits of God is seriously unorthodox." Samuel hacked a man to pieces in the Name of the Lord. In fact, he was outraged that the king of Israel had not done the hacking before he had arrived in the camp. What do we do with that one? Sounds eccentric to me! Joshua "met a man" whom he referred to as Yahweh Himself, 1200 years before Christ was born. The Apostle John told us that Isaiah saw Jesus 800 years before He was born. Philip told the story of how he was talking to an African politician in one place, and the next thing he remembered was that he was located miles away on a different mission. Eccentric? Unorthodox, or what? Wild, would you say? Some of these kinds of narratives may have or have not occurred since. But were they, or are they unsound or orthodox? Because things occurred in the gospels or in acts, we dare not even hint at their validity.

We are about to stare long and hard at one of the strongest, "unorthodox" men in the whole Bible. The divine conflicts Generated and fought by Elijah (and later Elisha) in God's expression of love and passion for the fidelity and continuance of His people show the

Almighty as more tender and exalted as I have ever perceived, even in the context of the New Testament.

We are, as I write, and as you read, one of the most unique human beings that ever walked the planet. Strange, weird, eccentric, and inexplicably, radically different – not only different from the rest of the world before or after him, but Elijah and Elisha were two of a pair and totally different from each other.

The first man is strange in his dress, his aloneness, and even within his race. He is said to be a "Tishbite". A man from Tishbe. Some scholars are not sure that the word refers to a geographical location or whether it simply means he was a "traveller". "Was he even Jewish?" Elijah ultimately mentored, tutored, and imparted all he had to a former farmer named Elisha. Elisha was expressly selected by Yahweh. The unorthodox manner of life and work, their power, and grace, with tinges of harshness that was mingled with gentleness, of the two of them make them stand out like suns in an otherwise deeply dark social sky. Elijah and Elisha were human beings with weaknesses and character flaws like everybody else, and yet, in a few criteria, they were clear sketches of Jesus Christ in His heavenly self.

These two men changed the course of Israeli and Jewish history, and as far as we understand, both achieved their impact while being alone with God.

GROUP ORTHODOXY CAN BRING A SAMENESS THAT REJECTS THE EXTREME.

Why is it that many (if not all) of the men and women who have taken their generation to a different level in God have strange "unorthodox" corners to their theology, character and Godly lifestyle? Why is it that most of these men of God had some sort of "quirky" dots and dashes holding their convictions tight? Quirks of unique perceptions of God and the unseen world were what pushed them into supernatural ministry, the supernatural ministry that attracted masses to Christ, to the church and its orthodoxy, the same church that, to a degree, rejected them both for their faults and failings. It was the awesome power of what sat on their lives that made them to be feared and awed.

The Bible teaches in the New Testament that gatherings and meetings for the mutual sharing of faith and spirituality is a necessity for soundness of heart, mind and soul. In the Old Testament there were indeed exhortations and commands given for the nation of Israel to gather and mix. But many of the generals of the faith were "lone rangers" with little or no close encouragement, apart from Yahweh Himself.

EXTREME ANOINTING, REVELATION AND ECCENTRICITY DOES NOT MEAN LACK OF ORTHODOXY.

Soon after my conversion to Christ and after I had settled into reading matter, magazines and journals that fed my hunger for God, the Bible and New Testament Christianity, I was somewhat dismayed that I was considered by some Christian folks to be drinking from soiled systems, profane pastors, and tainted teachers. As the years have passed, I am aware that such an attitude has continued with some. I remember one highly esteemed Pentecostal leader insisting that his members absolutely ignore a well-known American Evangelist who was holding meetings quite literally across the road from his own church base. However, no matter how loved and esteemed this Pentecostal leader was, I understand that many of his people went to hear the forbidden man of so-called extremism and thought he was most edifying.

Many of these Generals of God who have died and left a positive legacy are hailed, and praised and written about now – but were despised and rejected while they were alive. Smith Wigglesworth was one such character. With most of these people, their strange characteristics were interwoven with what many Christians would affirm as some very strange beliefs. Others were just followed and trailed by supernatural phenomena that only added to the mystique of their strangeness. You ask for examples?

ECCENTRICITY OF HEROES OF BREAKTHROUGH AND FAITH.

Charles Grandison Finney (August 29,1792 – August 16, 1875) was considered a downright heretic by many – until church leaders met him personally. When he visited Britain (1860), Spurgeon, to my understanding, did not in any way even acknowledge his visit. Those English church leaders who met him said they had never before encountered such grace and gentleness. The life, energy and innovation in Finney's meetings drove many ministers away. His penitent stool at the front of his meetings was considered wild and extreme to the contemporary Christian opinion of his day. He was one of the first to have "altar calls" at the end of his public addresses. He is known to have stopped a service and sent the congregation home for their lack of interest. "Come back when you are ready to receive." Orthodox? I have read much of Finney's works. Some of it I disagree with. Some of it I simply do not understand. Most of it would be acceptable to the majority.

Maria Woodworth Etter (July 22,1844 - September 16,1924). As well as moving in healing, prophecy and deliverance ministry that separated her from the vast majority of American ministers of her day, this lady had supernatural phenomena follow her wherever she went. We are talking of phenomena that did not seem to involve her directly but were popularly attributed to her on the grounds that strange things occurred wherever she preached. Empirical evidence pointed the finger at her as the causative factor of strange occurrences. People were sometimes transfixed, statue-like, some for 24 hours at a time. She had no explanation or teaching about the strange sight. But extreme faith, extreme commitment, and some extreme personal habits of discipline were part of her regime of holiness. Signs and wonders followed her preaching of the word. Many questioned her orthodoxy.

T.L. Osborn and A.A. Allen were welcomed to the UK for their renowned remarkable evangelistic results and the healing of the sick that was randomly plentiful in their mission gatherings. However, both in the USA as well as the UK, most pastors advised their "orthodox" people to stay away from these "extremists" during their lifetime. Their convictions about every sickness being instigated directly by demons were not received by Western Christian members and ministers. Whether I believe their teaching or not is irrelevant to my purpose. What I am saying is that I earnestly seek, pray and long for whatever it was that these men and women carried. They changed the lives of thousands towards Christ and left a lasting legacy. Both these men, called of God learned a lot of their convictions from a man named William Branham.

William Branham and Smith Wigglesworth were each educated only to an elementary level. They held to aspects of their faith that the rest of the body of Christ generally considered to be simply incorrect. But alongside these two giants with their lack of education, we have the likes of John Wimber, George Jeffreys and Charles Finney, who were great – some would add – "over-educated".

It is a fruitless pastime to throw the baby out with the bathwater. To be sure, there are many high profiled and divinely used people in the healing, deliverance, teaching and prophetic ministries. My question is, however, why did or do those in my list of "extremists," who moved in extreme power exhibit such an extreme visitation of grace on their lives if what they emphasise is considered strange, unbiblical and at times downright heretical by the main-stream body of Christ. Could it be that God Himself looks beyond those things that tend to offend vast swathes of senior high-profile Christian leaders.

Convictions and belief systems that verge from the "orthodox" are seen in issues like:

George Jeffreys was a Welsh preacher who birthed the Elim Pentecostal Church movement in the U.K., now a worldwide operation. He taught a difference between the Holy Spirit and the Spirit of Christ, something that few of his followers adhered to. I remember when I was at college, one of George Jeffreys's early adherents taught that very issue. The student lecture hall was something of a shouting match for nearly an hour. The "orthodoxy" of the class was insulted by the "unorthodoxy" of the teacher. Or was it the other way round?

Charles Grandison Finney was intellectually completely removed from the normal widespread Calvinistic theology of his day, denouncing orthodox Reformed teaching as ignorant and in error. It was like a single well-educated Christian telling the whole body of Christ that they were all wrong. I am neither embellishing nor exaggerating Finney's stance. He spoke assertively and authoritatively without any "conventional" theological training. His unique doctrinal deportment estranged him from Christians who had never met him. He was greatly loved by those who engaged with him.

John Wimber: Diverted from, "Healing in the atonement," and was only listened to because of the trail of the miraculous that he left behind him wherever he went. His gracious manner and the astute academic explanatory lectures he delivered won many people over to Christ. He was a "developed Quaker." Many Pentecostals and evangelicals had issues with his, "healing is not in the atonement" stance. He was belittled by all cessationists who knew him.

The sadly fallen and now well-known serial abuser TB Joshua held completely unique insights and mode of presentation. No conventional training in the slightest. This writer met this man and was impressed by how he taught soundly without any of the terminology or emphases that is the bread and butter of millions in the Western world. I never heard him refer to justification or sanctification, and yet those concepts were firmly taught. Normally classified as a Pentecostal I only once heard him speak or pray in tongues. He even dissuaded his people from speaking in tongues. But that is a discussion for another time. I simply acknowledge the man's strange corners of belief. And yet he was followed by a divine credential and approval that very few carry.

William Branham was another uneducated man of God. This man is probably the best example of strange Christian beliefs yet astonishing divine manifestations in much of what he said and did. He vilified the teaching of the Trinity, following the early Pentecostals that he mixed with early in his life and taught what was called the "Oneness teaching". He also taught something known as "the Serpent Seed", which, in a skeletal one-liner, taught that the serpent, the devil, had sexual intercourse with Eve, thus producing Cain. The man was constantly immersed in visionary experiences. His son testified that his father sometimes had 30-50 visions per day. He taught that every sickness was a demon. At first, he was deeply loved and treasured by the church worldwide but was later rejected because of his ever-deepening stray from orthodoxy. His Old Testament emphasis confused many. His healing ministry was clearly God sanctioned.

Alph Lukau is a contemporary prophet based at the time of writing in Johannesburg, South Africa. Concepts of authority and the supremacy of the Prophetic ministry are his heart's burden, issues that are so hard to swallow by the Christian masses. His authority over circumstances, sickness and even life are truly jaw-dropping. He goes where no prophet we know of has been.

A.A. Allen: Like William Branham, Allen taught that every sickness is a demon. His services and ministry were conducted in an almost music hall ambience.

Benny Hinn: Straining into a teaching role when many Christians find his claim to that gift somewhat questionable. Initially seen as unorthodox by masses, is in his senior years quieter and more widely accepted.

Tijo Thomas presents himself uniquely spiritualising the biblical narrative and its history, but with incredible insights and steering that have changed so many lives for the better.

Charles Finney, T.L. Osborn, William Branham, Oral Roberts, A.A. Allen, Henry's Glory meetings, Chard and Harry Greenwood, Morris Cerullo, Benny Hinn, Tijo Thomas, and Alph Lukau are just a few of the names of those who have earned my respect and reverence for their contribution to the body of Christ, and the personal load bearing truths that are the construct of my faith. Most of these men have well-known flaws and character warts that are commonly more highlighted than their anointing and gifting that took them where others have never been or are scared to go. I only list these people because of their general rejection by the body of Christ in their days.

There are, of course, biblical examples of unorthodox encounters with God: Enoch believing that he even could be translated, which Hebrews 11 tells us is what he had faith for. Unorthodox or what?

EXTREME VISION AND ANOINTING MAY SEEM HERETICAL TO A GROUP ORTHODOXY.

How did these people receive gift-producing revelations that mainstream Christian authorities declared as standing somewhere between theological error and downright heresy?

I discovered that the fullest and most comprehensive manifestations of all my Pentecostal convictions were seen in these "kind" of persons that generally were or are considered, by the main body of Christ, to be "extreme," "fringe" and some even had the general caucus of Christians labelling them as "heretics." "They are not subject to Christian or biblical orthodoxy," said one pastor. In those early days after my conversion in the late 1960's I was flummoxed by this kind of response. Today, I assert that orthodoxy is a formulation and organising of truth that fully intends to silence and eliminate any or all alternative thought. In the realm of the spirit, orthodoxy can tend to kill creativity and exploration. George Orwell said, "Orthodoxy is unconscious." And in the context of this comatose state, orthodoxy wakes up when the unconscious ears hear the rattle of any beliefs alien (or slightly different) to the status quo they claim to hold to.

What were the insights and revelations that birthed these anointings?

REVELATION DOES NOT BREAK FROM ORTHODOXY, BUT FROM MEDIOCRITY WITHIN ORTHODOXY.

Why were most of these people forced to become "parachurchs" in their field of service? Was it, is it just plain jealousy, or are there other reasons why church leaders generally have ubiquitously criticised and maligned these so-called "unorthodox para-church extremists?"

It is unique and divinely ordered revelations and/or visions that impact all these "unorthodox" captains of the faith. There are examples of these kind of "unorthodox" experiences which caused many biblical characters to be included in the sacred narrative.

Abraham had a visible visitation from God, with nothing that we, today would refer to as a body of beliefs. Yahweh appeared to Abram and spoke two or three sentences, and Abram's extravagant explorative and creative faith was birthed and exercised immediately. That birth of faith led him away from Mesopotamia, leaving his family and culture. God's words invited adventure on the part of Abram. The key and first word divinely given to Abraham was, "go!"

Moses was launched into greatness by drawing close to a burning bush. It's not exactly an orthodox means of finding one's calling. He saw Yahweh in the flame and heard an audible voice. After a lengthy "job interview," Yahweh's order was for Moses to "go".

Joshua and his loitering around the Tent while Moses spoke with visible Yahweh, face to face, transported the son of Nun to a future of sheer excitement, exploration, and achievement.

There are others with "unorthodox" experiences. Gideon and his visible angelic visitation. Samuel and his call at night, the voice of God sounding like Eli.

All these men were lifted to excellence and achievement while leaving mediocrity and non-achievement behind.

REVELATION FROM HEAVEN FACILITATES PEOPLE TO SEE FURTHER AND CHANGE THINGS FOR THE BETTER.

Men of power have often had extreme insights into things not held by the vast majority of Christian leadership. i.e., Angel sightings, visible coloured auras that define the illness or demons in people's lives, seer's visions, hearing audible voices, etc., as well as different interpretations of popular well-quoted scriptures, and strong emphases on truths and scriptures that others see as trivial or minor. I ask, seriously and openly: Do mantles of Holy Spirit power have to be accompanied by strange unorthodoxy?

SUPERNATURAL REVELATION AND VISION CAN ESTRANGE OTHERWISE ORTHODOX PEOPLE FROM THE GROUP.

Why is it that these "extreme" movers of power and healing carry and teach their own definition of sound doctrine and major load-bearing truths that are so different from the "normal, average" pastor?

Why do some of these far-reaching, ground-breaking men and women who carry a powerful sod-turning, "breaker" anointing stand so far apart from the well-read and accepted "Systematic Theology" pathways of thought? Could somebody tell me, please?

EXTREME REVELATION AND ANOINTING IS NOT ALWAYS GIVEN TO MASTERFUL COMMUNICATORS.

How is it that a small number of these men were so deeply profound and far-reaching in their gifting and yet so ineffective and unattractive in their preaching and teaching and their personal presentation?

We need to lay hold of sound doctrine and not be afraid of revelations that are not in anybody's "Systematic Theology volume." The very concept of a body of Theology to be set in concrete as an intellectual system is a totally human construct in search of tidiness, thoroughness, and uniformity amongst the masses. It may not be intended to hinder exploratory spiritual and intellectual research and growth, but ultimately, that is exactly what it will do. Understandably, a table of orthodox beliefs and practices are required for human equality and to fulfil a desire for a level plain of theology and grasp of sound faith for newcomers to take hold of.

The author of the first systematic theology, as far as I understand, is generally considered to be Augustine of Hippo (354-430 A.D). His work was entitled "De Doctrina Christiana" (On Christian Doctrine). This work is often cited as one of the earliest examples of a "systematic theology" in the Christian tradition. Augustine's book aimed to provide a comprehensive framework for understanding and interpreting Christian beliefs and practices. Original, widely read and generally accepted as far as history tells us. The dye was set for the future. Instead of leaving people to wrest the necessary truth from the scriptures themselves, church leaders were now imposing their own belief systems and interpretations onto their followers. "The City of God" by Augustine of Hippo while not a systematic theology in the modern sense, addresses theological issues and has had a profound impact on Western Christian thought also, even though it is extravagantly allegorical.

John of Damascus, in the 8th century, wrote a book entitled "Exposition of the Orthodox Faith", in which he attempted to set in order and demonstrate the coherence of the theology of the classic texts of the Eastern theological tradition. It was also a classic defence of icons in church buildings.

The Dark Ages left Western Europe's Christian thought somewhat less organised. Peter Lombard's 12th-century volume entitled, "Sentences" in which he thematically collected a great series of quotations gleaned from the early church fathers, became the basis of the medieval scholastic tradition of thematic commentary and explanation.

Throughout church history thereafter, there have been several significant systematic theologies that have shaped Christian thought and theology.

"Summa Theologica" by Thomas Aquinas (13th century) was Aquinas' magnum opus in a comprehensive work that sought to harmonize Christian theology with the philosophy of Aristotle. It is a key text in Catholic theology. Summa Theologiae best exemplifies this scholastic tradition. I struggle with the thoughts of Aquinas as expressed in English. However, as far as I can fathom his work, he is, strangely, a Roman Catholic as near to Charles Finney as it is possible to be (or, chronologically, I should say Finney is close to Aquinas). That is probably the impact of Aristotle on the two of them.

The Lutheran exegesis tradition of a thematic, ordered exposition of Christian theology emerged in the 16th century with Philipp Melanchthon's "Loci Communes" (Common places (of thought)), and was countered by the Calvinistic mentality, exemplified by John Calvin's "Institutes of the Christian Religion." This huge volume is a foundational text of Reformed theology and has had a significant influence on Protestant thought for centuries.

These are just a few examples of significant systematic theologies in church history. Each of these works has contributed to the development of Christian theology and has influenced generations of theologians and believers. There are literally, hundreds of "Systematic Theology" volumes on the streets in the twenty-first century. All seeking an orthodoxy to be accepted by the masses of Christians in the world, yet all being differently postured.

When orthodoxy becomes the norm and the rule within a company within the faith or society, there are various impacts on the individuals within the various groups of Christians. Here are some potential consequences, briefly bullet-pointing the good points as well as the negative.

1. Unity and cohesion. Positive

Orthodoxy being the norm can conceivably lead to greater unity and cohesion among believers as a unified group within a denomination, stream or group who adhere and subscribe to the established beliefs and practices as labelled as "orthodoxy". It can create a sense of belonging and shared purpose within a community.

2. Certainty and stability. Positive

Believers may find comfort and stability in following orthodox beliefs, as they provide a clear framework for understanding the world and one's place in it. This can indeed lead to a sense of purposeful certainty and security.

3. Social acceptance. Neither Positive nor Negative,

Adhering to orthodox beliefs can conceivably lead to greater social acceptance within the broader religious community. Believers who strictly hold to and declare the priority of conforming to the norm may be more readily embraced and supported by their peers.

4. Conformity and pressure. Negative.

However, there can also be pressure to conform to the stated and written orthodoxy, which may stifle individual expression and critical thinking. Some believers may feel constrained or oppressed by rigid adherence to established doctrines.

5. Exclusion and marginalisation. Negative.

Those who do not fully adhere to some of the orthodox beliefs may face exclusion or marginalisation within the Christian community. This can lead to feelings of isolation and alienation for individuals who hold the slightest of non-conforming beliefs,

6. Intellectual stagnation. Negative.

A focus on orthodoxy as the norm may discourage critical enquiry and intellectual exploration within the community of believers. This can hinder the development of new ideas and interpretations, potentially leading to intellectual stagnation.

7. Conflict and division. Negative.

Differences in interpretation or practices within the community can lead to conflict and division among believers. Disagreements over orthodoxy may result in schisms or factions within the religious group.

8. Spiritual growth or stagnation

While orthodoxy can provide a strong foundation for spiritual growth for some believers, for others, it may lead others to a sense of spiritual stagnation or a lack of personal growth if there is no room for questioning or personal exploration.

Overall, the impact of orthodoxy as "the norm" on believers can vary depending on the individual, the specific religious community, and the broader cultural context in which they exist. It is important for believers to critically reflect on the implications of group orthodoxy and to consider how it may influence their personal beliefs, values, and experiences.

While Elijah and Elisha played vitally important roles in the ongoing history of Israel and in the prophetic tradition, their contributions were more focused on prophecy, moral guidance, and divine intervention rather than systematic theological analysis and organisation. However, their statements and activities show an utterly new dimension in issues they believed. The two of them entered areas of authority, power, and attitudes toward people and life that were extreme, to say the least. Prepare to be challenged.

The prophets Elijah and Elisha are known for their remarkable and sometimes extremely eccentric behaviours, as recorded in the Bible.

42

WHY SHOULD CHRISTIANS READ THE OLD TESTAMENT?

The Old Testament, often referred to as the Hebrew Bible, holds a foundational place in the Christian faith. While many modern Christians may prioritize the New Testament, viewing it as the primary source of their faith and practice, the Old Testament is essential for a holistic understanding of Christianity. Scholars like Walter Brueggemann, along with other theologians, emphasize the significance of the Old Testament in enriching the Christian faith, providing historical context, revealing God's character, and offering moral and ethical guidance. This essay explores these aspects to elucidate why Christians should engage deeply with the Old Testament.

One of the most compelling reasons for Christians to read the Old Testament is its historical context. The Old Testament provides the backdrop against which the New Testament unfolds. Understanding the narratives, laws, prophecies, and poetry of the Old Testament equips Christians to grasp the richness of the New Testament message.

Walter Brueggemann, a leading scholar in Old Testament studies, highlights that the Old Testament is not merely a collection of ancient texts but a vital part of the story of God's engagement with humanity. It narrates the covenant relationship between God and Israel, showcasing how God's promises and actions throughout history set the stage for the coming of Christ. For instance, the themes of exile and return, justice and mercy, and the longing for a Messiah resonate deeply throughout both Testaments, enriching the Christian understanding of Jesus' mission.

Moreover, the Old Testament provides insights into the early Christian community. The apostles and early followers of Jesus were steeped in Hebrew Scriptures, and their teachings are often grounded in Old Testament texts. By engaging with these writings, Christians can better appreciate the foundations of their faith, including crucial doctrines such as creation, sin, redemption, and the nature of God.

The Old Testament serves as a profound revelation of God's character and attributes. It portrays God as creator, sustainer, and redeemer, emphasizing His faithfulness, justice, and mercy. Through the narratives of figures such as Abraham, Moses, and David, the Old Testament illustrates God's desire for a relationship with humanity and His willingness to intervene in human affairs.

Brueggemann points out that the Old Testament reveals a God who is both transcendent and immanent, a deity who is beyond human comprehension yet actively involved in the world. The stories of Israel's struggles, triumphs, and failures reflect the complexities of faith and obedience. For instance, the lamentations of the Psalms articulate the human experience of suffering and doubt, allowing believers to connect with God in deeply personal ways.

Furthermore, the prophetic books challenge readers to understand God's concern for justice and righteousness. Prophets like Amos and Micah call for social justice, highlighting that true worship must be accompanied by ethical living. This emphasis on justice is foundational for Christian ethics, underscoring the relevance of the Old Testament in contemporary discussions about morality and social responsibility.

The Old Testament is replete with moral and ethical teachings that remain relevant today. The laws given to Israel, particularly in the books of Exodus and Leviticus, may seem distant to modern readers, but they encapsulate principles of justice, mercy, and community living that are essential for Christian life.

Brueggemann emphasizes that the Old Testament laws were not merely rules but a means of shaping a community that reflected God's character. The call to love one's neighbour, care for the marginalized, and pursue justice resonates throughout both Testaments. For example, Leviticus 19:18 states, "You shall love your neighbour as yourself," a commandment that Jesus later reiterates as central to the law and the prophets.

Moreover, the wisdom literature, including Proverbs and Ecclesiastes, offers insights into the human condition, relationships, and the pursuit of a meaningful life. These texts provide practical guidance on living wisely in a complex world, addressing issues such as integrity, humility, and the fear of the Lord. In a time when moral relativism is prevalent, the ethical teachings of the Old Testament provide a steadfast foundation for believers seeking to navigate life's challenges.

Another critical reason Christians should read the Old Testament is its profound narrative of hope and redemption. The Old Testament is filled with covenant promises that point toward future fulfilment. The prophecies of a coming Messiah, articulated in texts like Isaiah, foreshadow the arrival of Jesus Christ.

Brueggemann notes that the Old Testament's narrative arc is one of continual hope despite the recurring themes of sin and judgment. The cycles of disobedience and repentance in Israel's history ultimately lead to a longing for restoration and reconciliation with God. This theme is particularly evident in the prophetic literature, where the promise of a new covenant and a coming Savior is articulated.

Understanding these themes enriches the Christian's appreciation of Jesus' role as the fulfillment of Old Testament prophecies. For instance, the suffering servant in Isaiah 53 finds its ultimate expression in the crucifixion and resurrection of Christ. By engaging with these prophetic texts, Christians can deepen their understanding of the significance of Jesus' life, death, and resurrection, recognizing that the story of redemption is woven throughout the entirety of Scripture.

Engaging with the Old Testament is not merely an intellectual exercise; it is a spiritual practice that invites Christians to encounter God through His Word. The richness of the narratives, poetry, and wisdom literature can lead to transformative experiences that deepen one's faith.

Brueggemann and other scholars encourage readers to approach the Old Testament with openness and curiosity, recognizing that it speaks powerfully to contemporary issues. The lamentations of the Psalms can provide solace in times of sorrow, while the calls for justice in the prophets can inspire action in the face of societal injustices.

Moreover, the Old Testament invites Christians into a communal reading of Scripture. Engaging with these texts within the context of a faith community fosters discussions about identity, purpose, and the nature of God. By reading the Old Testament together, believers can share insights, challenge assumptions, and grow in their understanding of God's character and His call on their lives.

In conclusion, the Old Testament is an indispensable part of the Christian faith that offers historical context, reveals God's character, provides moral and ethical guidance, and narrates a profound story of hope and redemption. Scholars like Walter Brueggemann highlight the richness of these texts and their relevance to contemporary believers.

Christians are called not only to read the Old Testament but to immerse themselves in its narratives, teachings, and promises. By doing so, they can deepen their faith, foster a more profound understanding of God's work in history, and engage meaningfully with the moral challenges of the present. As believers explore the depths of the Old Testament, they will find a treasure trove of wisdom and insight that profoundly enriches their spiritual journey and enhances their relationship with God.

43

WHAT'S THE TAKEAWAY ?

OK! OK! OK! Assuming you have read the whole caboodle; as the person who wrote the whole caboodle, I have to challenge myself notwithstanding asking all my readers with the question: What is there to take away from this book before I put it on my bookshelf (or give it to a second-hand bookshop) or give it to a friend.

Looking for the uncommon response and treating the cliché answers as one would treat leprosy, here is a list of my major conclusions gleaned from this book.

Praying alone, long, hard and repetitively for things around the world to change is not an option.

Learning to authentically, deeply pray is the main life or death journey. It cannot and must not be avoided.

Being immersed in praying over some scary verses of scripture to be fulfilled in your life or in society is not to be shied away from.

Deny and break the power of thought processes that keep you where you are in God forbidding change.

Own what you believe and drive your faith "system." Never allow theological doctrinal certitudes to grip you.

Don't allow theological ideas that you don't understand to restrain you. You are talking to Him who suggested that you speak to mountains and mingled that statement with "All things are possible." The Master Himself said that, not me.

Develope your listening practice (dare I say technique) and follow what you hear from God by praying it through. Try telling God, "I am not closing my prayer until you talk to me." And see what happens.

Make it a life-or-death issue to hear from God. Get to your knees with a "hear God or I die" mentality. This is where stuff takes place that turns "Sauls" into "Pauls" and "Simons" into "Peters". It is what changes sand foundations into solid, immovable rock. It will also totally wreck your life of set appointments.

The time you spend in whatever posture you take to pray in is about to greatly increase.

Live with an attitude of submission to Christ to the degree that the goose pimples and shivering that you can feel while on your knees in prayer remain when you rise to your feet and hit the streets. It is the presence of God that you live in that will change the world and all around you.

There is an inner fight to be open with Christian friends and to be independent with what you get from your prayer, the deeper you go. That can conceivably be a problem.

Loose yourself from group demands while being a positive force in any group you are a part of.

Be ready for your friends in Christ to raise their eyebrows with things you say.

Constantly invest yourself in bringing light and healing to all you meet and mix with.

Whatever your age, fearlessly face and defy death and all its traditional fears, and confrontations. Read all that the scripture says about it. Master it before your last day comes, even if it's possibly half a century away.

Be prepared to see, hear and sense some strange demonic and/or angelic stuff while praying. That should be normal and routine.

We are surrounded by other worlds and dimensions and the Bible suggests that the deeper in God you go, the more likely you are to visit some of them, or they might visit you.

Stay real! Stay authentic! Be yourself. But prepare to change.

Self-promotion is from the pit and could negate all that you are pursuing. Don't even dare to put your toe in that cess pool.

Never ever even play with the idea that "you have achieved". There is eternally more to pursue. You are a God chaser, not a trophy achievement promotion.

Abhor cliches from the Christianese language dictionary. Constantly seek the uncommon in Christ.

Don't be afraid of others labelling you as "eccentric". Most emulated men and women of God were labelled as having "eccentricities".

Dreams and aspirations from God, about God, towards God can be embarrassing to discuss and share. Be careful who you share it with.

Seek the outlook and worldview of Elijah.

Go for it!

PROPHETS THROUGHOUT THE HEBREW BIBLE.

1. Moses — Deut. 18:9-22.
2. "Man of God" — 1 Sam. 2:27-36
3. Samuel — 1 Sam. 1 – 16, 19, 21, 25, & 28
4. Saul "among the prophets
5. Gad — 1 Sam. 22;2 Sam. 24;1
6. Nathan — 2 Sam. 7.1 Kings 1;
7. Ahijah — 1 Kings 11:26-40; 1 Kings 12:1-20;
8. Prophet Shemaiah — 1 Kings 12:21-24; 2 Chron. 11:1-4; 2 Chron. 12
9. Man of God from Judah — 1 Kings 13:1-32
10. Seer/Prophet Iddo — 2 Chron. 9:29-30; 2 Chron. 12:15 2 Chron.
11. Prophet Oded I & His Son Azariah — 2 Chron. 15
12. Prophet Hanani — 2 Chron 16.
13. Prophet Jehu — 1 Kings 16:1-3. 2 Chron 19:1-23
14. Prophet Elijah — 1 Kings 17-19 &21. 2 Kings 1-2. 2 Chronicles 21
15. Other Unnamed Prophets — 1 Kings 20
16. Prophet Micaiah — 1 Kings 22:1-38; 2 Chron. 18
17. Prophet Jahaziel — 2 Chron. 20:13-30
18. Prophet Eliezer — 2 Chron. 20:35-37
19. Prophet Elisha — 2 Kings 2 – 9 & 13
20. Prophet Zechariah I — 2 Chron. 24:17-22; 2 Chron. 26:3-5
21. Unnamed Prophets. — 2 Chron. 25:1-24
22. Prophet Jonah — 2 Kings 14:23-27
23. Prophet Oded II — 2 Chron. 28:1-15
24. Every Prophet & Seer — 2 Kings 17
25. Prophet Isaiah — 2 Kings 8-20; 2 Chron.26:22; 2 Chron 32
26. Unnamed Prophets — 2 Kings 21:10-15
27. Prophetess Huldah — 2 Kings 22; 2 Chron. 34
28. Seer Jeduthun — 2 Chron. 35:15
29. Prophet Jeremiah — 2 Chron 35-36
30. Prophets Haggai/Zechariah. — Ezra 5-6
31. Prophet Isaiah

32. Prophet Jeremiah
33. Prophet Ezekiel
34. Prophet Daniel
35. Prophet Hosea
36. Prophet Joel
37. Prophet Amos
38. Prophet Obadiah
39. Prophet Jonah
40. Prophet Micah
41. Prophet Nahum
42. Prophet Habakkuk
43. Prophet Zephaniah
44. Prophet Haggai
45. Prophet Zechariah
46. Prophet Malachi

CHRONOLOGY OF THE BIBLICAL PROPHETS

Prophet Name	Prophet to king (Reign/Time Frame BC)	Comments
Man of God	Priest Eli (Time of Judges/Samuel)	Unnamed Prophet
Samuel.	Time of Judges & King Saul (1031-1011)	
Gad.	King David (1011-971)	
Nathan	King David (1011-971)	
Ahijah	King Jeroboam of Israel. (931 – 910)	
Shemaiah	King Rehoboam of Judah (931 – 913)	
Man of God from Judah	King Jeroboam of Israel (931 – 910)	Unnamed Prophet
	Contemporary with Prophets Ahijah & Shemaiah	
Oded I / Azariah	King Asa of Judah (911 – 870)	
Hanani	King Asa of Judah (911 – 870)	
Jehu	King Baasha of Israel (909 – 886)	
	King Jehoshaphat of Judah (873 – 848)	
Elijah	King Ahab of Israel (874 – 853)	
	King Ahaziah of Israel (853 – 852)	
	King Jehoram of Judah (853 – 841)	
Other Prophets	King Ahab of Israel (874 – 853)	Unnamed Prophets
Micaiah	King Ahab of Israel (874 – 853)	
Jahaziel	King Jehoshaphat of Judah (873 – 848)	
Eliezer	King Jehoshaphat of Judah (873 – 848)	

Elisha	King Joram of Israel (852 – 841)	
	King Jehu of Israel (841 – 814)	
	King Jehoash of Israel (798 – 782)	
Zechariah I	King Joash of Judah (835 – 796)	
	Prince Uzziah of Judah	Taught Uzziah as Youth
Unnamed Prophets	King Amaziah of Judah (796 – 767)	
Jonah	King Jeroboam II of Israel (793 – 753)	
Oded II	Reign of King Pekah of Israel (740 – 732)	Prophet in Samaria
Isaiah	King Uzziah of Judah (790 – 739)	
	King Hezekiah of Judah (715 – 686)	
Unnamed Prophets	King Manasseh of Judah (696 – 642)	
Huldah	King Josiah of Judah (640 – 609)	Prophetess
Jeduthun	King Josiah of Judah (640 – 609)	
Jeremiah	King Josiah of Judah's Death (609)	
	King Jehoiakim of Judah (609 – 597)	
	King Jehoiakin (Jehoiachin) of Judah (597)	
	King Zedekiah of Judah (597 – 586)	
Haggai	Rebuild Temple in Jerusalem (516) Dedicated	Temple
Zechariah II	Rebuild Temple in Jerusalem (516) Dedicated	Temple

B.	**Prophets who wrote.**		
	Prophet's Names	**Prophet to King (Reign / Time Frame BC)**	**Comments**
	Prophets Before Exile:		
	Jonah	No Record in Scripture (862 Estimate)	Prophet to Nineveh
	Obadiah	Queen Athaliah of Judah (841 – 835)	ProbableTimeFrame
	Amos	King Jeroboam II of Israel (793 – 753)	
		King Uzziah of Judah (790 – 739)	
	Hosea	King Jeroboam II of Israel (793 – 753)	
		King Uzziah of Judah (790 – 739)	
		King Jotham of Judah (750 – 731)	
		King Ahaz of Judah (735 – 715)	
		King Hezekiah of Judah (715 – 686)	
	Isaiah	King Uzziah of Judah (790 – 739)	
		King Jotham of Judah (750 – 731)	
		King Ahaz of Judah (735 – 715)	
		King Hezekiah of Judah (715 – 686)	

	Micah	King Jotham of Judah (750 – 731)	
		King Ahaz of Judah (735 – 715)	
		King Hezekiah of Judah (715 – 686)	
	Nahum	Prior to Fall of Nineveh (612)	
	Habakkuk	King Josiah of Judah (640 – 609)	ProbableTimeFrame
	Zephaniah	King Josiah of Judah (640 – 609)	
	Jeremiah	King Josiah of Judah (640 – 609)	
		King Jehoiakim of Judah (609 – 597)	
		King Jehoiakin (Jehoiachin) of Judah (597 – 597)	
		King Zedekiah of Judah (597 – 586)	
		Exiles in Babylon & Egypt (After 586)	(overlap into Exile)
Prophets During Exile:			
	Daniel	King Jehoiakim of Judah (3rd Year of Reign = 606)	
		to	
		King Darius of Persia (1st Year of Reign = 521)	
		King Jehoiachin of Judah (5th Year of Reign = 592)	

385

		to	
		25th Year Babylonian Exile / 14th Year After Jerusalem Fell (572)	
	Prophets After Exile:		
	Haggai	King Darius of Persia (2nd Year of Reign = 520)	
	Zechariah	King Darius of Persia (2nd & 4th Years of Reign = 520 & 518)	
	Malachi	No Record in Scripture (397 Estimate)	Probable Time Frame

BIBLIOGRAPHY

Re: Elijah.

Elijah and the secret of his power. By F.B. Meyer

Elijah: Faith and Fire. By Priscilla C. Shirer

The Days of Elijah by John Noble

Elijah: A Man of Heroism and Humility (Great Lives Series Book 5) by Charles R. Swindoll

Elijah (The Jacob Da Nesta Saga Book 1) by S. A. Haycock and Sam Glaister

The Life of Elijah by A. W. Pink.

Lessons From Elijah by Andrew Wommack

"Elijah: A Prophet for Our Times. David Wilkerson. Thomas Nelson. 2010

"Elijah: The Prophet of Fire". Herbert Lockyer. Kregel Publications. 1998

"The Life of Elijah". Charles Swindoll. Moody Publishers. 1999

"The Prophet Elijah: His Life and Times". David E. Garland. Jewish Publication Society. 1992

"Elijah: The Man Who Stood Up to Kings". John MacArthur. Harvest House Publishers. 2011

"Elijah: A Story of Courage". Catherine Mackenzie. David C. Cook. 2006.

"The Prophet Elijah". Michael D. Coogan. Brill. 2009

"Elijah: A Biblical Hero". John W. Wright. Fortress Press. 2015

"Elijah and Elisha: The Prophets of Israel". Robert D. Anderson. Abingdon Press. 1993

"The Story of Elijah". Nancy I. Sanders. Christian Focus Publications. 2008

"Elijah: The Coming of the Prophet". William H. Shea. University of Nebraska Press 1998

"Elijah: The Prophet Who Defied a King". John E. McKinley. Zondervan. 2005

"Elijah: A Spiritual Biography". John A. T. Robinson. Paraclete Press. 2018

"The Life of Elijah". William H. Allen. Hurst & Co. 1894

"Elijah: A Commentary on the Book of Kings". John M.W. Wilcox. Harper & Bros. 1904

"The History of Elijah". John H. Hinton. Hinton & Sons. 1833

"Elijah the Prophet". William H. Hutton. E. & J. Bumpus. 1895

"The Life and Times of Elijah". George W. McCready Price. The Review and Herald Publishing Association. 1943

"The Prophet Elijah". John J. McMahon. R. & T. Washbourne. 1890

"Elijah: The Prophet of Fire". Edward J. Young. Eerdmans. 1950

"The Prophet Elijah: His Life and Times". John S. Wright. The United Methodist Publishing House. 1897

"Elijah: The Man Who Stood Up to Kings". William C. Dix. American Baptist Publication Society. 1892

"The Life of Elijah". Joseph D. H. Smith. Williams & Norgate. 1899

"Elijah, the Prophet of the Old Testament". John B. F. Watson. Harper & Brothers. 1897

"Elijah: The Prophet of the Wilderness". William E. Channing. Charles C. Little and James Brown. 1838

"The Life and Prophecies of Elijah". Benjamin H. DeWitt. The American Tract Society. 1875

"The Ministry of Elijah". Robert H. Smith. The Christian Literature Company. 1890

"The Prophet Elijah: His Life and Work". A. H. B. L. Thomas. Smith, Elder & Co. 1895

"Elijah: A Study of the Prophet". William T. M. Wylie. The Religious Tract Society. 1884

"The Life of the Prophet Elijah". William H. Baker. The Sunday School Union. 1893

"The Drama of Elijah". C. H. Spurgeon. Passmore & Alabaster. 1890

"The Prophet Elijah: A Novel". Robert J. Morgan. Archway Publishing. 2016

"Elijah: A New Translation". Michael Fishbane. Jewish Publication Society. 2010

"Elijah: The Man Who Knew God". John W. Wylie. National Geographic. 2008

"The Life and Times of Elijah". William H. Allen. CreateSpace Independent Publishing Platform. 2013   "Elijah: The Man and His Message". Charles R. Swindoll. Broadman & Holman Publishers. 2000

Re: Both Elijah and Elisha.

Elijah and Elisha. The Mantle for God's People. Russell M. Stendal.

Lessons from Elijah and Elisha by Alan Toms and Hayes Press

Elijah and Elisha: One Prophetic Ministry by Stephen Kaung

Study the Prophets: Elijah and Elisha., Ronald George MacIntyre

Elijah and Elisha, by Franklyn J. Andreen

Elijah and Elisha: The Mantle for God's People.

Re: Elisha.

Gleanings from Elisha. By Arthur W. Pink.

Why Prophet Elisha Died Sick and How to Avoid It. Amb Promise Ogbonna

Elisha: The Man of God (Understanding the Old Testament) by Hamilton Smith

Available for God's Purpose: Lessons from the Life of Elisha

by Bill Crowder

Elisha: His Early Ministry by Friedrich Wilhelm Krummacher, Edward Bickersteth, et al.

The History of the Prophet Elisha. By William Plaskett Dothie

Re: General Research

Dreams and Visions of Destiny, Barbie Breathit.

Miracles: What are they, why they happen, and how can they change your life? Eric Metaxas

Prophets and Personal Prophecy. Hamon. Dr Bill. Destiny Image Publishers. 1987.

A History of Israel. Volume 1. Robinson, Theodore H. Oxford at the Clarenden Press. 1957.

Ellicott's Bible Commentary, Volume 1. Ellicott, Charles. Excursus H.

M.B. Van't Veer writes, (My God is Yahweh, p. 34)

Undesigned Coincidences in the Old and New Testament, J. J. Blunt

Secrets of the Seer: 10 keys to activating Seer encounters, by Jamie Galloway

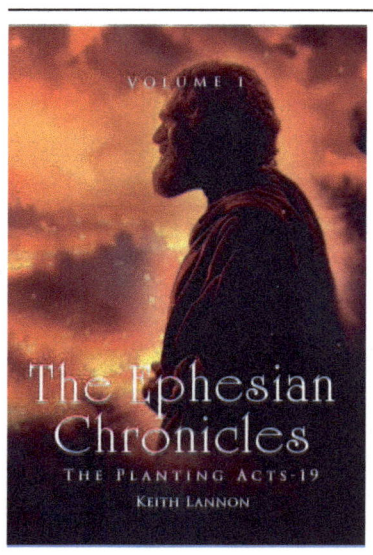

Volume 1. The Ephesian Chronicles. The Planting. Acts 19.

By Keith Lannon

The narrative of the life of Saul of Tarsus - aka the Apostle Paul - holds timeless significance for every generation, serving as a vital cornerstone in preserving the full spectrum of biblical truth deposited with Christ's followers until He returns. His experiences and convictions inspire the global church to boldly articulate the message that the Master entrusted to His followers.

In a world yearning for authentic expression of Christian truth, the call to share the unfiltered words of Christ, free from the constraints of modern religiosity, weighs heavily on the global body of Christ. Paul fearlessly preached in environments where his message faced such strong opposition. This book invites readers to embrace the Holy Spirit's call to embody the spirit and actions of Christ's Great Command to "go into all the world", and to emulate Paul's leadership at the peak of his prophetic evangelisation of the Roman world.

In examining Paul's mission to Ephesus, as detailed in Acts 19, Keith Lannon explores both the physical logistics and psychological dynamics, as well as the practical down to earth planning that challenged Paul's leadership in navigating the manifestation of the miraculous and engaging with the demonic culture that dominated Ephesus around 54 AD. Paul's openness to the gifts, energies, and visions derived from his relationship with the Holy Spirit serves as a powerful model for believers today. Join us on this transformative journey to rediscover the essence of Paul's legacy and its relevance for our time. Prepare for conceptual confrontation.

An insightful read of probably Paul's greatest mission. With devoted team members and friends, an entire subcontinent is taken with the gospel of Christ. Surely the peak of apostolic ministry.

Available now on line:

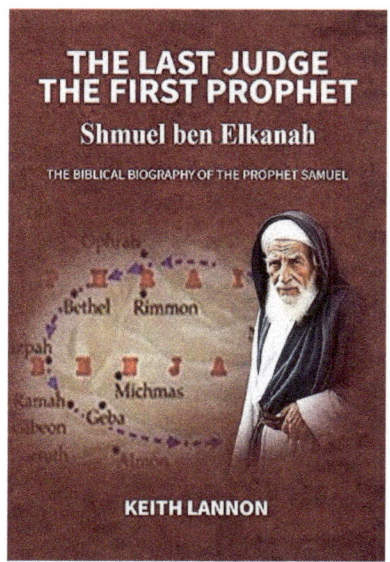

The Last Judge, The first Prophet.

Biography of the Prophet Samuel.

By Keith Lannon

Immerse yourself in the profound life and teachings of the revered prophet Samuel with this comprehensive volume. Meticulously crafted over years of dedicated research, it blends academic rigor with spiritual insight to offer a captivating portrayal of his journey. Seamlessly weaving historical context with devotional depth, this work presents a compelling narrative that is both accessible and enriching.

Designed to resonate with both scholars and seekers alike, its narrative style invites readers to delve into the complexities of faith while navigating the intriguing tapestry of Samuel's life. Whether you're a seasoned Bible student or a casual reader, this volume promises to captivate your imagination and deepen your understanding of biblical history.

A timeless treasure, it stands as a testament to the enduring relevance of Samuel's story and the profound impact of his teachings. Engaging, thought-provoking, and spiritually enriching, this work is destined to become a classic in the realm of biblical literature. Dive into its pages and embark on a transformative journey through the life and legacy of one of history's most influential prophets.

Meet Keith Lannon, a native of Manchester, England, whose passion for exploring the timeless wisdom of the biblical narrative has spanned over five decades. With a background in preaching, teaching, editing and writing, Keith has spent years delving into the depths of biblical relevance for twenty-first century living.

Keith was born in 1949 and is the eldest sibling of seven, all of whom are now in their senior years. Keith now lives in Derby, England.

This book is Keith's third publication on the world market, and he assures us he has more to come.

Keith's life's journey (now in his 76th year) has taken him far and wide, sharing his insights and wisdom across continents. From the bustling cities of the United States to the vibrant landscapes of Africa and all across Europe, Keith's unique presentations have captivated audiences, earning him high-profile invitations to speak to crowds numbering at times in the thousands. He has pastored in the UK and Africa. He claims now he is busier than he has ever been.

Invites for ministry should be addressed to: keithlannon49@gmail.com

www.ingramcontent.com/pod-product-compliance
Lightning Source LLC
Chambersburg PA
CBHW061733070526
44585CB00024B/2647